UNDERSTANDING PICTURES

There are many ways to picture the world—Australian 'x-ray' pictures, cubist collages, Amerindian split-style figures, and pictures in two-point perspective each draw attention to different features of what they represent. The premise of *Understanding Pictures* is that this diversity is the central fact with which a theory of figurative pictures must reckon.

Lopes argues that identifying pictures' subjects is akin to recognizing objects whose appearances have changed over time. He develops a scheme for categorizing the different ways pictures represent—the different kinds of meaning they have—and he contends that depiction's epistemic value lies in its representational diversity. He also offers a novel account of the phenomenology of pictorial experience, comparing pictures to visual prostheses like mirrors and binoculars.

The book concludes with a discussion of works of art which have made pictorial meaning their theme, demonstrating the importance of the issues this book raises for understanding the aesthetics of pictures.

Understanding Pictures

DOMINIC LOPES

CLARENDON PRESS · OXFORD

1 6 AUG 2007

This book has been printed digitally and produced in a standard specification in order to ensure its continuing availability

OXFORD
UNIVERSITY PRESS

Great Clarendon Street, Oxford OX2 6DP

Oxford University Press is a department of the University of Oxford.
It furthers the University's objective of excellence in research, scholarship,
and education by publishing worldwide in

Oxford New York

Auckland Cape Town Dar es Salaam Hong Kong Karachi
Kuala Lumpur Madrid Melbourne Mexico City Nairobi
New Delhi Shanghai Taipei Toronto
With offices in
Argentina Austria Brazil Chile Czech Republic France Greece
Guatemala Hungary Italy Japan South Korea Poland Portugal
Singapore Switzerland Thailand Turkey Ukraine Vietnam

Oxford is a registered trade mark of Oxford University Press
in the UK and in certain other countries

Published in the United States
by Oxford University Press Inc., New York

ISBN 0-19-927203-4

For
Anita Macfarlane and Anthony Lopes

ACKNOWLEDGEMENTS

No first book is a solo effort. This one began as a thesis for the D.Phil. degree at Oxford University in 1992. I am grateful to the Social Sciences and Humanities Research Council of Canada for awarding me a Doctoral Fellowship at a time when there was little other material incentive to pursue graduate studies. The advice of Adrian Cussins and Timothy Williamson was particularly useful at crucial stages in writing the thesis, and the criticisms of my examiners, William Child and Paul Snowdon, led to some rethinking that shaped this volume. Above all, I was most fortunate to have benefited from the guidance and teaching of John Campbell and Patrick Gardiner. Their enthusiasm for my work and their different yet complementary insights into it were a constant stimulus and encouragement.

My debts to those who eased the transition from thesis to book are many. A grant-in-aid of research from Indiana University Kokomo defrayed the cost of picture research and permissions, while a faculty fellowship enabled me to devote the summer of 1993 to writing Chapter 11. The introduction was written during a visit to the Institute for Advanced Study in Bloomington, and I would like to thank Henry Remak and his staff for making my stay there a productive and pleasant one. My thanks also go to Lynn Perrill for teaching me the art of grant-writing, to Jenny McCoy for her efficient way with paperwork, to Lauren Keach at the Indiana University Fine Arts Library for her picture-sleuthing, and to Peter Momtchiloff and Jennifer Scott at Oxford University Press for their help guiding this book through the publication process. I am indebted to the Press's reviewers, as well as to Víctor Krebs, Robert Strikwerda, Crispin Sartwell, and Stephanie Ross for taking the time to read through my revisions in whole or in part—I hope I have done their suggestions justice. My final debt I know will be forgiven: to my brother damian lopes, for a steady and nourishing diet of kind words and good cheer.

D.M.L.

Lafayette, Indiana
January 1995

CONTENTS

LIST OF ILLUSTRATIONS

Introduction

COMPARE Canaletto's painting of the Piazza San Marco, reproduced in Figure 1, with the following passage from Luigi Barzini's book *The Italians*:

Loiterers discuss grave matters and wave their hands to emphasize some important point. Some are opera singers without a job, waiting for an engagement to drop from the sky, to sing *Rigoletto* or *Trovatore* in the provinces, abroad, in South America, anywhere. Other strollers are visibly from the country, red-faced, fat, solid. . . . Handsome and well-dressed young men stroll there with feline steps, to look disdainfully at women; handsome and well-dressed women stroll languorously to look at and be looked at by men. . . . The noise and the gestures fill the empty space.[1]

For all they have in common—in representing Venice's famous public place, in vividly and fancifully evoking its character, and, perhaps, in entertaining us—it is the difference between Canaletto's picture and Barzini's description that lies at the heart of what follows. If pictures represent, they do not represent in the same way as descriptions. Yet, as manifest as this difference is, it is far from obvious how to explain it.

Let me begin by drawing some distinctions and, as often happens when distinctions are drawn, introducing some special terminology. I will then reflect briefly upon what I intend to look for in a theory of how pictures represent, raising some questions about the aesthetics, history, and anthropology of pictures that a theory of picturing should keep, if only peripherally, in its sights.

Explaining Depiction

How can I claim, as I just did, that it is far from clear how pictures represent? Surely the difference between pictorial and linguistic representation is plain: pictures represent because they look like what they

[1] Luigi Barzini, *The Italians* (New York: Atheneum, 1964), 72.

Fig. 1. Canaletto, *Piazza San Marco, Looking South-East,* 1742–4

represent. When I look at *Piazza San Marco*, I have an experience of what it represents, and this experience is like seeing the piazza itself. The marvel of pictorial representation is that it replicates visual experiences of objects; descriptions do not have this power. Admittedly, we experience pictures *as of* their subjects. Our intuitive concept of a picture runs something like 'a two-dimensional representation that looks like what it represents', and I am willing to let this serve as a working definition of 'picture'.[2] Nevertheless, the idea that 'looking like' explains depiction harbours a serious error, for it is precisely the fact that when looking at a picture we experience what it represents that needs explaining.

This error is masked by a failure to make certain distinctions. First, I call the real-world entities a picture represents its 'subject'. In doing so, I depart somewhat from ordinary usage in so far as a fictive picture, according to my definition, has no subject—there are no real-world entities that a picture of a manticore represents.[3] But the principal advantage of my choice of terminology is that it encompasses not only objects but also scenes, events, and states of affairs. *Piazza San Marco*'s subjects include San Marco's basilica (an object), the piazza (a scene), people gesticulating (events), and the fact that people gesticulate in Venice (a state of affairs).

Of course, pictures are objects in the world, too. They have physical properties that vary with their physical composition, size, age, and the like. Among these is a privileged set of visual properties, those by means of which pictures represent their subjects. I shall speak of these properties as making up pictures' 'designs'. An incomplete list of pictorial design properties would include marks, directions, boundaries, contours, shapes, colours, hues, relative contrasts between light and dark, and also textures, such as smoothness of surface or invisibility of brushwork. Design properties are typically laid down in paint, ink, charcoal, or some other substance, on a flat surface. (However, the image of a slide projected on a screen shows that pictorial colours and shapes need not be comprised of any pigmented substance.)

Distinct from both a picture's subject and its design is its 'content'. The content of a representation of any kind, whether mental, linguistic,

---

[2] This will serve only as a working definition. The word 'four' contains four visible elements, f o u r, and so looks like what it denotes, but it is not a picture.

[3] Since fictive pictures purport to represent real objects, ordinary talk of pictures' subjects embraces the things they purport to represent as well as the things they do represent. This violates my definition of 'subject'.

pictorial, or musical, consists in the properties it represents the world as having. Pictorial content, by extension, consists in the properties a picture represents the world as having. The content of a picture, if we grasp it aright, determines the content of our experience of the picture. When we experience a picture in the right way, we have an experience which represents the world as having the properties the picture represents it as having. It is because *Piazza San Marco* represents a basilica that, when we look at the picture, we have an experience as of a basilica.

Content is not easily confused with design. A picture's line, shading, colour, and textural properties are rarely properties it ascribes to its subject. *Piazza San Marco* does not represent San Marco's basilica as a few centimetres in height, though that is the height of the brush strokes comprising its design. But there is a much greater temptation to equate a picture's content with its subject, confusing properties the picture ascribes to the world with properties the world has. What is wrong with this is that a picture can have a content that misrepresents its subject, attributing properties to it that it does not have.

It is the equation of content with subject that underlies our erroneous intuition that pictures represent because they 'just look like' their subjects. While they need not do so, the contents of pictures frequently match properties of their subjects, and, as a result, the contents of our experiences of pictures frequently match the contents of our experiences of actual scenes. These matches acquire a paradigmatic stature in our pre-theoretic conception of depiction: we conceptualize our experiences of pictures as like our experiences of their subjects. However, noticing that a picture's content matches its subject or that our experience of a picture matches our experience of its subject is no explanation of how the picture comes by that content. The task of a theory of pictorial representation is to explain how it is that pictures come to have content in the first place. The common-sense view that pictures represent because they 'just look like' their subjects simply takes depiction for granted.

An explanation of how pictures come by their contents, thereby enabling them to give rise to experiences as of certain scenes, must begin with an examination of the relationship between design and subject. A genuine resemblance theory of depiction, for instance, holds that a picture has a content as of its subject because its design resembles its subject—but more of this in the next chapter. For the present let us take care always to distinguish between design, content, and subject, explaining content by means of design, subject, and the relation between them.

Figurative and Abstract Pictures

Some readers might have some misgivings about my characterization of pictures as representing objects and scenes. A guiding principle of this book is that pictures come in many varieties, and this diversity is something which a theory of picturing must take into account. But, in apparent violation of this principle, I am proposing to limit my discussion to what are commonly called 'figurative' pictures.

The red cows and Chinese horses of Lascaux, *The School of Athens*, the royal visages engraved on notes of legal tender, doodles, maps, inkblots, Ansel Adams vistas, suprematist compositions, mythological scenes, family snapshots, Pollock drips, Mondrian grids, and psychology textbook representations of illusions all count as pictures. Of these, maps, vistas, banknotes, and philosophical group portraits are figurative (and in this respect may be classed with descriptions), while drips, grids, and many doodles are not figurative but 'abstract'.

In overlooking abstract pictures, I do not mean to endorse the view that abstract pictures are not representational. It is true that abstractions do not represent objects and scenes as do still lifes or landscapes, but abstractions may represent in other ways. Pictures such as Rothko's coloured clouds or Rorschach ink-blots may *express* subjective psychological states—of anxiety, exhilaration, conflict, mystical union, and the like. Others *make manifest* features of the process of their production, as a Pollock drip painting manifests the direction and force of the artist's movements, the liquidity and stickiness of the paint, and the effects of gravity.[4] Expression and manifestation are species of representation in so far as they draw our attention to features of the world—subjective mental states in one case and processes of making in the other.[5]

Whatever the prospects for bringing such pictures within the representational fold, I propose to sweep this issue under the rug and avail myself of the traditional, intuitive division of pictures into those that represent physical objects and scenes and those that do not. By no

---

[4] See Nelson Goodman, *Languages of Art: An Approach to a Theory of Symbols*, 2nd edn. (Indianapolis: Hackett, 1976), ch. 2; and Patrick Maynard, 'Drawing and Shooting: Causality in Depiction', *Journal of Aesthetics and Art Criticism*, 44 (1985), 115–29, from which I borrow the term 'manifestation'.

[5] Of course, expression and manifestation are not found only in abstract pictures. A picture may express psychological states or manifest the history of its production by representing objects and scenes.

means do I reject the principle that a complete account of pictures should explain abstract pictures as well as figurative ones. I merely restrict myself to the less ambitious task of attempting to explain pictures that, like descriptions (though in their distinctive way), represent objects, properties, and states of affairs. I henceforth follow standard philosophical practice in using the terms 'pictorial representation' and, more conveniently, 'depiction' to apply only to figurative representation.

This is not to say that I assume that the line dividing the figurative from the abstract is always sharp. Looking at a picture like Pollock's *Out of the Web*, in which the ghosts of figures linger, we may be unsure whether anything is depicted. But our uncertainty does not impeach the principle that every picture either does or does not depict an object, scene, or state of affairs. A theory of depiction should provide a more or less effective procedure for deciding whether any given picture represents some subject and, if so, what. It will do so by explaining how pictures with certain designs acquire contents as of certain objects or scenes.

Art Pictures, Demotic Pictures

Some readers may wish to divide pictures along aesthetic lines. Pollock's drips and *The School of Athens* are works of art; doodles and family snaps are (generally) not. No theory of depiction can afford to ignore pictures' aesthetic potential.

The fact that pictures can sometimes be works of art, having properties that capture and hold our aesthetic interest, imposes a burden on a complete theory of pictorial representation. Whatever account we supply of how pictures represent their subjects should lay a foundation for an explanation of how it is that the fact that a picture does represent objects and scenes can be aesthetically interesting.[6] In addition, if our aesthetic engagement with pictures differs from our aesthetic engagement with other kinds of representations (e.g. novels or songs), we will want to know what it is about *pictorial* representations that occasions a *pictorial* aesthetic. There is an ancient view (with modern adherents) that works of art are representational, bearing certain kinds of meaning. The challenge for this representation theory of art is to explain how

---

[6] I therefore contest radically 'formalist' conceptions of art according to which artworks' representational properties are never relevant aesthetically.

different representational media, bearing different kinds of meaning, can make for different kinds of art.[7]

I do not attempt to trace out fully and systematically the aesthetic implications for the theory of depiction I propose. Nevertheless, Chapter 11 is designed to serve, in a limited capacity, as a model for uncovering the roots of a pictorial aesthetic in pictorial representation.

Although we should be aware of the contribution that a theory of representational pictures can make to a theory of art pictures, we must not take the tie between accounts of pictures and art pictures too seriously. Theories of depiction have traditionally been the province of aesthetics, so it is no surprise that they have been influenced by the concerns of those whose main interest is art. The principal danger of this 'aestheticization' of depiction has been a neglect of the vast majority of representational pictures—heads of state engraved on banknotes, polaroids of Space Mountain, maps, architectural elevations, and the like—which do not qualify as works of art. These I call 'demotic' pictures, since they are a product of the people rather than the art world.

In my view, a theory of depiction should take demotic pictures as fundamental, while also providing the basis for an explanation of how pictures can transcend the commonplace and enter the realm of the aesthetic. This parallels methodology in the philosophy of language, which begins by attempting to explain ordinary linguistic communication, and only then tries to shed light on metaphor, fictional narrative, and other modes which are parasitic on ordinary language but also underwrite its aesthetic potential.[8]

A central claim of this book is that pictures are at bottom vehicles for the storage, manipulation, and communication of information. They put us in touch with our physical environment, especially our visual environment, often parts of it that are beyond our reach, across space or time. Pictures share language's burden in representing the world and our thoughts about it. And this function of pictures is at the forefront in the demotic rather than the aesthetic.

---

[7] Modern adherents include Arthur Danto, *Transfiguration of the Commonplace: A Philosophy of Art* (Cambridge, Mass.: Harvard University Press, 1981); and Richard Wollheim, *Painting as an Art* (London: Thames and Hudson, 1988). Wollheim predicates a theory of art pictures on a theory of pictorial representation. A work of art is a work in which meaning is thematized; a work of pictorial art is not just a picture in which meaning is thematized, but a work in which a specifically pictorial kind of meaning is thematized.

[8] For a recent theory of depiction that disregards this stricture, see Kendall Walton, *Mimesis as Make-Believe: On the Foundations of the Representational Arts* (Cambridge, Mass.: Harvard University Press, 1990). I critique Walton's approach in Ch. 4.

Moreover, giving pride of place to non-art pictures lends some jus-
tification to my strategy of limiting my account of pictures to figurative
ones. One source of resistance to that strategy stems from the fact that
it is among works of pictorial art that we find most examples of abstraction. A theory of figurative representation therefore comprises only part
of a complete theory of art pictures, and should be developed from the
outset alongside theories of expression and manifestation.[9] But demotic
pictures are almost exclusively figurative. So to the extent that we seek
an account that takes demotic pictures as paradigmatic, it seems reasonable to proceed with a theory dedicated to figurative pictures.

Explaining Pictorial Diversity

The pioneering study of theoretical issues in pictorial representation
was a book written by an art historian, E. H. Gombrich's *Art and
Illusion*.[10] The greater part of Gombrich's legacy to philosophical research on pictures, as we shall see in Chapter 2, is the illusion theory
of depiction. Yet Gombrich's primary concern was with the problem of
why pictorial representation has a history—and, for that matter, an
anthropology. The importance of this for accounts of how pictures
represent has not been recognized.

The problem of the history of depiction arises, for Gombrich, in the
following way. To begin, Gombrich endorses the standard view that an
explanation of depiction will depend on facts about perception. When
we look at pictures, we enjoy visual experiences of what is not there—
experiences of Venetians strolling about the Piazza San Marco or a
mandolin on a table, as the case may be. This suggested to Gombrich
that pictures represent objects and scenes by triggering perceptual illusions that induce experiences as of those objects or scenes. But while
artists have always claimed to copy what they see, the pictures of
different cultures and different eras represent the world in strikingly
different ways. Egyptian tomb paintings, medieval miniatures, ukiyo-e
prints, north-west coast First Nation totems, the cows and horses at

---

[9] However, my hunch is that we will get the aesthetics of figurative pictures right only
once we recognize that they function in the first place as conveyors of information and
seek to ground our aesthetic interest in them in this fact. Abstraction distracts us from this
point.

[10] E. H. Gombrich, *Art and Illusion: A Study in the Psychology of Pictorial Representation*, 2nd edn. (Princeton: Princeton University Press, 1961).

Fig. 2. Kwakiutl, Thunderbird, painting from house front

Lascaux, the collages of Picasso and Braque, all illustrate not only the diversity but also the cultural embeddedness and historical development of depiction.[11] Hence Gombrich's problem: how can depiction have historical and cultural dimensions if pictures are perceptual and perception is ahistorical and universal across cultures?

The traditional response to this question simply assumes the superiority of Western post-Renaissance canons of realistic representation, putting pictorial diversity down to either a taste for non-figurative ornamentation or a lack of technical sophistication. Hoping to avoid this response, with its overtones of Whig history, Gombrich argued instead that pictures are 'conceptual' as well as perceptual. By this he meant that pictures are like language in so far as design–subject correlations are more or less arbitrary—brown paint can be and was used to represent green grass, for example. Gombrich called different sets of design–subject correlations 'schemata'. Egyptian tomb paintings belong to one schema, impressionist canvases belong to a second, and north-west coast First Nation split-style drawings to a third (e.g. Fig. 2). Pictorial schemata, like languages, are conventional. The split style is the convention prevalent among the Kwakiutl, while cubism was conventional in the Parisian art world between the wars.

---

[11] The pictures reproduced in this book illustrate this diversity. Interestingly, most of these are art pictures. This is due in large measure to the relative freedom of those who make art to explore diverse modes of representation, but it is also due to a tendency, especially in recent years, to aestheticize the historically or culturally exotic.

The history of depiction and its cultural embeddedness are therefore the result of a tension between its perceptual and conceptual origins. Changes in the way people represent things are sometimes attempts to correct the prevailing schemata so as to achieve a closer match with visual experience; sometimes they represent a pull towards the 'primitive' and the conceptual.

I have argued elsewhere that Gombrich's account of depiction fails in its aim to provide a basis for rich historical or anthropological explanations of pictures.[12] On the one hand, Gombrich maintains a monolithic conception of an ideal match between pictures and objects. This means that artists interested in enhancing pictures' perceptual aspect have their goal set out for them: the route of the march towards a better match is predetermined. Moreover, as pictures approach illusionism, they reflect fewer particularities of the context in which they were made, so that illusionistic art is beyond social explanation.[13]

On the other hand, if the adoption of a schema in a context is a matter of convention, then choices of schemata are arbitrary, for conventions are arbitrary.[14] And to say that it is an arbitrary matter what schema is used in a context is to forestall any explanation of why particular schemata are suited to particular contexts. The Kwakiutl, on this view, use the split style simply because it is customary among them to do so, just as Britons drive on the left for no other reason than that it is better that they all drive on the same side of the road and it is customary among them to drive on the left. If schemata are arbitrary, then there can be no explanation of the adoption of a schema in a context that refers to its suitability for the needs of picture-users in that context.

Gombrich's account explains why depiction is diverse and why it is possible for pictures to belong to different modes or schemata of representation. But it cannot explain why particular schemata prevail in particular contexts, since what is conceptual in depiction is arbitrary, and what is perceptual is predetermined. What we want to be able to

<hr />

[12] Dominic Lopes, 'Pictures, Styles, and Purposes', *British Journal of Aesthetics*, 32 (1992), 330–41. See also Norman Bryson, *Vision and Painting: The Logic of the Gaze* (New Haven: Yale University Press, 1983).

[13] Of course, illusionistic art thrives only in certain cultural and technical conditions. But it hardly explains why a schemata was adopted at a particular place and time merely to assert that it had become possible to adopt it.

[14] For the classic argument that conventions are arbitrary, see David Lewis, *Convention* (Cambridge, Mass.: Harvard University Press, 1969). For an argument that depiction is not conventional, see Sect. 6.5.

explain is what it is about the style invented by Alberti that answered to forces at work in Renaissance Europe, and what it is about split-style pictures that suits them to the purposes of the Kwakiutl. This is the merest sketch of Gombrich's problem—how pictures, if they are grounded in perceptual processes, can reflect features of culture. My aim has been not to assemble a decisive refutation of Gombrich, but rather to illustrate that different theories of depiction have different implications for how we can explain pictures as social and historical artefacts. A theory of depiction must identify the features that pictures have in virtue of which they have a history and an anthropology. It must explain, first, how pictures can belong to different schemata or styles or modes of representation and, second, how pictures in those schemata, styles, or modes can be more or less suited to particular times and places.

Perceptual or Symbolic?

In describing Gombrich's model of the perceptual and social determinants of pictorial meaning, I have touched on two schools of thought concerning pictorial representation. According to one, pictures depend on perceptual processes. Perceptualism takes seriously our intuition that what distinguishes pictures from other kinds of representations—what distinguishes Canaletto's painting from Barzini's prose—is that pictures 'look like' their subjects. The alternative to perceptualism is any theory that stresses analogies between pictorial representation and other kinds of symbols, particularly linguistic ones. Linguistic analogies give us access to the sophisticated tools of the philosophy of language, enabling us to study what I call the 'logic' of pictures. Their drawback is that they threaten to assimilate pictures to descriptions.

Although perceptualism and the symbol theory seem at loggerheads, I am in sympathy with Gombrich's attempt to reconcile them in a way that retains the advantages of each. My own view is that convergence is natural in light of recent advances in our understanding of perception, cognition, and language. In particular, we now know enough about the visual mechanisms pertaining to object recognition to see that they possess the right kind of flexibility and the right kind of structure to explain how we recognize objects in pictures. At the same time, it has become apparent to many philosophers of language that linguistic understanding is intimately bound up with the exercise of perceptual capacities. I have found Gareth Evans's conception, in *The Varieties of Reference*, of the links between language, cognition, and perception a particularly illuminating model for what might be called a perceptual theory of pictorial symbols.[15]

Parts One and Two of this book review and assess perceptual and symbolic accounts respectively. Although the best versions of each have flaws, a careful analysis of their relative strengths and weaknesses offers clues as to what a successful theory should ultimately look like. In Part Three, I introduce and defend my 'aspect-recognition theory' of depiction, a hybrid incorporating perceptual elements within a symbolic framework. I believe that this theory is equipped to ground rich historical and anthropological explanations of pictures. Finally, in Part Four, I use my conception of pictures' distinctive power to communicate certain kinds of information to show how pictorial representation can be aesthetically interesting.

[15] Gareth Evans, *The Varieties of Reference*, ed. John McDowell (Oxford: Oxford University Press, 1982).

PART ONE
Pictures as Perceptual

I

Representation and Resemblance

RESEMBLANCE is deeply implicated in our intuitive understanding of what it is to be a picture. When asked how the pictures it contains represent things, any visitor to the local art gallery will readily agree with Samuel Johnson's commonsensical definition of a picture as a 'resemblance of persons and things in colours'. Unlike Barzini's words, Canaletto's deft applications of pigment to canvas do indeed look like what they represent. What sets pictures apart from other kinds of representations is that they resemble their subjects. Does this fact explain how pictures represent?

1.1 The Independence Challenge

Nobody denies that visual resemblance has something to do with pictures; nor does anybody advocate severing the intuitive link between pictures and resemblance.[1] Nevertheless, it is by no means self-evident that resemblance explains depiction. According to the resemblance theory, identifying what a picture represents is a matter of recognizing a similarity between its design and its subject. But to deny that we understand pictures by noticing similarities is not to deny the intuitive significance of resemblance for depiction. Design–subject similarities may well be invisible until we know what is represented, and the fact that a picture depicts an object may itself explain our noticing similarities between them.

Resemblance's grip on our intuitions is so firm, though, that to give fair consideration to this point, we would be wise to set pictures aside for a moment and concentrate on other representations with imitative elements. For instance, while resemblance plays a role in the sign languages used by the deaf, it does not follow that it explains how they represent.

[1] Even Nelson Goodman, the arch anti-perceptualist, grants that pictures resemble their subjects. See Goodman, quoted in E. H. Gombrich, 'Image and Code: Scope and Limits of Conventionalism in Pictorial Representation', in *The Image and the Eye: Further Studies in the Psychology of Pictorial Representation* (Oxford: Phaidon, 1982), 284.

Fig. 3. American Sign Language—*left*: 'duck'; *middle*: 'rabbit'; *right* 'truth'

The hand shapes, movements, and positions making up sign languages fall into three categories.[2] Some, like the American Sign Language (ASL) sign for 'truth', obviously do not visually resemble what they stand for (see Fig. 3). Understanding these signs neither depends upon nor promotes any perceived similarity between them and their referents.[3] Other signs we can grasp just by noticing their resemblance to what they signal; the ASL sign for a duck can be understood just by noticing its resemblance to a duck.[4] When a similarity can be seen between a sign and its referent without first knowing its meaning, the similarity is 'representation-independent'. The third class of signs consists of those whose similarity to their subjects is evident only once we know what they refer to. Only once you know what the sign for a rabbit stands for do you see its resemblance to a rabbit. Its resemblance to its referent is 'representation-dependent'.

In the case of pictures, some design–subject resemblances are obviously representation-dependent. Only once we learn that streaked lines behind a figure represent movement do we notice how they capture the

---

[2] See Trevor Pateman, 'Transparent and Translucent Icons', *British Journal of Aesthetics*, 26 (1986), 380–2; and Margaret Deuchar, 'Are the Signs of Language Arbitrary?', in Horace Barlow, Colin Blakemore, and Miranda Weston-Smith (eds.), *Images and Understanding* (Cambridge: Cambridge University Press, 1990), 168–79.

[3] Often lack of resemblance between sign and signified can be attributed to the impossibility of manually imitating what is signed. This is not the case with the sign for truth: if, for instance, truth is correspondence with reality, then parallel lines drawn through the air visually resemble truth.

[4] Such signs *can* be but *need not* be interpreted by noticing what they resemble. ASL signs are not normally interpreted by noticing resemblances; signers do not communicate by playing elaborate games of charades.

Fig. 4. Running rabbit

appearance of the background of a fast-moving object that we are following with our eyes (see Fig. 4). Likewise, the wavy lines drawn emanating from a pie are not just conventional symbols for the pie's smell and warmth—they seem, almost paradoxically, to look like its smell and warmth. Resemblance so dominates our conception of depiction that just about anything a picture represents, it seems to resemble. As Nelson Goodman puts it, 'resemblance and deceptiveness, far from being constant and independent sources and criteria of representational practice, are in some degree products of it'.[5]

The resemblance theory holds that we understand what pictures represent by recognizing their similarity to their subjects. But while intuition tells us that pictures resemble their subjects, it is unable to distinguish representation-dependent from representation-independent resemblances. Seeing a resemblance between Constable's *Wivenhoe Park* and its subject may be a consequence of first knowing that it represents a manorhouse, in the way that seeing a rabbit in two fluttering hands depends on knowing the meaning of the sign. Resemblance is inextricably connected to depiction, but it remains to be seen whether we understand pictures by noticing resemblances or notice resemblances as a result of understanding pictures.

As a consequence, resemblance theorists must heed what I call the 'independence challenge'. An adequate resemblance theory of depiction must avoid merely appealing to the intuitive connection between depiction and resemblance. It must specify those representation-independent resemblances in virtue of which we identify pictures' subjects. Not all resemblances need be representation-independent, for seeing what a picture represents may draw viewers' attention to further resemblances that they would not have noticed otherwise.[6] Nevertheless, those similarities which viewers must notice in order to identify the picture's

---

[5] Goodman, *Languages of Art*, 39.
[6] I thank Crispin Sartwell for this observation.

subject must be representation-independent. After all, to claim that pictures represent because they are seen to resemble in certain respects and then to allow that they are seen to resemble in those respects because they represent would be patently circular.

1.2 Objective Similarity

What is the record of the resemblance theory in addressing the independence challenge? Traditional versions of the theory hold that there are objective similarities between pictures' design properties and properties of their subjects, and it is by recognizing these similarities that their subjects are identified.

A number of notorious worries dog this enterprise. To begin with, the relations of depiction and resemblance are logically quite different. Resemblance, unlike depiction, is reflexive—all things resemble themselves, but nothing depicts itself. And resemblance, unlike depiction, is also symmetric—if the left of the pair of central figures in *The School of Athens* resembles Aristotle in certain respects, then Aristotle resembles that figure in the fresco in those respects; but although that part of the fresco depicts Aristotle, this does not mean that he depicts part of it. (Incidentally, that resemblance does not imply symmetrical representation does not mean that symmetrical representation is impossible. One might imagine two pictures drawn simultaneously, each of the other.)

More seriously, whatever design–subject similarities turn out to be salient for pictorial representation, some pictures will be less similar to their professed subjects in salient respects than to other objects. We need not look far afield for examples. The bulk of pictures familiar to many of us (unfortunately) are reproductions in posters, magazines, and art books. Prints from the same plate, photographs from the same negative, expert forgeries of old masters, and photographic reproductions share with each other whatever visual properties could be considered salient for representation, and differ from each other in few other respects, but they typically do not depict what they reproduce. (Pictures that do depict what they copy merit special consideration, provided in Chapter 11.)

With sufficient ingenuity I suspect that both these difficulties can be finessed. The last one is more worrying, however. If the resemblance view is to meet the independence challenge, it must provide a fairly specific account of what similarities are salient for resemblance. These similarities must be unique to pictures, since they distinguish pictures from all other representational media. They must also be uniform, lest viewers be driven to take into account the peculiarities of individual pictures or groups of pictures in violation of the independence constraint. However, as a cursory survey of a variety of pictures from different times and places reveals, pictures in different styles share a number of disjoint sets of properties with their subjects. The capacity to see how an ukiyo-e print, a Byzantine icon, a cubist collage, or a Kwakiutl totem each resembles its subject seems to depend at least in part on a familiarity with how each kind of picture represents.

A promising remedy for these difficulties makes use of the fact that pictures are human artefacts specifically designed for communication, and concludes that what they represent is as much a matter of artists' intentions as of resemblance. Thus a picture represents an object if and only if, first, it resembles it in salient respects, and second, it was made with an intention to represent its subject by resembling it in those respects.[7] Aristotle does not depict any part of *The School of Athens*, though he resembles part of it, because the picture is intended to represent the philosopher, not vice versa. Likewise, multiple prints of a photograph resemble each other more than they resemble their subject, but they depict the latter because they are intended to represent only it.

At first glance, the intentionalized resemblance theory responds to the independence challenge with aplomb, by providing an account of the properties that pictures share uniquely and uniformly with their subjects: salient resemblances are simply intended resemblances. This appears to reconcile resemblance with the diversity of depiction. Pictures in different styles of representation—from Egyptian profile style to cubism—resemble their subjects in those respects intended in their contexts.[8] Our familiarity with the similarities typical of a style is a familiarity with the intentions of artists working in that style. As plausible as this seems, however, it will not do.

On the one hand, to be guided by knowledge of how a picture is intended to resemble its subject is to seek representation-dependent similarities. If a picture's resemblance to its subject cannot be noted without first knowing how that picture is intended to resemble its subject, then the claim that pictures are interpreted by recognizing what they resemble, independently of what they represent, has been relinquished.

---

[7] See Jerry A. Fodor, *The Language of Thought* (New York: Crowell, 1975), 182–3.

[8] James W. Manns, 'Representation, Relativism, and Resemblance', *British Journal of Aesthetics*, 11 (1971), 281–7.

On the other hand, if the claim is no more than that pictures are intended to represent their subjects in a standard and familiar set of ways, then talk of intended resemblance is superfluous. We still require an account of the particular salient similarities that pictures are standardly intended to share with their subjects. Statues, carpet or wallpaper samples, and a host of other representations are intended to represent things by resembling them in certain respects, though not in the same respects as pictures. The resemblance theory has not met the independence challenge until it has specified the salient resemblances characteristic of depiction and shown them to be representation-independent.

1.3 Internalizing Similarity

Rather than further pursuing the prospects for a unique, uniform specification of objective similarities between pictures' designs and their subjects, I believe that it is more profitable to examine in some detail an alternative version of the resemblance theory recently proposed by Christopher Peacocke.[9] Peacocke's strategy is to explain depiction not by means of objective similarities between pictures and objects, but by means of *subjective* similarities between our experiences of each. This strategy is reasonable, because any objective similarity which explains how we interpret pictures is likely to be an experienced similarity. The prospects for an objective resemblance theory of depiction are advanced if it can be shown that pictures are experienced as similar to their subjects.

As it happens, Peacocke's version of the similarity theory does not adequately answer the independence challenge. The main reason is that it makes the mistake that Ruth Millikan, writing about theories of mental representation, calls 'internalizing content'.[10] Since Peacocke's is but one instance of a venerable way of understanding the relation between pictures and visual perception, we can learn something about both by studying where Peacocke goes wrong. In the end we will see the need for a constraint to be heeded by any adequate theory of depiction.

One of the merits of Peacocke's account is that it provides a theoretical apparatus that can be used to probe the objective and subjective properties of experience. The key to this apparatus is a distinction between what Peacocke calls 'sensational' and 'representational' properties

---

[9] Christopher Peacocke, 'Depiction', *Philosophical Review*, 96 (1987), 390–1.
[10] Ruth Garrett Millikan, 'Perceptual Content and Fregean Myth', *Mind*, 100 (1991), 439–59.

of experience.[11] Representational properties of experience are those that experience represents the world as having; its sensational properties are those that reflect what it is like to have the experience. Thus, whereas a visual experience of nearby and far-away trees may represent both as the same size in physical space, it is a sensational property of the experience that one tree occupies a larger area of the visual field than the other. Similarly, an envelope viewed from different angles is invariably represented as occupying a rectangular portion of physical space, though from many angles it is experienced as occupying irregular rhomboidal regions of the visual field. A rectangular shape is a representational property of a visual experience of the envelope; a rhomboidal shape is its sensational property.

A corresponding distinction can be made between two kinds of content possessed by perceptual experience. The representational content of experience is comprised of properties that it represents the world as having, such as the physical size of the tree or the rectangular shape of the envelope. The sensational content of experience consists of properties that capture what it is like to have the experience.[12] In our examples, the sensational contents of visual experiences include sizes in the visual field of nearby and far-away trees and irregular shapes in the visual field presented by an envelope seen from different angles.

In both these examples, the concept of the 'visual field' figures as part of a causal explanation of subjective features of visual experience. The visual field is an imaginary plane interposed between scene and viewer which, together with facts about the behaviour of light, causally explains the sensational properties of visual experiences. The nearby tree's larger size in sensational space and the different shape experiences of the rectangular envelope are determined by the rules governing the projection of light on to this imagined interposed plane, the visual field.

One advantage of introducing the notion of the visual field as a theoretical entity figuring in causal explanations is that it is immune to objections that subjective similarities are 'private' experiences.[13] According-ing to one version of the resemblance theory (the version championed

---

[11] Christopher Peacocke, *Sense and Content* (Oxford: Oxford University Press, 1983), 5–6; and *idem*, 'Depiction', 385.

[12] Peacocke reserves use of the expression 'content of experience' for representational contents of experience.

[13] See Bryson, *Vision and Painting*, 38–43. For a related use of the private-language argument to critique the view that object recognition consists in matching mental images, see Evans, *Varieties of Reference*, 289–96.

by Tolstoy), pictures represent because they replicate in their viewers the *same experiences* as their makers enjoyed. But, as Wittgenstein would have insisted, the criteria for understanding a picture cannot be privately assessable. A viewer understands a picture not because it triggers the 'right' experience, but because she is able to correctly identify its subject, where correct identification is assessed by performance. 'Right' experience is neither necessary nor sufficient for right identification.

Peacocke does not fall into this trap. The sensational contents of experience are not private because they are visual field properties, and the visual field is an explanatory construct. The notion of an imaginary interposed plane makes the identity conditions for sensational properties of experience inter-subjectively available.

According to Peacocke, pictures are experienced as similar to their subjects at the level of sensational properties. Experience does not represent *Salisbury Cathedral* as similar in shape to Salisbury Cathedral—after all, Constable's painting is seen to be flat, and the cathedral itself to be robustly three-dimensional. What the painting does do is present a shape in the visual field that is experienced as similar to one which the cathedral itself might present. As Peacocke puts it, pictures must be F-related ('field-related') to their subjects. Something is F-related to an object only if it is presented in a region of the visual field which is experienced as similar in shape to a region in which the object could be presented when seen from some point of view.[14] And if regions of the visual field are *experienced* as similar, then they *are* similar, since experienced properties are visual field properties by definition.[15]

With the F-relation in hand, Peacocke proposes that a picture depicts an object only if it is intended successfully that in intended viewing conditions it is F-related to that object. By 'intended viewing conditions' Peacocke means conditions required for viewing any picture, such as the availability of adequate lighting and unobstructed visibility. Thus, experiencing a picture as similar to its subject does not depend on first determining what features the artist intends experiences of picture and subject to share—as I have argued, such a requirement would make experienced similarity representation-dependent. Salient similarities are not simply intended similarities, they are similarities in the visual field.

The F-relation promises to meet the independence challenge by specifying how pictures resemble their subjects in a way that avoids merely

---

[14] Peacocke, 'Depiction', 386–7.

[15] Similarity in the visual field does not, however, entail experienced similarity. Countless objects present similar shapes in the visual field that go unnoticed by most perceivers.

appealing to intuition. Peacocke's contribution is to locate pictorial similarity not in the objective properties of pictures and their subjects but in our internal, visual field representations of each. But does visual field similarity in fact explain how we experience pictures as like their subjects, independent of knowledge of what they depict? The promise of the F-relation is undermined, I believe, in light of Ruth Millikan's warnings about the dangers of 'internalizing content'. Internalizing content is a manœuvre sometimes made in the hope of explaining mental states, including perceptual ones. To internalize content is to hypothesize an inner vehicle or mental intermediary with properties mirroring those of the content of the state we hope to explain. There is nothing amiss with postulating mental intermediaries to explain mental states; doing so is probably essential to understanding cognition. However, internalizing content involves not only postulating mental intermediaries but also projecting selected properties of the states to be explained on to the mental intermediaries thought to explain them. This is legitimate provided that there are independent reasons for ascribing the same properties to the mental intermediary and the state it explains. But when content is internalized illegitimately, without an independent defence of the ascription of selected properties of the state to be explained to the mental intermediary, we are prone to mistakenly take the postulated sharing of properties between vehicle and content as an explanation of that content.

A notorious example of internalizing content illegitimately is the attractive yet erroneous 'inner pictures' theory of vision. Some philosophers hoped to explain veridical visual perception by supposing that we see by means of pictures in the head, these pictures possessing key properties of what we see. But inner picture theorists simply postulated inner states with properties of the visual experiences they wished to explain, and then took this sharing of properties between inner and outer to explain vision. This illegitimately internalizes visual experience. Michael Dummett exposes another case of internalizing content in his critique of 'explanations' of assertoric force as an external, verbal reflection of a psychological state of judgement.[16] Internalizing content evidently produces inadequate, often illusory, explanations that harbour, and rely upon, significant intuitive appeal.

The F-relation fails to meet the independence challenge, because it

---

[16] Michael Dummett, *Frege: Philosophy of Language*, 2nd edn. (London: Duckworth, 1981), 362–3.

illegitimately internalizes content. Peacocke posits the visual field as an inner vehicle to serve as the backdrop for selected properties of visual experience, and then takes experienced similarities to depend on similarities in regions of the visual field. Only having so internalized the notion of the visual field does it make sense to say that we experience a picture as like its subject because they are similar in the visual field. I argue that, on the contrary, experienced pictorial similarity does not entail similarity in visual field properties.

The best way to see this is to begin by considering pictures which clearly satisfy the F-relation. *Salisbury Cathedral* presents shapes on an imagined interposed plane which are approximately congruent with shapes which its subject could project on to such a plane. There is a reason for this. Constable knew and acted on the principle that a picture's surface should be treated as equivalent to an imagined plane interposed perpendicular to the line of sight between artist or viewer and subject on to which the subject is projected. Given the rules of optical projection, pictures so treated will present shapes on the visual field similar to those presented by their subjects seen from some point of view.

In effect, the F-relation holds for pictures made in accordance with Alberti's rule directing artists to treat every picture as a transparent surface on which the outlines of objects seen through it may be inscribed. Alberti advises painters 'to present the forms of things seen on [the picture] plane as if it were of transparent glass'.[17] Dürer's woodcut of an artist at work illustrates what Alberti has in mind quite literally (Fig. 5). This method is effective because of the laws of optics governing the projection of light on to plane surfaces: 'he who looks at a picture, done as I have described, will see a certain cross-section of a visual pyramid' presenting rays of light equivalent to those which might be presented by the object itself.[18] Albertian pictures satisfy the F-relation because the definition of the visual field and Alberti's recipe for drawing in perspective are one and the same.

It follows that pictures not produced in accordance with Alberti's rule will not satisfy the F-relation. Pictures which are projections on to interposed planes that are either not flat or not perpendicular to the line of sight between artist and subject conform to the F-relation only in special conditions—when viewed from oblique angles or in bent mirrors

---

[17] Leon Battista Alberti, *On Painting*, trans. John R. Spencer, rev. edn. (New Haven: Yale University Press, 1966), 51.　　　　　　　　　　　　　　　　　[18] Ibid. 52.

(Fig. 6). Perhaps the best-known example of such an 'anamorphic' picture is the skull which stretches across the floor in Holbein's *Ambassadors* (Fig. 7).[19] The visual field shapes presented by anamorphs obviously do not resemble those presented by their subjects from any viewpoint, but nevertheless they 'look like' and are identifiable as of their subjects. One might reply that the F-relation need hold only for anamorphs when viewed under special, intended conditions (e.g. from oblique angles or in curved mirrors), but I would point out that such trick pictures are actually meant to be seen from both 'special' and 'ordinary' viewpoints, since the effect produced by the former depends on noticing a contrast with the latter.

In any case, caricatures deliberately violate Alberti's rule. There is no point of view from which Baroness Thatcher presents a shape in the visual field similar to that presented by a Gerald Scarfe caricature, which, needless to say, depicts her none the less. Peacocke recognizes that he must account for such flagrant disregard of the F-relation. Conceding that they are not F-related to their subjects, he proposes instead that caricatures are F-related to correspondingly distorted hypothetical three-dimensional models of their subjects.[20] Scarfe's caricature represents the Baroness because it is F-related to something like a *Spitting Image* puppet, and the puppet represents her.

One difficulty with this is that it hardly seems useful to postulate hypothetical models for all of the large body of pictures which are not perspectival projections of their subjects. How could the split-style pictures of the Kwakiutl be reproduced, hypothetically or otherwise, in three dimensions (see Fig. 2)? And even if appropriate models can be envisioned, it remains mysterious how the relationship between them and the objects they model can stand less in need of explanation than that between pictures and their subjects. A three-dimensional construction based on Picasso's cubist portrait of Ambroise Vollard may be experienced as similar to the art dealer in some sense, but not in the sense that it is presented in a region of the visual field similar in shape to that in which he could be presented from some point of view (Fig. 8). What reason do we have to suppose that the relationship between *Vollard* and Vollard is not irreducibly pictorial?

Finally, some pictures render objects and scenes in ways that can only be represented in two dimensions. No animal or three-dimensional

[19] Jurgis Baltrušaitis, *Anamorphic Art*, trans. W. J. Strachan (Cambridge: Chadwych–Healey, 1977), reproduces a wealth of fascinating examples.
[20] Peacocke, 'Depiction', 397.

Fig. 5. Albrecht Dürer, Artist drawing on a 'picture-window'

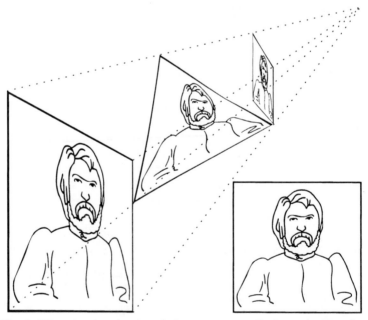

Fig. 6. 'Distortions' on interposed planes not perpendicular to the line of sight

Fig. 7. Detail, Hans Holbein, *The Ambassadors*

model of an animal presents shapes in the visual field resembling those shown in an Australian 'X-ray' picture (Fig. 9). And the trident illusion looks both two- and three-pronged in a paradoxical way not explicable by the F-relation (Fig. 10). It is certainly not the Albertian projection of a trident, actual or hypothetical.

Though each of these pictures violates the F-relation, I think we would be reluctant to deny that they are pictures which do, in some relevant sense, resemble what they depict. That many of the examples I have just given disregard the canons of perspective representation indicates the F-relation's commitment to Alberti's equation of the picture surface with an interposed plane.

But F-relation problems are not limited to spatial representation. Analogous difficulties arise in the case of colour. Pictures are generally experienced as similar in colour to their subjects. This might be explained by saying that a picture must present a region of the visual field

Fig. 8. Pablo Picasso, *Portrait of Ambroise Vollard*, 1910

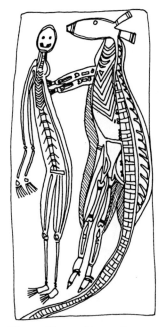

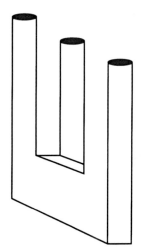

Fig. 9. X-ray picture of man
and kangaroo, after native
Australian bark painting

Fig. 10. Trident illusion

experienced as similar in colour to the colour which might be presented
by its subject seen under certain conditions of lighting. For example, in
an academic landscape, foreground grass is painted with brown paint;
yet it is experienced as similar to grass because in the twilight lighting
conditions once considered ideal for painting nature scenes, grass is
indeed experienced as brown in colour.[21]

Nevertheless, the colours which may be used to represent grass are
not constrained by the chromatic version of the F-relation: nothing in
principle prevents red paint from being used to depict green grass.
Granted, paintings which represent objects as 'miscoloured' are often
perceived as misrepresenting their subjects, as are Andy Warhol's Day-
Glo portraits of Marilyn Monroe and Elvis Presley. But untrue colours
do not always look awry. Matisse's use of rose skin tones shows that

---

[21] Grass is brown-toned when seen through a 'Claude glass', a darkened mirror used
to replicate twilight lighting conditions in academic painting.

colours used to represent skin may depict and may be experienced as similar in colour to skin, even though skin is not normally experienced as that colour.

Pictures are experienced as like their subjects in some respects, under some conditions, but not necessarily in the way the F-relation requires. They may be experienced as similar to their subjects under Albertian conditions, anamorphic conditions, caricatural conditions, cubist conditions, split-style conditions, and countless others. Peacocke has failed to identify a similarity that is representation-independent. The allegedly representation-independent notion of visual field similarity depends in fact on internalizing Alberti's conception of picturing. Experienced similarity holds only between pictures and objects as they may be seen in pictures.

Does the F-relation at least explain those pictures which do conform to Albertian principles? I doubt it. Once we have seen how our understanding of pictorial similarity depends on internalizing the Albertian conception of depiction by identifying the picture surface with the visual field, we may wonder whether there is any reason to postulate the visual field as a mental representation with the properties of Alberti's interposed plane.

Peacocke introduced the F-relation in the first place to explain visual experiences like those of the trees and the envelope. Yet, far from providing independent evidence for the visual field, experiences of this kind may be a symptom of our ability to view the world as if seen on a picture surface. James J. Gibson has urged that the visual field 'is simply the pictorial mode of visual perception, and it depends in the last analysis not on conditions of stimulation but on conditions of attitude. The visual field is a product of the chronic habit of civilized men of seeing the world as a picture.'[22] We experience the nearby tree as bigger than the distant one because we are able to experience objects as if they were pictured.

Unexpected support for Gibson's claim comes from cross-cultural research in pictorial perception. When shown pictures, such as Figure 11, containing ambiguous depth cues, 'unsophisticated African subjects',

[22] James J. Gibson, 'The Visual Field and the Visual World', *Psychological Review*, 59 (1952), 149–51. See also *idem*, 'The Information Contained in Pictures', in Edward Reed and Rebecca Jones (eds.), *Reasons for Realism* (Hillsdale, NJ: Lawrence Erlbaum, 1982), 269–83.

Fig. 11. Drawing used to test pictorial depth perception

as they are described, apparently do not see depth.[23] Of course, these people can interpret pictures, since they identify man, spear, elephant, antelope, and landscape. What they do not do, at least at first, is recognize that the elephant is distant and elephant-sized, rather than nearby and minuscule. The reason may lie in a failure to treat certain contents of experience in the special way Albertian perceivers do.

It is possible that, having internalized picturing as part of our visual conception of the world, we routinely perceive the world as if it were pictured. If so, then it is not the visual field but our mastery of the Albertian canons of depiction which explains why we are willing to say that trees at variable distances are different in size or that a rectangular object has different shapes from different viewpoints.

The appeal of the F-relation reflects its connection to a pictorial tradition which still dominates our conceptions of pictorial representation and vision. According to this tradition, a correctly made picture is one treated as an imagined interposed plane. But to identify the picture surface with the Albertian plane and the Albertian plane with the visual field is to internalize the Albertian picture surface as the visual field. And if we explain subjective properties of visual experience in terms of Albertian depiction, then it should come as no surprise that Albertian pictures seem to be explained in terms of subjective properties

[23] See Jan B. Deregowski, 'Illusion and Culture', in R. L. Gregory and E. H. Gombrich (eds.), *Illusion in Art and Nature* (London: Duckworth, 1973), 161–91. For an excellent review of the literature, see Rebecca K. Jones and Margaret A. Hagen, 'A Perspective on Cross-Cultural Picture Perception', in Margaret A. Hagen (ed.), *The Perception of Pictures* (New York: Academic Press, 1980), 2: 193–226.

of experience. But it is a mistake to use visual field similarity to explain depiction, Albertian or otherwise.

1.4 The Diversity Constraint

There is something to be learned about vision and visual concepts from this conclusion. If pictures are, as few would deny, visual representations whose meaning we grasp at least in part through visual processing, then vision must be flexible enough to accommodate depiction's diversity. We can visually identify the subjects of pictures that violate the F-relation in a great variety of ways. Cubist pictures, split-style pictures, pictures in axonometric or reversed perspective, pictures which distort their subjects to ridicule them—none of these are experienced as similar to their subjects as seen on a visual field, yet we can see what each represents. If pictures are visual objects, then their diversity shows that vision must be more dynamic and flexible than we might at first imagine.

I impose the following constraint on an adequate theory of depiction. Such a theory must explain the full range of pictorial styles and types, not just the Albertian pictures that some consider to be the epitome of picturing. It should explain how Constable's *Salisbury Cathedral*, the cubist *Vollard*, and the Kwakiutl split-style picture all depict their subjects. In recognition of the multiplicity of ways pictures represent, I call this the 'diversity constraint'.

As I believe my discussion of Peacocke's theory shows, failing to explain the diverse range of pictorial styles, to specify similarities that all pictures share with their subjects, is tantamount to failing to meet the independence challenge.

1.5 Resemblance Relativized

The phenomenon of pictorial diversity is one of the central themes of Gombrich's *Art and Illusion*. Gombrich argues that the diverse history of pictorial representation, from Lascaux to medieval book illustration, Renaissance perspective, and impressionism's colour experiments, belies the myth of the innocent eye. The eye is not innocent, because depiction cannot be explained by perception alone; sight is informed by the cultural and the cognitive.[24] Although Gombrich endorses a perceptual

---

[24] Gombrich, *Art and Illusion*, 298.

theory (to be discussed in Chapter 2), that theory is independent of his ideas about the cultural education of the art-perceiving eye. Can the resemblance theory take advantage of Gombrich's insights about the cultural and cognitive dimensions of depiction?

One might think that if there is an indefinite number of ways that pictures can be (experienced as) similar to their subjects, with no single similarity in common, then pictorial resemblance is relative to context. On this view, every picture belongs to a 'system of representation', defined by a characteristic set of salient similarities.[25] The paintings of Lascaux, Old Kingdom Egypt, and Byzantium, the Kwakiutl bird, and the 1910 *Vollard* each belong to a different system; each resembles its subject in respects determined by its system.

No picture is seen with an innocent eye, because we come to pictures primed with beliefs, expectations, and attitudes about systems of representation. Gombrich called these beliefs the 'mental set' or 'cognitive schema' making up the 'beholder's share' in interpreting pictures. Identifying what any given picture represents involves recognizing its similarity to its subject in respects associated with its system of representation. Different systems of depiction establish different networks of salient similarities; these similarities are visible only in light of the appropriate mental set, and correctly interpreting a picture requires the ability to see how it resembles its subject in respects defined by its system.

On this account, resemblance is relative, but not, it is hoped, representation-dependent. Noticing similarities between a picture and its subject requires knowledge of the picture's *system*, not of what the picture represents. Once they recognize that *Vollard* is a cubist picture, viewers can go about seeking typically cubist similarities between the picture and familiar objects. If they are successful in seeing what the picture resembles in a cubist manner, they will have identified its subject. What a picture represents is determined by what it resembles, and what it resembles is determined by its system.

By relativizing pictorial resemblance to system of representation, this view honours the diversity constraint. Picasso's cubist portrait of Vollard and the more traditional one reproduced in *The Vollard Suite* represent the art dealer by resembling him within different systems of

[25] See Manns, 'Representation, Relativism, and Resemblance', 281–7; Patrick Maynard, 'Depiction, Vision and Convention', *American Philosophical Quarterly*, 9 (1972), 243–6; Karen Neander, 'Pictorial Representation: A Matter of Resemblance', *British Journal of Aesthetics*, 27 (1987), 213; and David Novitz, 'Picturing', *Journal of Aesthetics and Art Criticism*, 34 (1975), 144–55.

representation, one cubist, the other Albertian. This explains what the two portraits have in common—they resemble and portray Vollard—and how it is they differ—they resemble Vollard in different ways, consistent with different systems of representation.

This also explains why pictures in unfamiliar systems can sometimes strike us as artificial, stylized, or even distorted. Such judgements are the result of trying to interpret a picture relative to the wrong system. What is jarring in our experience of the cubist *Vollard* is a consequence of the misapprehension that it should resemble Vollard in the way the 1915 *Vollard* does. Similar misclassifications are at the root of the infamous responses to Duchamps's *Nude Descending a Staircase* as 'a hurricane in a shingle factory' and to the murals in San Francisco's Rincon Annex Post Office as distorted because 'our ancestors did not have square heads'.

However, saying that a picture's similarity to its subject is seen in light of the system it belongs to is not enough to answer the independence challenge. We must also be sure that identification of its system is independent of knowledge of its subject. But how do we identify a picture's system?

The short answer is that we tell a picture's system by looking at it. A cubist picture, surely, looks cubist; an ukiyo-e picture looks ukiyo-e; and an impressionist one looks impressionist. The longer answer notes that if a picture's system depends on its visual properties, these can be either representational or non-representational properties.

Pictures' non-representational visual properties may be classed as representationally 'invariant' because variations in them make no difference to what is represented.[26] Impressionism, for instance, is characterized by the use of fuzzy lines, but since all impressionist pictures have fuzzy lines, fuzziness of line holds no representational significance for impressionism. Few systems, however, are distinguishable by their invariant, non-representational properties, and none by non-representational properties alone.

The alternative is that we identify a picture's system by means of its representational properties. As Karen Neander puts it, identifying a picture's system involves 'taking note of what is represented'.[27] But if this is right, then identifying a picture's system depends on first identifying its subject. Consider one of Scarfe's drawings. Is it a caricature

[26] Kendall Walton, 'Categories of Art', *Philosophical Review*, 79 (1970), 334–67.
[27] Neander, 'Pictorial Representation', 217.

of Baroness Thatcher or an Albertian portrait of Cyrano's kinswoman? In trying to grasp what a picture such as this represents, we are guided by our knowledge that caricatures exaggerate selected features of their targets, and so seek a similarity between the huge, imperiously pushy nose in the drawing and the sharp, slightly imperious nose of Thatcher.[28] But how can we identify the picture as a caricature in the first place, without first seeing that it represents a woman with an immense nose? The problem is that if detecting a picture's resemblance to its subject depends on ascertaining its system, and if ascertaining its system requires us to identify what it represents and how, then a picture's resemblance to its subject is representation-dependent. Relativizing resemblance to system of representation fails to meet the independence challenge. Pictures may resemble their subjects relative to their system, but this fact does not explain how we interpret them.

1.6 The Phenomenology Constraint

Where does this leave the phenomenon of pictorial resemblance? There is no denying that pictures are experienced as resembling what they represent. I have urged, however, that any use of this fact to explain how pictures represent must show that pictures represent by means of representation-independent similarities. Three versions of the resemblance theory, postulating objective resemblances, subjective resemblances, and system-relative resemblances, have failed to meet this challenge. There is no reason to suppose, especially in light of the diversity of depiction, that we interpret pictures by noticing representation-independent similarities.

Let me reiterate that this is not to deny that pictures are experienced as in some sense like their subjects. My position is nicely expressed in Max Black's assessment of the resemblance theory as, 'uninformative, offering a trivial verbal substitution in place of insight. . . . The objection to saying that some paintings resemble their subjects is not that they don't, but rather that so little has been said when only this has been said.'[29]

---

[28] See Stephanie Ross, 'Caricature', *Monist*, 58 (1974), 285–93.
[29] Max Black, 'How Do Pictures Represent?' in Maurice Mandelbaum (ed.), *Art, Perception, and Reality* (Baltimore: Johns Hopkins University Press, 1972), 122.

I conclude that if we do not understand pictures by noticing resemblances, then we notice resemblances as a result of understanding pictures. An adequate theory of how pictures represent their subjects should explain how we experience them as looking like their subjects. I call this second constraint on a theory of depiction the 'phenomenology constraint'.

2

Depiction and Vision

RATHER than reducing depiction to noticing similarity, some perceptual theories try to capitalize on the complexity and variability of vision itself. The two theories described in this chapter offer alternative characterizations of the relationship between viewers' experiences of pictures and ordinary visual perception. According to the illusion theory, pictorial experience is a special case of ordinary visual experience. I express this by saying that, on the illusion theory, pictorial experience is 'continuous' with ordinary visual experience. According to the seeing-in theory, by contrast, pictorial seeing is a distinctive kind of seeing, because seeing things in pictures is 'discontinuous' with seeing them in the flesh. Neither theory, I argue, is adequate; an adequate perceptual theory must blend features of each.

2.1 The Illusion Theory

According to the illusion theory, pictures represent by taking advantage of ambiguities or failures in visual discrimination so as to cause viewers to have visual experiences as of their subjects.[1] Gombrich, the leading proponent of the illusion view, argues that 'just as a knock against the eye makes us see sparks and a strong glare an after-image, so the experienced manipulator, whether conjuror, artist or scientist, has been able to find out how to predict and trigger certain non-veridical visual experiences through the arousal of visual sensations'.[2]

Illusions, including those generated by pictures, trigger non-veridical visual experiences, but Gombrich does not mean to imply that they delude. As he repeatedly insists, it is the eye, not the mind, that is

---

[1] See Gombrich, *Art and Illusion*; *idem*, 'Illusion and Art', in R. L. Gregory and E. H. Gombrich (eds.), *Illusion in Nature and Art* (London: Duckworth, 1973), 193–243; Terence Wilkerson, 'Representation, Illusion, and Aspects', *British Journal of Aesthetics*, 18 (1978), 45–58; and Catherine Wilson, 'Illusion and Representation', *British Journal of Aesthetics*, 22 (1988), 211–21.

[2] E. H. Gombrich, 'Mirror and Map', in *The Image and the Eye*, 180.

deceived by pictures. Looking at a picture, one need not falsely believe that one sees a piazza in order for the picture to represent one. Nor is having a false belief sufficient for depiction. For example, I might be convinced that Astarte lives in the temple, but this does not explain why the temple idol depicts her. Pictures deceive in a special way. They cause illusions because when we look at them we see something which is not a piazza or a manor-house but which nevertheless causes us to have visual experiences characteristic of seeing piazzas or manor-houses. Having such an experience need not, though it sometimes may, lead one to believe that there is a piazza or a manor-house.

Even so, there is a connection between illusion and delusion. The illusion theory holds that a picture of a piazza produces a visual experience characteristic of looking at a piazza. This must mean that it causes an experience of a kind that the piazza itself might cause. To deny this is to accept that the picture might simply cause whatever sort of experience a *picture* of a piazza might prompt, and this would not explain how the picture represents a piazza. And what is an experience of a kind that the piazza itself might cause but one that would, under suitable conditions, lead one to believe, perhaps mistakenly, that one sees a piazza? As I construe it, then, the illusion theory states that a picture depicts such-and-such if and only if there are circumstances in which a viewer looking at the picture might, on the basis of her experience of it, come to believe she sees a such-and-such. Pictorial experience is 'continuous' with ordinary perceptual experience in the sense that our visual experience of an object in a picture is of a kind with our experience of the object itself.

The *possibility* of delusion is a consequence of the continuity of pictorial experience with ordinary experience. Since pictures cause experiences of a sort that, under the right conditions, could elicit true beliefs, they might, under other conditions, result in false beliefs. For example, a picture depicts Derek Parfit outside the Palazzo Ducale only if it causes an experience that, were the viewer in sight of him, could give rise to the true belief 'I see Parfit outside the Palazzo Ducale'. Such an experience could also, under the right conditions, cause me to falsely believe that I see Parfit outside the Palazzo Ducale. Illusion, to repeat, entails the potential to delude.

One problem with the illusion view is that, though it is a fair description of our experience of many pictures, it shares a flaw with resemblance theories in overlooking pictures' diversity. Pictures made according to Alberti's directions are illusionistic because, with the aid of peep-holes, mirrors, and other laboratory apparatus, they might give rise to experiences that lead one to believe that their subjects are there. But surely there are no plausible circumstances in which competent viewers could mistake line-drawings, stylizations, or many modern figurations for the objects they represent. How could anyone having the experience they have when looking at the Kwakiutl picture in Figure 2 be inclined to believe that they are seeing a bird? Could viewers of Picasso's 1910 portrait of Vollard (see Fig. 8) come to believe, on the basis of their viewing, that Vollard is there? Each of these pictures causes an experience as of its subject, but neither causes experiences that its subject itself might have caused.

The responses to pictorial diversity that were available to the resemblance view are also available to the illusion view. One is to dilute the notion of what it is to have an illusory experience. In order to account for pictures like the 1910 *Vollard* or the Kwakiutl bird, we might abandon the requirement that an illusory experience of an object be one that the object itself might have produced. However, this concession leaves the illusion theory without substance. What could it be to have an illusionary experience of an object if it is not to have an experience that the object could have evoked?

The response favoured by Gombrich in *Art and Illusion* is that pictures in diverse systems of representation give rise to illusionistic experiences in relation to the appropriate 'mental set' and background beliefs. But this response ultimately reduces understanding pictures to having the right mental schema, so that pictorial interpretation becomes a matter of belief, rather than experience. Given suitable beliefs about cubist pictures and the objects they represent, my experience of a cubist picture might be one capable of leading me to believe that its subject is there. As Max Black remarks, this is 'only a misleading way of making the obvious point that if we have learned how Picasso in his cubistic period painted a woman, we shall *know* that the painting is of a woman'.[3]

2.2 The Denial of Twofoldness

That the illusion theory violates the diversity constraint is sufficient reason to reject it. But the theory's commitment to the continuity of

---

[3] Black, 'How Do Pictures Represent?', 117.

pictorial experience with ordinary perceptual experience generates a further difficulty, one that indicates the need for an additional constraint on any adequate theory of depiction.

A theory of depiction must explain two aspects of our experience of pictures. We experience pictures as two-dimensional designed surfaces, but we also experience them as of their subjects. Gombrich characterizes the relationship between these two aspects of pictorial experience in a way that has provoked some discussion, but ultimately raises serious doubts about the illusion theory.

To have an illusionistic experience is to have the kind of experience which could, under the right conditions, cause one to believe that a picture's subject is there. Obviously, this experience must be one which is incompatible with *simultaneous* experience of the picture's physical surface features. If, in looking at a picture, I experience its design—a flat array of marks, textures, and colours—I am surely not having the sort of experience which could lead me to believe that I am looking at the robust three-dimensional surfaces of a philosopher in Venice. For this reason, illusionistic experience of a picture's subject cannot occur simultaneously with experience of its design.

For the illusion theory, the paradigm (or perhaps the ideal) of pictorial experience is *trompe-l'œil*.[4] In successful *trompe-l'œil*, information about a picture's design properties is impossible or difficult to obtain. It is no accident that among the most effective *trompe-l'œil* pictures are ceiling paintings, such as Pozzo's decoration of the vaults of St Ignatius's Church in Rome, whose surfaces are out of easy reach. In the absence of information about their designed surfaces, such pictures prompt experiences exclusively as of their subjects, and so are much more likely to deceive viewers. This is not to say that *trompe-l'œil* pictures are always deceptive; only that they are more likely to deceive viewers because they thwart awareness of their physical features.

Gombrich accepts that ordinary pictures differ from *trompe-l'œil* pictures in that ordinary pictures produce both illusionistic experiences as of their subjects and experiences of their marked, coloured surfaces. But he believes that ordinary pictures, like *trompe-l'œil*, cannot produce both experiences at the same time. Experience of a picture's subject cannot be at one and the same time experience of its surface, because

---

[4] Michael Polanyi, Foreword to M. H. Pirenne, *Optics, Painting and Photography* (Cambridge: Cambridge University Press, 1970), p. xvi, argues that awareness of a picture's design is exclusive of awareness of what it represents, and vice versa. Polanyi supports this claim by generalizing the case of *trompe-l'œil* to all pictures.

Fig. 12. Duck–rabbit

that would spoil the illusion—the experience would not be one that might lead us to believe that the picture's subject is there. We can only switch back and forth between experiences of subject and surface. Gombrich's description of Kenneth Clark's attempt to 'stalk' an illusion illustrates this nicely:

Looking at a great Velasquez he wanted to observe what went on when the brush-strokes and dabs of pigment on the canvas transformed themselves into visions of transfigured reality as he stepped back. But try as he might, stepping forward or backward, he could never hold both visions at the same time, and therefore, the answer to his problem of how it was done always seemed to elude him.[5]

Gombrich enlists further support for the non-simultaneity of the two aspects of pictorial experience from the phenomenon of attention switching, illustrated by the philosophers' mascot, the duck–rabbit (Fig. 12). Just as we can experience this picture as either a duck or a rabbit, but not both at the same time, so we must switch attention between experiences of pictures' designs and contents. However, as some readers of Gombrich have noted, switches in attention between two contents are not analogous to switches in attention between design and content. That the duck and the rabbit cannot be seen simultaneously does not show that the duck cannot be experienced together with the picture's design or that the rabbit cannot be experienced together with the same design. It is a grave mistake to suppose that no picture may be experienced

[5] Gombrich, *Art and Illusion*, 6.

simultaneously as a marked, coloured, textured surface and as what it represents. Some pictures, like the Velázquez, undoubtedly support Gombrich's conception of pictorial experience; others clearly do not. Richard Wollheim, a no less acute observer of pictures than Gombrich, writes that we are often 'led to marvel endlessly at the way in which line or brush stroke or expanse of colour is exploited to render effects or establish analogies that can only be identified representationally'.[6] Wollheim is right to insist that simultaneous awareness of a picture's content and design is central to the experience of many pictures. The use of colour in a picture such as Titian's *Flaying of Marsyas* sets up a tension between surface colour and represented colour, and an integral component of experiencing such a picture is noticing and attempting to reconcile this tension. Likewise, in some of Van Gogh's pictures, emphatic brush strokes and impasto compel viewers, with varying degrees of success, to try to reconcile the two aspects of their experience. An experience which is simultaneously that of design and content Wollheim calls 'twofold'.

Remember that it is the illusion theory's commitment to the continuity of pictorial experience with ordinary visual experience that obligates it to deny the possibility of twofoldness. An illusionistic experience of an object is an experience that the object might cause. So unless it is possible to experience the Piazza San Marco as a flat, varnished surface, an experience as of *Piazza San Marco*'s design is not part of illusionistic experience. But if we abandon the claim that pictorial experience is continuous with ordinary perceptual experience—that an experience of a picture is the kind of experience that could lead the viewer to believe that the picture's subject is there—then we have abandoned the illusion theory.

Twofoldness is a fact. That the illusion theory proves to be incompatible with twofoldness shows that it is operating with a mistaken conception of pictorial experience. Any theory of depiction which does not allow that pictorial experience may be simultaneously an experience of looking at a decorated surface and an experience of looking at what that surface represents contravenes what I shall call the 'twofoldness constraint'. Note that in keeping with the possibility of pictures like the Velázquez that Clark tried to stalk, the principle that no theory should be inconsistent with twofoldness is a deliberately weak one.

---

[6] Richard Wollheim, 'Seeing-as, Seeing-in, and Pictorial Representation', in *Art and its Objects*, 2nd edn. (Cambridge: Cambridge University Press, 1980), 216.

2.3 The Seeing-In Theory

The patronage of one Renaissance painter, scientist, and humanist has assured the prominence of another perceptual theory of depiction. In his handbook *On Painting* Leonardo da Vinci advised students to stimulate their visual imaginations by free-associating upon irregular shapes of stains on walls. He wrote:

if you look at any walls soiled with a variety of stains, or stones with variegated patterns, when you have to invent some location, you will therein be able to see a resemblance to landscapes graced with mountains, rivers, rocks, trees, plains, great valleys, and hills in many combinations. Or again you will be able to see various figures darting about, strange-looking faces and costumes, and an endless number of things which you can distil into finely-rendered forms.[7]

You can see horses in clouds, red and green after-images in the McCullough grid, the ghosts of figures in Pollock's *Out of the Web*, and whole scenes in the stained walls of Leonardo's workshop.

Wollheim calls this phenomenon 'seeing-in', and proposes that pictures' subjects are seen in the marks, colours, and textures of pictures' surfaces. The difference between seeing a face in a cloud and seeing one in a picture is that the latter is governed by an intentional standard of correctness. We see a picture correctly when we see in it the scenes that the artist intended to be seen in it. A representation depicts *x* if and only if a suitable viewer is able to see *x* in it, and it is in virtue of this fact that the picture is intended to represent *x*.[8]

The seeing-in theory of depiction accommodates not only twofoldness but also pictures' diversity and phenomenology. We experience *Piazza San Marco* as similar in certain respects to the place which is its subject, because we are able to see the piazza in the drawing. Moreover, we are able to see things in pictures belonging to diverse representational styles. To grasp what Figure 2 represents just by looking at it is, at the very least, to see a bird in the picture. Finally, seeing one thing in another implies a simultaneous, or twofold, experience of the surface in which something is seen and of the object seen in it.

Wollheim is explicitly pessimistic about the possibility of any detailed account of seeing-in. 'Seeing-in', he writes, 'is triggered off by the presence within the field of vision of a differentiated surface. Not

---

[7] Leonardo da Vinci, *On Painting*, trans. Martin Kemp and Margaret Walker (New Haven: Yale University Press, 1989), 222.

[8] Wollheim, 'Seeing-as, Seeing-in'; see also *idem, Painting as an Art*, chs. 1 and 2.

all differentiated surfaces will have this effect, but I doubt that anything significant can be said about exactly what a surface must be like for it to have this effect.'⁹ An analysis of depiction in terms of seeing-in may well be true, but at the very least it stands incomplete. This admission can give rise to a serious objection. Without an account of the perceptual basis of seeing-in, what is there to rule out the possibility that seeing-in is not a perceptual process at all? Compare the seeing-in theory with a convention theory of depiction, which holds that pictures are symbols with conventional meanings, as are linguistic symbols.¹⁰ Since identifying what symbol a picture is, is necessary for grasping what it symbolizes, such a theory *a fortiori* satisfies the twofoldness constraint. Moreover, recognizing that pictures are visual symbols, the convention theorist might allow that, as a matter of fact, pictures depict things only if those things can be seen in them—Goodman makes just such a concession.¹¹ But the symbol theorist will also insist that what explains seeing-in has to do not with facts about vision but with our mastery of pictorial symbol systems. Anything can be seen in anything else, and we see a piazza in Canaletto's canvas because it is a piazza symbol. Only once you know what a picture symbolizes, do you see its subject in it. In other words, the convention theorist might advocate a 'cognitive' conception of seeing-in over a 'perceptual' one.

Since I have some doubts about the viability of a non-perceptual convention theory of depiction, I am inclined to grant that perceptual mechanisms do underlie seeing-in. Nevertheless, Wollheim's scepticism about the possibility of giving an account of these mechanisms means that the only content his theory is left with lies in the claim that seeing-in is a distinctive kind of seeing.

In particular, seeing-in is to be contrasted with the more common and general phenomenon of seeing-as, which is continuous with ordinary seeing.¹² Wollheim claims that seeing-in differs from seeing-as in three ways. My view is that since the first two differences are spurious, the weight of the distinction between the two kinds of seeing falls on the third difference, the fact that seeing-in, unlike seeing-as, is twofold.

⁹ Wollheim, *Painting as an Art*, 46, see also 359–60 n. 5.
¹⁰ Jenefer Robinson, 'Some Remarks on Goodman's Language Theory of Pictures', *British Journal of Aesthetics*, 19 (1979), 70–1.
¹¹ Nelson Goodman, *Problems and Projects* (Indianapolis: Bobbs–Merrill, 1972), 123.
¹² The classic discussion of seeing-as is Ludwig Wittgenstein, *Philosophical Investigations*, trans. G. E. M. Anscombe, 2nd edn. (Oxford: Basil Blackwell, 1958), 193–214.

Fig. 13. Jean Siméon Chardin, *Soap Bubbles*, *c.*1733–4

Wollheim argues, first, that seeing-as and seeing-in have different kinds of contents. The contents of seeing-in include states of affairs as well as particular objects and properties. Thus in Chardin's *Soap Bubbles* I see not only particular objects, including a bubble, a man, and a child, but also that the man is blowing a bubble to divert a child (Fig. 13). The contents of seeing-as, by contrast, are always particular objects and properties, never states of affairs. I can see Chardin's picture as a soap bubble, as a man, and as a child, but I see that a man is blowing the bubble to divert a child *in* the picture.

It is true that seeing-in and seeing-as have different grammars, as it were. 'I see . . . in *P*' can be completed with a proposition, whereas 'I see *P* as . . .' cannot be. But this does not show that the experiences on which these statements are based have different kinds of contents—unless we adhere to the implausible principle that grammatical differences always have philosophical implications.

An examination of ordinary, non-pictorial experience shows, I think, that the differences between seeing, seeing-as, and seeing-in do not reflect differences in their contents, but rather differences in how those contents are related to perceivers.

To say that the experiences of seeing-in and seeing-as have distinct contents is to say that one represents the world as satisfying kinds of properties that the other does not. But, in ordinary vision, what more is there to the experience of seeing a state of affairs than there is to the experience of seeing the things which, related to each other, constitute that state of affairs? Surely, the contents of the experiences of seeing that a man blows a bubble and seeing a man and a bubble in a certain relation with each other are one and the same.

The difference between seeing states of affairs and seeing things lies not in the experience, but in the way that the experience is related to perceivers. First, seeing a state of affairs, unlike seeing things, puts a perceiver in a position to judge whether or not the state of affairs obtains. Second, seeing that a state of affairs obtains requires that the perceiver have concepts of the objects, properties, and happenings comprising the state of affairs. Seeing that a man is blowing a bubble requires possession of the concepts 'man', 'bubble', and 'blows', whereas seeing a man blowing a bubble does not. You can see a man blowing a bubble without knowing what a bubble is; you cannot see *that* he is blowing a bubble without a concept of a bubble.[13] In sum, the experiences of seeing a man blowing a bubble and seeing that a man is blowing a bubble have the same contents, but when I see that a man is blowing a bubble, my conceptual and epistemic relation to my experience changes.

Corresponding points can be made about the content of pictorial experience. There is nothing more to the content of the experience of

[13] Cf. Fred Dretske, *Seeing and Knowing* (Chicago: University of Chicago Press, 1969), 4–77; *idem*, 'Conscious Experience', *Mind*, 102 (1993), 263–83; and Alec Hyslop, 'Seeing Through Seeing-in', *British Journal of Aesthetics*, 26 (1986), 371–9.

seeing that a man is blowing a bubble *in* a picture than there is in seeing the picture *as* a man blowing a bubble. The difference between them lies in how they are related to the conceptual resources and epistemic stances of the picture's viewers—to the role they play in viewers' larger cognitive lives.

The second contrast that Wollheim draws between seeing-as and seeing-in is that the former is bound by the 'localization requirement': when *x* is seen as *y*, some part of *x* must be seen as *y*. By contrast, there need be no part of a picture *in* which I see that a mob of people is angry or that a man is blowing bubbles and a child is being amused. However, this point depends on the previous one; seeing-as is necessarily localized only if its content is necessarily particular and non-propositional. If it is possible to see a picture *as* a man blowing a bubble for the amusement of a child, then there will be no proper part of the picture seen as bubble blowing and child diversion; seeing-as will not be bound by the localization requirement.

The weight of the argument that seeing-in is a distinctive kind of seeing rests by default on the final point of contrast between seeing-as and seeing-in: namely, that twofoldness is a property of the latter, but not the former. Wollheim observes that one cannot at one and the same time see *x* as *y* and be aware of the features of *x* which sustain seeing *y*—it is necessary to switch attention between *x* and *y*. Yet seeing *x in y* means simultaneously attending to the features of *x* which sustain an experience of *y* in it. Pictorial seeing is discontinuous with other varieties of seeing, because it alone provides for the possibility of twofold experience.

But if it is to distinguish seeing things in pictures from all other kinds of seeing, twofoldness is not merely a possibility, it is essential. Wollheim writes that, when looking at pictures, 'it is not just permitted to, but required of, me that I attend simultaneously to object and medium'.[14] Let us call the position that twofoldness is *essential* to pictorial experience 'strong twofoldness', and correspondingly, the position that twofoldness is merely *consistent* with pictorial experience, 'weak twofoldness'.

2.4 Strong Twofoldness

Unless it can be shown that pictorial experience is strongly twofold, there is no basis for the claim that seeing-in, the seeing applicable to

---

[14] Wollheim, 'Seeing-as, Seeing-in', 213.

pictures, is a distinctive kind of seeing. But while twofoldness is un-doubtedly a feature of pictures, it is arguable whether it is essential to depiction.

One argument that Wollheim gives for strong twofoldness is moti-vated by normative standards for the appreciation of pictures. It is a virtue of pictures that their viewers get caught up in noticing the way marks, colours, and textures on their surfaces produce representational effects, and this can only be explained by the fact that when we look at pictures we attend both to their design properties and the objects seen in them.[15] Wollheim compares painting with poetry, the appreciation of which mandates simultaneous awareness of both the sound and the meaning of words.

The obvious objection to this is that it invalidly generalizes from what is required of experience of one class of pictures to all pictures: it takes art pictures—indeed, art pictures of a particular 'painterly' style—as paradigmatic. Is twofoldness a necessary, let alone desirable, feature of anatomy textbook illustrations, magazine advertisements, or family snapshots? Moreover, it is doubtful that twofoldness is a virtue of all art pictures, or is essential to a pictorial aesthetic. From the fact that appreciation of some pictures requires twofoldness, it does not follow that appreciation of all pictures does. To deflate the analogy with liter-ature, some pictures may be less like poetry and more like prose, in which the sound of words is of little or no importance compared with their meaning.

A second consideration in favour of strong twofoldness is the need to explain the phenomenon of perceptual constancy.[16] When a picture is viewed from an oblique angle, the shapes of the objects represented are not experienced, as the rules of optics would predict, as distorted. A likely explanation of this constancy of represented shape is that the viewer is aware not only of what is represented but also of the orienta-tion of the surface on which it is represented, so she is able to compen-sate accordingly.

However, there are a number of problems with the hypothesis that perceptual constancy supports strong twofoldness. To begin with, the

[15] See also Michael Podro, 'Depiction and the Golden Calf', in Norman Bryson, Michael Ann Holly, and Keith Moxley (eds.), *Visual Theory: Painting and Interpretation* (New York: Harper Collins, 1991), 163–89.

[16] Michael Kubovy, *The Psychology of Perspective and Renaissance Art* (Cambridge: Cambridge University Press, 1986), contains an excellent discussion of perceptual con-stancy and the historical development of techniques that enhance it.

information that the visual system requires to compensate for surface orientation may be made available through switches of attention, rather than through simultaneous twofold attention. Moreover, supposing perceptual constancy does require that vision maintain continuous contact with pictures' surfaces, it does not follow that viewers must be 'visually aware' of their design features. The required information may be processed along with a wealth of other visual information at a 'subpersonal' level.

In any case, perceptual constancy is not essential to depiction. After all, someone viewing Pozzo's ceiling in the church of St Ignatius in Rome from a mark in the middle of the nave sees a lofty architecture of columns and arches reaching for an open sky in which the heavenly host appears. Granted, when viewed from any other position, the columns and arches warp and tilt alarmingly, no doubt because design information necessary to compensate for the viewing angle is unavailable.[17] But this proves only that information about a picture's surface is necessary for perceptual constancy, not that constancy is a prerequisite for depiction. When seen obliquely, Pozzo's ceiling still depicts, and is experienced as of, cherubs and columns, albeit rather twisted ones. And if perceptual constancy is not necessary for depiction, the argument that twofoldness is necessary for constancy does not show that it is essential to depiction.

Wollheim's third reason for endorsing strong twofoldness is that seeing-in is a distinctive kind of seeing because it has a distinctive phenomenology. Twofoldness is the mark of this phenomenology. However, the existence of *trompe-l'œil* pictures—pictures, experiences of which are experiences of their subjects, but which typically preclude experiences of their design properties—is incompatible not only with strong twofoldness but also with the hope that pictures always have a distinctive phenomenology. *Trompe-l'œil* demonstrates that what it is like to see an object in a picture need not be discontinuous with what it is like to see that object itself in plain sight.

In defense of strong twofoldness, one might respond that pictures do have a distinctive phenomenology, but that *trompe-l'œil* pictures do not share this phenomenology because we do not see them *as pictures*. We do not see a *trompe-l'œil* as a picture because, by definition we see only what it represents. Twofoldness, the argument goes, is essential only to seeing pictures *as pictures*. But it simply begs the question to assert that

---

[17] See Pirenne, *Optics, Painting and Photography*, 81–4.

twofoldness explains the distinctive phenomenology of our experiences of pictures seen as pictures, if what we mean by seeing pictures as pictures is seeing them in a way that excludes *trompe-l'œil*. What we are trying to understand is what it is to see a picture as a picture, and there is no reason to deny that we see *trompe-l'œil* pictures as pictures. A theory of pictorial experience must embrace *trompe-l'œil* together with more painterly forms of depiction.

None of Wollheim's three arguments for strong twofoldness prevails. But, as I have argued, strong twofoldness is all that distinguishes seeing-in from other forms of seeing and all that gives substance to the seeing-in theory. There is therefore no reason to believe that seeing-in is a distinctive kind of seeing. The seeing-in theory is vacuous. This does not mean that we do not see things in pictures, but the fact that we do so does not explain how they depict. Indeed, seeing-in may be acknowledged by theories, such as the symbol theory, which reject perceptual explanations of depiction altogether.

2.5 The Twofoldness Constraint

This discussion of the illusion and seeing-in theories and their competing analyses of the twofoldness of pictorial experience suggests the following synthesis. Some pictures, *contra* Gombrich, are experienced simultaneously as designed surfaces and as of their subjects; other pictures, *contra* Wollheim, preclude twofoldness.

Pictures may be thought of as arranged along a spectrum, at one end of which lie *trompe-l'œil* pictures, experiences of which are experiences of their subjects, but which generally preclude, or at least suppress, experiences of decorated, marked, and painted surfaces. At some intermediate point on the spectrum lie pictures which afford one kind of experience or the other, but not both simultaneously. Gombrich's conception of depiction, taking Kenneth Clark's experiences stalking an illusion in a Velázquez painting as its model, gravitates towards this middle ground. At the other extreme lie pictures typical experiences of which are simultaneously experiences of their subjects and experiences of flat, pigmented surfaces. Van Gogh's wheat fields, de Kooning's Woman series, and Lichtenstein's Ben Day-dotted paintings congregate at this pole, which may be described, very loosely, as 'painterly'. Experiences of these pictures may properly be described as twofold.

An advantage of the notion of such a spectrum is that it construes twofoldness as a matter of degree. It is not the case, as Gombrich and Wollheim maintain, that twofoldness is all or nothing. Rather, we may ask of any picture to what extent it fosters or inhibits simultaneous experience of its content and its design.

It is tempting to conflate the spectrum of twofoldness with the diverse range of pictorial styles. It would seem that Albertian pictures gravitate towards the illusionistic, and that what Gombrich called 'conceptual' pictures gravitate towards the painterly. However, this would be a mistake. An Albertian picture may allow for a twofold experience— I find this to be a strange effect of photo-realist painting—and a non-Albertian one may not.

Wollheim outlines a notion of what he calls 'naturalism', which has to do with the relation between experiences of a picture's surface and its subject. In particular, naturalism comes about through a reciprocity between the two aspects of our experience of certain pictures.[18] Such a notion of naturalism is plausible, but it is quite independent of 'naturalism' understood as referring to pictures made in accordance with Albertian prescriptions.[19] When they look at pictures like Figure 2, the Kwakiutl may experience a naturalistic reciprocity between surface features and representational features.

Let me close by revising the twofoldness constraint to take into account the distinction between its strong and weak versions, rejecting the former. An adequate perceptual theory of depiction should explain the full range of our experience of pictures, including those which are twofold, those which require a shift in attention from content to design and back again, and those rare pictures whose contents we experience even when their designed surfaces are not visible.

---

[18] Wollheim, *Painting as an Art*, 73.

[19] I argue elsewhere that judgements of the 'realism' of some systems, such as Alberti's, depend on contextually variable conceptions of the kinds of contents that pictures should have. See Dominic Lopes, 'Pictorial Realism', *Journal of Aesthetics and Art Criticism*, 53 (1995).

PART TWO
Pictures as Symbols

3
Goodman's Symbol Theory

I BEGAN by enquiring how we can explain the difference between Canaletto's pictorial representation of a Venetian piazza and Barzini's linguistic one. Part One surveyed three versions of the obvious answer to this question: namely, that, unlike words, we see what pictures represent. I have nowhere denied that pictures might visually resemble their subjects, or cause experiences of a kind their subjects could cause, or enable us to see their subjects in them. But I have given reasons to doubt that resemblance, illusion, or seeing-in explain depiction, for they fail to accommodate the diversity and twofoldness of depiction. Since perceptual theories have reached an impasse, it is not unreasonable to take seriously the proposal that a theory of depiction should take as its starting-point not the differences between pictures and language but their similarities.

Since this proposal is likely to meet with some incredulity on the part of committed perceptualists, I begin by considering the implications of the language model for perceptual theories of depiction. Only then do I turn to what is justifiably the most prominent symbol theory of depiction, Nelson Goodman's in his book *Languages of Art*.

3.1 Pictures and Symbols

It is natural to be apprehensive about using language as a model for depiction. Comparisons between pictures and language flagrantly contradict our intuitions about their differences. But nobody claims that pictures are just the same as linguistic utterances. Whether our apprehensions are warranted depends on precisely what features of language and depiction are taken to be analogous. That pictures are like language in certain crucial respects need not trample our sense of their differences.

Let me briefly illustrate how making links between pictures and language can be either obfuscatory or enlightening. One important property of language is captured in Frege's dictum that the fundamental unit of linguistic meaning is the proposition, something that is true or false.

But Gombrich insists that 'a picture can no more be true or false than a statement can be blue or green'.[1] Assuming that this is correct, we will shed no light on depiction by construing pictures as propositional.[2] If language is essentially propositional and pictures are not, then pictures cannot be usefully modelled on language's propositional structure.

Contrast this with a second way of modelling pictures upon language. One fact about language given prominence by some theorists is that linguistic utterances are used to perform speech-acts—they are used to make assertions, issue warnings, and the like. Clearly, we can learn something about pictures by examining how they might be used to perform similar acts. Just as I can communicate my belief about corruption in local politics by saying to you 'The mayor takes kickbacks', so I can also do so by drawing and displaying a cartoon of the mayor carrying a briefcase bulging with banknotes. Both an utterance and a picture can be used to perform what is perhaps the very same 'speech'-act.

Propositionality does not model depiction well; speech-act theory might. The lesson is that the value of any language model of depiction depends on what features of language we incorporate in the model.

Language models of picturing fall into two categories, depending on how friendly they are to perceptual theories of picturing. 'Antiperceptualist' linguistic models of depiction are those which are incompatible with perceptual theories of depiction, whereas 'compatibilist' models do not rule out the possibility that pictures can be explained perceptually.

Apprehension about language models of depiction rests on the assumption that linguistic models are invariably anti-perceptual. Sceptics typically believe that explaining depiction on the model of language infects pictures with the arbitrariness commonly thought to be the hallmark of language. However, there exist linguistic models of depiction which emphasize links between pictures and certain features of language without obviously excluding perceptual theories.

Take the speech-act model just mentioned. The suggestion that pictures are used in acts such as making assertions or issuing warnings is

---

[1] Gombrich, *Art and Illusion*, 89.

[2] The claim that pictures cannot have propositional content has been challenged by numerous theorists. See Marcia Eaton, 'Truth in Pictures', *Journal of Aesthetics and Art Criticism*, 39 (1980), 15–24; and Carolyn Korsmeyer, 'Pictorial Assertion', *Journal of Aesthetics and Art Criticism*, 43 (1985), 257–65. Nevertheless, it seems that propositional contents are not fundamental in depiction as they are in language. See Sects. 4.3 and 4.4 and Ch. 6.

not incompatible with perceptual explanations of depiction. David Novitz, for instance, analyses the ways in which pictures are used in communicative acts, but also holds that what acts a particular picture can be used to perform depends in part on what it resembles.[3] A picture may be used to inform voters of corruption at city hall in part because it resembles the mayor carrying a money-bag.

In *Languages of Art* Goodman argues that just as words, descriptions, and sentences are symbols belonging to languages, so pictures are symbols in systems of representation. At a minimum, symbol systems consist in sets of marks (or designs) together with principles mapping them on to domains comprised of their subjects. Letters, words, texts, musical scores, pictures, diagrams, maps, models, dances, and plays are all symbols correlated with sounds, objects, states of affairs, theories, and even other symbols.[4] Pictures are obviously symbols on this definition because they belong to systems in which their designs are correlated with other objects. I shall call any theory of depiction modelled upon such a conception of symbolization a 'symbol theory'.

The claim that pictures are symbols in this sense is not incompatible with perceptual explanations of depiction. Nothing in the symbol model rules out pictures being correlated with, and standing for, their subjects because they resemble them or provide for illusionistic experiences of them or enable us to see things in them. Indeed, some perceptual theorists happily grant that pictures are symbols—they are simply symbols whose symbolic function is mediated in crucial ways by perceptual processes.[5] A theory of depiction may, without inconsistency, explain pictures as both symbolic and perceptual.

As well as proposing that pictures belong to symbol systems, Goodman adds that the principles of correlation constituting pictorial symbol systems are *not* governed by perceptual processes. Depiction is arbitrary relative to perceptual facts: 'almost anything may stand for almost anything else'.[6] As notorious as it has proved to be, however, Goodman provides little if any argument in support of this thoroughgoing anti-perceptualism. *Languages of Art* proceeds with extraordinary insouciance from a critique of the resemblance theory of depiction to the claim that what a picture symbolizes is a matter of what symbol system or language it belongs to, as if the resemblance theory were the only

---

[3] Novitz, 'Picturing'.
[4] Goodman, *Languages of Art*, p. xi.
[5] e.g. Wollheim, *Painting as an Art*, 361 n. 23.
[6] Goodman, *Languages of Art*, 5.

possible perceptual theory. For this reason, Goodman's adherence to an incompatibilist version of the symbol model is merely tendentious.[7]

In this section I have wanted merely to demonstrate that there are a variety of ways to model depiction on language, some compatible with perceptual explanations of picturing, others not. The compatibilist option is often overlooked, and this oversight feeds our apprehensions about linguistic models of depiction. Yet the compatibilist suggestion that pictures belong to systems of symbols is Goodman's central insight. It is, I believe, an insight critical to the development of an adequate *perceptual* theory of depiction. Only once we have recognized what the language model has to offer does it become possible to rethink the perceptual mechanisms that account for how pictures symbolize.

3.2 Seven Theses

In no small measure, the suggestiveness of *Languages of Art*, or at least those chapters concerning depiction, derives from an abundance of novel thoughts conjoined with an absence of cohesive supporting argument.[8] I have encapsulated Goodman's views on depiction in seven theses. The failure to recognize that not all these theses entail or are entailed by the others poses certain dangers for readers of *Languages of Art*. Those who try unsuccessfully to systematize Goodman's views will be tempted to dismiss them for their lack of logical cohesiveness. Others, who wrongly assume them to form a coherent structure, will be tempted to take the implausibility or falsity of some to impeach all. Succumbing to either temptation is unfortunate, I think, because some of what Goodman says is salvageable.

The seven theses divide naturally into two groups. The first four describe the semantic or logical structure of depiction, categorizing the relations of correspondence that hold between pictures and their subjects. These theses stress analogies between pictures and other symbol systems, including language. The remaining three theses are designed to account for the differences between pictures and other kinds of symbols.

(1) Depiction is denotation in a pictorial symbol system. This thesis establishes three points central to Goodman's symbol theory of depiction.

---

[7] Some of those inspired by Goodman have sought to remedy this by arguing that pictures are conventional, hence arbitrary; however, Goodman himself rejects this tactic. I discuss the convention theory in Sect. 6.5.

[8] This section draws on Goodman, *Languages of Art*, 3–43, 127–73, 225–32.

First, like all representations, pictorial representations denote, refer to, stand for, or symbolize objects—I shall use these expressions interchangeably. Denotation or reference is a relation holding between a symbol and some object, and is governed by two conditions. A picture denotes an object only if that object exists, and it denotes *a* provided that if *b* is identical to *a*, it also denotes *b*. Of course, there are pictures that do not denote only individuals. A picture of an emu in a dictionary denotes no individual emu but rather each and every emu 'distributively'.

Second, like all representations, pictures denote in symbol systems: depiction is system-relative. Just as sentences have meaning only in the context of a language, so pictures refer only in the context of a system of depiction. A symbol system is a set of designs correlated with a field of reference, a set of subjects. Philosophers of language will recognize in this the familiar conception of an interpreted language as an ordered pair consisting of a set of characters and a function or 'principle of correlation' mapping characters on to objects in a domain, the language's or system's 'extension'. Different pictorial symbol systems have different principles of correlation mapping picture-symbols on to the domain. This means that a design denoting one object in one system may refer to something completely different in a second system, or nothing at all in a third. In other words, visually indistinguishable pictures may depict different subjects in different systems, and pictures which 'look' extraordinarily different but belong to different systems may in fact depict the same subject, each relative to its system. Every picture is ambiguous until its system is fixed.[9]

Finally, to depict, a representation must not only denote in a system, it must denote in a *pictorial* symbol system. After all, *Piazza San Marco* folded up in a certain way is a picture and may denote an airplane, but it would not depict one. Likewise, a portrait of the Duke of Wellington might, in the context of a military briefing, denote the fleet; but it does not follow that it depicts the fleet. While they represent an airplane and the fleet, they do not represent them in pictorial symbol systems, so they do not depict them. What, then, is a pictorial symbol system, and what distinguishes such a system from other kinds of systems? Goodman answers these questions in theses (5), (6), and (7).

(2) Depiction is predication in a pictorial symbol system. Pictures not only denote, they are also predicates applied to what pictures denote.

---

[9] Of course, a picture may also be ambiguous *within* a system, if it denotes two or more objects in the system's extension.

For instance, *Piazza San Marco* not only denotes a church, it depicts the church as Byzantine. According to Goodman, predicates classify things by labelling them. Linguistic expressions such as 'is a tourist' or 'is Byzantine' are labels which classify objects into kinds—things which are tourists and things which are Byzantine. And just as objects can be classified by means of linguistic labels, so they can also be classified by pictures. Thus *Piazza San Marco* classifies its inhabitants as loiterers, as gesticulators, as under the observation of four stone horses (we can continue in this vein almost indefinitely).

Predicates are themselves classifiable into different kinds, according to what they label. *Piazza San Marco* and the expression 'is Byzantine' can each be classified under the labels 'is a Byzantine-classifying-picture' and 'is a Byzantine-classifying-expression'. This long-winded way of labelling labels can be abbreviated to provide a convenient way of characterizing kinds of pictures. *Piazza San Marco*, for instance, can be characterized as a Byzantine-picture and a gesticulating-loiterer-picture.

Denotation, as we saw, may be either singular or distributive, but predication must not be confused with distributive denotation. Through predication, a picture can represent a class without denoting any member of the class. As the *Pioneer* space probe hurtles through the void towards distant planets, it carries to their inhabitants a picture meant to represent an ideal or typical pair of humans—a visual analogue of the literary figure 'Everyman', who is neither a single person nor in fact every person (Fig. 14). Similarly, the generic 'happy face' icon denotes neither a particular happy person nor all happy people; it is a happy-face-picture.

Interestingly, pictures need not predicatively represent classes through avoidance of detail. It is true that the *Pioneer* astronauts are drawn in a stylized manner, no doubt to facilitate interpretation by extraterrestrials. But the figures of peasants in Figure 15, though finely detailed, represent generic types, not individuals. Pictorial predicates, perhaps unlike linguistic ones, can give an impression of referential particularity.

The phenomenon that Goodman calls 'representation-as' is a special case of pictorial predication. A picture representing an object which is *F* may or may not represent it *as F*. Thus Wellington was a soldier, but a picture of him may represent him as either a soldier or a civilian. Indeed, with representation-as comes the potential for misrepresentation—a picture can represent something which is not *F* as *F*. James Gillray's cartoon denotes Wellington and represents him as a soldier, but it also represents him as a boot, which he certainly was not (Fig. 16).

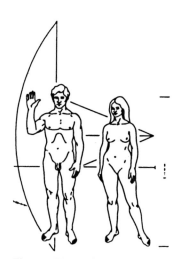

Fig. 14. Plaque from *Pioneer* space probe

Fig. 16. James Gillray, Cartoon of Wellington

Fig. 15. Pieter Bruegel the Elder, *The Peasant Dance*

To put the point intuitively, predication has to do with *how* a picture represents its subject. A picture can depict the same object in many ways or many objects in the same way. The difference between the engraving that once decorated £5 notes and Gillray's cartoon is not a difference in what each denotes, for each denotes the Duke of Wellington; rather, it is a difference in what properties each represents its common subject as satisfying.

Goodman's preference for an ontology bereft of properties leads him to resist saying that an F-picture is one representing something as having the property F. So far, I have accommodated Goodman's metaphysical scruples by talking of predication as classifying through labelling, but since his nominalism has no substantive implications for his views on depiction, I henceforth treat pictorial predication as represented property possession. In other words, we may say that *Piazza San Marco* is a Byzantine-church-picture because it represents the basilica of San Marco as having the property of being Byzantine. The set of predicates that a picture complies with, or the properties it represents the world as satisfying, comprise its 'predicative content'.

Again, what label a picture is or what properties it represents things as having depends on the system to which it belongs. A given design may be classified as an F-picture in one system and a G-picture in another system; in a third system it may fail to label anything. As in the case of his account of denotation in a system, the question of how pictures are classified in specifically pictorial systems will be taken up in the final three theses.

(3) Independence: denotation and predication in a symbol system are independent of each other. One of the central aspects of Goodman's views on depiction is that he posits two independent kinds of representation. We may say on the one hand what a picture refers to and on the other what properties it ascribes to its subject.

Whereas in language, reference and predication are indicated by conventional signs, no such signs distinguish pictorial denotation from pictorial predication. Pictures have no marks indicating what they denote and what properties they represent. As Goodman notes, 'saying that a picture represents a soandso is . . . highly ambiguous as between saying what the picture denotes and saying what kind of picture it is'.[10] The distinction between denotation and predication is evident only in their logical differences.

    [10] Goodman, *Languages of Art*, 22.

Pictorial predication need meet neither of the conditions placed on denotation. Remember that a picture denotes an object only if that object exists, and it denotes *a* provided that if *b* is identical to *a*, it also denotes *b*. But from '*P* is an *F*-picture' we may infer only that *P* exists, not that there is anything that is *F*. Gillray's caricature is a soldier-as-a-boot-picture, although 'is a soldier and a boot' applies to nothing. As we shall see, this point is important for Goodman's view of fictional representation.

And whereas a picture denoting an object denotes everything identical to that object, predicative content is 'intensional' in the sense that although it permits substitution of some, it need not permit substitution of all, coextensive predicates. Thus, if all *F*s are *G*s and *P* is an *F*-picture, it does not follow that *P* is a *G*-picture. Of course, some pictures do permit substitution of coextensive predicates—sheep are sources of wool, and a sheep-picture is also a source-of-wool-picture—but this is the exception rather than the rule.[11] The lion is the mascot of St Jerome, but it does not follow that a picture of Churchill as a lion also represents him as St Jerome's mascot.

Beyond cataloguing the logical differences between pictorial reference and pictorial content, Goodman argues that the one is independent of the other. 'The denotation of a picture no more determines its kind', he writes, 'than the kind of picture determines the denotation.'[12] It is easy to see why pictorial predication is not determined by denotation. We saw that a picture of an *F* need not represent it as *F*. The more radical claim is that what a picture denotes does not depend on what kind of picture it is. Of course, a picture may denote an *F*, yet not be an *F*-picture. But the independence thesis claims more than this. It claims that what a picture denotes has nothing to do with the properties it represents its subject as having. In Chapter 5 I will consider whether Goodman is right about this.

(4) Fictional depiction is pictorial predication. Thesis (1) is clearly not true of all pictures. Fictional pictures—of Charlie Brown, Pallas Athena, or Bigfoot—violate the first condition on denotation because they purport to denote objects which turn out not to exist. At best, fictional pictures can be said to denote nothing, the empty set. This generates the additional problem that since pictures of Athena and Bigfoot denote the

---

[11] I thank Paul Snowdon and Bill Child for this point and the example illustrating it.
[12] Goodman, *Languages of Art*, 26.

same thing, namely the empty set, we have no account of the obvious fact that to depict one is not the same as to depict the other.

Goodman's solution to this conundrum is that fictive pictures represent what they purport to denote by predication. '*P* represents *a*' is interpreted as denotational just in case *a* exists, otherwise it should be interpreted as equivalent to '*P* is an *a*-picture'. That a picture represents Bigfoot means not that it denotes Bigfoot, which it cannot, but rather that it is a Bigfoot-picture. And while it is true that a picture of Bigfoot denotes what a picture of Athena denotes, namely nothing, the empty set, they differ in so far as one is a Bigfoot-picture and the other an Athena-picture.

Although fictive denotation is a species of predication, this does not detract from the fact that fictive pictures belong to denotative systems and purport to denote. Goodman writes that 'the rule correlating symbols with denotata may result in no assignment of any actual denotata to any symbol . . . elements become representations only in conjunction with some such correlation, actual or in principle'.[13] But, as we shall see, the notion that a system consisting wholly of fictional pictures can still be denotative is puzzling when we remember that in thesis (1) Goodman defined denotative systems as systems of symbols having extensions.

Theses (1)–(4) characterize the main logical features of depiction. Pictorial symbol systems consist of referring symbols and predicates; these are independent of each other, and fictional pictures are predicative. These are the features that pictures have in common with all representations, including linguistic ones.

But given that reference and predication are common attributes of pictorial and verbal symbol systems, what distinguishes pictures from descriptions? What distinguishes Canaletto's painting from Barzini's description? What, in sum, makes a symbol system *pictorial*? A compatibilist response to these questions is that the principles of correlation and classification governing pictorial symbol systems depend on a perceptual mechanism such as noticing resemblance. This is not Goodman's response.

(5) Entrenchment: pictorial principles of correlation and classification are merely habitual. This thesis embodies Goodman's anti-perceptualism.

---

[13] Goodman, *Languages of Art*, 228.

The principles of correlation determining what objects pictures denote are arbitrary, as are the principles governing predication by pictures. 'Almost any picture may represent almost anything', because 'given picture and object there is usually a system of representation, a plan of correlation, under which the picture represents the object . . . and there are countless alternative systems of representation and description. . . . The choice among systems is free.'[14] In the right system, Constable's *Wivenhoe Park* could depict a pink elephant.

The principles of correlation underlying a system are entirely a matter of the habits and practices of the system's users. When principles of correlation defining a system enter into the practices of picture-users in a context, the system becomes 'entrenched' in that context. However, Goodman's symbol theory is not a convention theory of depiction. Conventions are rules, and Goodman is sceptical about pictorial practices (or any symbolic practices) being rule-governed. What is habitual resists codification—'borderlines shift and blur, new categories are always coming into prominence, and the canons of classification are less clear than the practice'.[15]

(6) Pictorial resemblance and realism are matters of a system's entrenchment in a context of use. According to thesis (5), pictorial systems may become entrenched in the representational practices of picture-users in a context. Goodman adds that pictures in entrenched, familiar symbol systems are those judged in that context to be 'realistic' and so to resemble what they are of to a relatively high degree. Thus a picture's realism depends on the standardness of its system in a context of use: 'realism is relative, determined by the system of representation standard for a given culture or person at a given time'. As old standards atrophy and give way to new systems which subsequently gain familiarity, previously unrealistic pictures can become realistic. To illustrate this idea, Goodman cites Picasso's riposte to a complaint that his portrait of Gertrude Stein did not resemble her: Picasso is reported to have said, 'No matter; it will.'[16] While the 1915 *Vollard* is entrenched and so deemed realistic, the 1910 one may become entrenched, and subsequently be deemed realistic.

Resemblance also derives from systemic standardness: 'that a picture

---

[14] Ibid. 39–40.
[15] Ibid. 23.
[16] Ibid. 37. For a critique of Goodman's account of realism, see Lopes, 'Pictorial Realism'.

looks like nature often means only that it looks the way nature is usually painted'.[17] Pictures resemble their subjects, but they do so in ways that vary from system to system and cannot be reduced to constant, objective standards. Thus a picture depicts in a symbol system, and a picture which depicts in a relatively familiar symbol system is judged highly similar to what it depicts, in respects determined by the system. Resemblance in pictures is a product, not a precondition, of depiction.

(7) Formalism: pictorial symbol systems are distinguished by the formal properties of analogicity and relative repleteness. If pictorial systems are not distinguished by their reliance on perceptual principles of correlation, and if, as is surely the case, entrenchment is as likely to be a property of many representational media as of pictures, then the question which introduced thesis (5) remains unanswered. What distinguishes pictorial systems from other types of representation?

One might think, as Goodman suggests early in *Languages of Art*, that a picture is simply a representation with certain design properties. The general idea is that something which represents by possessing certain colour and texture properties is a picture, while something that represents by possessing certain modelling properties is a sculpture, and something that represents through sound properties is a linguistic utterance or musical representation. But this is only a partial answer. It does not do justice to the differences between depiction and other types of representation. Pictures are not different from words simply because they are made of colours. Possessing certain design properties no more highlights what is distinctive about depiction than possessing sound properties gets to the heart of describing.

Instead, Goodman proposes that pictorial symbol systems possess two formal properties which linguistic systems do not: analogicity and relative repleteness.[18] Analogue systems are 'dense' rather than 'notational'.

A symbol system is made up of a set of designs, marks, or sounds, 'characters' to which the designs, marks, or sounds belong, and a domain of compliants, objects to which characters refer. The 'syntax' of a system concerns the organization of designs into characters; its 'semantics'

---

[17] Goodman, *Languages of Art*, 39.

[18] Goodman's notion of analogicity has fomented some discussion. See esp. Kent Bach, 'Part of What a Picture Is', *British Journal of Aesthetics*, 11 (1971), 119–37; David Lewis, 'Analog and Digital', *Noûs*, 5 (1971), 321–7; and John Haugeland, 'Analog and Analog', in J. I. Biro and R. W. Shahan (eds.), *Mind, Brain and Function* (Brighton: Harvester, 1982), 213–25.

concerns the relationship of characters to compliants. Syntactically, a notational system is disjoint and differentiated because no design, mark, or sound belongs to more than one character, and it can be determined in principle what character any design, mark, or sound belongs to. Linguistic symbols are syntactically notational, because language-bearing sounds and marks are ordered into a finite number of disjoint and differentiated characters. Any mark or sound that is an instance of one character is an instance of no other, and it is possible in principle to determine what character any mark or sound belongs to, if it belongs to any.

A syntactically *dense* system is not notational. It provides for a dense ordering of characters such that for every two there is provision for a third (and hence indefinitely many). Pictures belong to syntactically dense systems, because any difference in a picture's design properties makes for a different character in the system, and there is no way to tell whether a given design belongs to one character or another. It should be emphasized that while picture systems *provide for* an indefinite number of characters such that between every two on any ordering there is a third, there need not be an indefinite number of pictures for depiction to be dense.

Depiction is also semantically dense rather than notational. A semantically notational system is unambiguous, disjoint, and differentiated; no character has more than one compliant, no two characters share a compliant, and it is in principle possible to tell what any character complies with. Musical scores are notational with regard to pitch, because there is a one-to-one correspondence between notes marked on the staff and pitches, and it is possible to determine what pitch any note complies with. By contrast, a non-notational system provides for a dense ordering of objects in its extension; for every two compliants the system provides for a third (there need not actually be a third), and it is not always possible to tell to which character a compliant belongs. Music notation is dense with respect to tempo, since it provides for a tempo intermediate between every two notated tempos, and tempos shade off into each other.

Depiction is analogue, because it is both semantically and syntactically dense. Imagine some images of trees. Let one image's design be slightly larger than another, a third intermediate, a fourth intermediate to the second and third, and so on. Minuscule differences in height make each picture a different character in the system; moreover, each image may correspond with a difference in the tree's represented height, no difference in height being too small to be represented. Again, we need not suppose that there are an indefinite number of designs or compliants: a system is dense if it provides for a dense ordering.

Analogicity does not suffice to distinguish depiction from other forms of representation—examples of non-pictorial analogue systems include line-graphs representing temperature and EEG read-outs. Goodman adds that pictures, unlike other dense systems, are 'relatively replete'. Repleteness has to do with the number of design properties which have representational relevance in a system. Thickness of line, for instance, makes a representational difference in a drawing but not in a line-graph. One system is replete relative to a second if the design properties with representational relevance in the second are included among those with relevance in the first. Thus repleteness is a matter of degree: pictures are replete relative to other forms of representation, such as graphs, because some properties have representational significance in pictures but not in graphs.

In sum, pictures represent objects in just the way that all other symbols do, by denotation and predication within a system. What distinguishes pictorial systems from other systems is not principles of correlation reliant on perceptual mechanisms. Pictures differ from other systems in their formal properties; they are analogue and relatively replete.

3.3 A Brief Assessment

Let me pause to take note of the virtues of Goodman's theses. How well do they accommodate the diversity, twofoldness, and phenomenology constraints?

First, the structure of picture systems described in the first two theses as a set of designs and an extension is compatible with twofoldness: we see pictures' designs and, in the case of those in familiar systems, experience them as like what they denote. Theses (1) and (2) also accommodate the diversity of depiction with consummate ease. It is not implausible to think of some of the pictures discussed in Chapter 1, including drawings in the caves at Lascaux, Byzantine icons, medieval book illustrations, the Kwakiutl bird, Picasso's cubist *Vollard*, and Albertian projections, as belonging to different symbol systems. Moreover, it is because they represent within systems that pictures in some novel systems can initially appear artificial and stylized.

Thesis (5) supports pictorial diversity of a more radical kind: almost any picture may represent almost anything. However, it must be said that Goodman gives no argument for anti-perceptualism beyond his refutation of the resemblance theory. He pays scant attention to real-world pictorial symbol systems. The only example he provides of systemic difference is a highly implausible one—there is no known system of depiction in which *Wivenhoe Park* represents a pink elephant. The phenomenon of pictorial diversity as we actually find it across cultures and periods certainly presents problems for established perceptual explanations of picturing, but it does not show that the principles of correlation governing depiction and classification are arbitrary and are not constrained by perceptual processes. There is, then, no evidence that pictorial systems are as diverse as thesis (5) suggests. Theses (1) and (2) may suffice to account for the range of systems of depiction. I will take up the claim that systems of depiction are arbitrary in Chapter 6, where I hope to ascertain the limits of pictorial diversity.

As an explanation of the phenomenology of pictorial experience, the idea that perceived resemblance is a consequence of entrenchment is incomplete at best. Thesis (6) does have this virtue. The claim that pictures represent arbitrarily is highly counter-intuitive, and any theory which undercuts our intuitions in this way should offer an account of why we are so mired in error. The entrenchment account of pictorial resemblance provides just such an 'error theory'. It is because depiction is a matter of deeply entrenched habits that our pictorial practices come to seem natural and, having been naturalized, acquire the intuitive force of necessary truths.

Nevertheless, entrenchment does not explain the nature of pictorial experience. First, pictures in unfamiliar systems can be experienced as of their subjects—witness the effect on Renaissance viewers of the innovations of Alberti and his colleagues. Furthermore, nothing precludes non-pictorial symbol systems from being well entrenched, yet no amount of familiarity with one's native language, for example, suffices for linguistic tokens to seem to resemble (sound like?) what they refer to. Goodman concedes that non-pictorial symbols can be entrenched, and that 'no amount of familiarity turns a paragraph into a picture'.[19] He concludes that the essential feature of depiction is not its entrenchment but its analogicity and relative repleteness. However, analogicity does not explain how we see pictures as their subjects.

---

[19] Goodman, *Languages of Art*, 231.

Consequently there is a gap between what Goodman holds is the distinctive mark of depiction, namely possession of the formal properties of analogicity and relative repleteness, and what he thinks explains judgements of resemblance, namely a high level of entrenchment.

We must jettison either the view that pictures have a distinctive phenomenology or the explanation of their phenomenology as a side-effect of familiarity. The latter seems more reasonable.

The final point to note about Goodman's theses is that the four semantic theses entail none of the second group of three substantive theses. If it is true that pictures denote or label in systems, each governed by certain principles of correlation, it by no means follows that systems of depiction are arbitrary, merely habitual, and independent of perceptual facts. Nor does it follow that pictures are distinguished from other symbol systems by the formal properties of analogicity and relative repleteness.

3.4 The Competence Constraint

A constant source of resistance to any attempt to model depiction on language lies in certain facts about our mastery of pictorial representation. Our ability to interpret pictures, so the objection goes, differs in crucial respects from our ability to interpret denotative linguistic expressions. If this is so, then Goodman's symbol theory of depiction is unable to explain the distinctive character of pictorial competence.

Our competence with pictorial representation manifests itself in two interesting and useful ways. First, we do not need to learn the meaning of unfamiliar pictures in the way we must learn the meaning of unfamiliar words. Competence in depiction consists in an ability to understand almost any picture of a familiar object at a glance: depiction is 'generative'. Being able to interpret some pictures generates an ability to interpret any other picture, provided that one knows what the object it represents looks like.[20]

Goodman's insight that pictures belong to systems is not only consistent with this pictorial generativity, it also explains its structure. As we have seen, the subjects of pictures belonging to unfamiliar systems are not always evident to us at a glance. Think of your first encounter

---

[20] On generativity, see Flint Schier, *Deeper into Pictures: An Essay on Pictorial Representation* (Cambridge: Cambridge University Press, 1986), ch. 3.

with a cubist or split-style picture, and how difficult it was to puzzle out its subject. If research on the perception of pictorial depth cues across cultures is correct, then interpreting Albertian pictures also requires some learning. But once unfamiliar systems are mastered, any picture in the system can be understood with ease. The implication is that depiction is only partially generative between pictorial systems. Competence in Albertian depiction does not carry with it complete competence in split-style depiction. Depiction is generative, however, *within* pictorial systems. Once viewers are able to interpret some split-style pictures, they have mastered the system and can interpret any picture belonging to it.

Our competence in interpreting pictures is manifest in a second way when they are used to show us what *unfamiliar* objects look like. This is the point of pictures in advertisements, children's alphabet books, and Audubon field guides. As Wollheim remarks, 'children who are not as yet able to recognize things in pictures learn to recognize them through pictures . . . a picture-book is not only a mirror of, it is also a guide to, the world'.[21] Being able to grasp an A-is-for-aardvark-picture or a Q-is-for-quagga-picture conveys an ability to visually identify aardvarks or, were they not extinct, quaggas.

Thus the second direction in which pictorial competence runs is from picture to object, for looking at a picture of an unfamiliar object often confers an ability to visually identify that object. I call this aspect of pictorial competence 'transference', to convey the idea that an ability to identify depicted objects often quite usefully carries over into an ability to identify seen objects.[22] Transference differs from generativity in the following way. A system is generative when familiarity with the system plus a knowledge of an object's appearance enables viewers to grasp any picture of that object in the system. A system provides for transference when familiarity with the system endows viewers with the ability to recognize a novel picture's subject, sight unseen.

Perceptual theories are appealing in part because they seem to explain the generativity and transference of depiction inherently. If pictures resemble their subjects, then knowing what an object looks like and how pictures resemble things adds up to knowledge of what a picture of that object will look like. And if we do not know what an

[21] Richard Wollheim, 'Nelson Goodman's *Languages of Art*', in *On Art and the Mind* (London: Allen Lane, 1973), 298.
[22] In *Painting as an Art*, Wollheim uses the term 'transfer' as equivalent to what I have been calling 'generativity'.

object looks like, a picture that resembles it teaches us what it looks like, in case we encounter it. Thus the thought that pictorial competence is generative and transferable is not uncommonly taken as proof that depiction is at bottom perceptual.[23]

Moreover, it is widely held that the generativity of depiction refutes symbol theories. Generativity is incomprehensible if pictures are like linguistic expressions, because, as one commentator puts it, 'with words it is unfortunately the case that we must learn in a tiresome way what each refers to one-by-one'.[24] A glance, by contrast, usually reveals a picture's content. Likewise, Wollheim insists that generativity must baffle adherents of the 'semiotic' theory of depiction: it is as if 'knowing that the French word *chat* means a cat, and knowing what dogs look like, I should, on hearing it, be able to understand what the word *chien* means'.[25]

These pronouncements obviously assume that any linguistic model of depiction necessarily infects depiction with the arbitrariness of language, and it is this arbitrariness that is incompatible with the facts about pictorial competence. One of my aims in this chapter has been to challenge the assumption that symbol theories of depiction modelled on language are incompatible with perceptual theories of depiction. I believe it is enlightening to compare pictures with linguistic expressions, without sacrificing perceptual explanations of pictorial competence.

It is also worth pointing out, however, that our competence in many 'arbitrary' symbol systems, including language, is manifest through generativity and transference. Any symbol system allows for generativity and transference when the system is rule-governed and competence in the system consists in grasping the rules governing the system. Take, for example, standard musical notation.[26] Mastery of a suitable sample of symbols, including markings for pitch, duration, tempo, and dynamics, enables readers of music to interpret novel scores of familiar or unfamiliar music. Thus musical notation is both generative and transferable.

Of course, it is crucial to the usefulness of knowing a language that it also possesses these features. Once English-speakers have mastered

[23] See Robert Schwartz, 'Representation and Resemblance', *Philosophical Forum*, 5 (1974), 499–512, for a discussion of this presumption in the psychological literature on depiction.

[24] Wilson, 'Illusion and Representation', 212.

[25] Wollheim, *Painting as an Art*, 77.

[26] Schwartz, 'Representation and Resemblance', 501–2.

the grammatical and lexical fundamentals of English, they are able to understand novel utterances and learn about features of the world through them. A sentence such as 'The quagga is a wild horse which looks part zebra and part donkey' can be understood with a knowledge of English grammar and the meanings of the individual words, thus providing a means to identify quaggas.

Musical notation and language are arbitrary symbol systems in so far as any set of marks could stand for any musical or linguistic phrase. Given suitable principles of correlation, Constable's *Wivenhoe Park* could represent the theme from *The Godfather*, or the theme from *The Godfather* could count as a statement of the first law of thermodynamics. But provided that there are sufficient regularities governing the symbols *within* a system, learning some symbols may suffice for being able to interpret any symbol in the system.

The amount that must be learned about a system before competence is achieved varies from system to system. Competence in a language requires many years of study; competence in number systems is easily acquired; the representational system used by analogue thermometers, which correlates the height of a column of mercury with temperature, is learned at a glance.

In sum, the claim that pictures are arbitrary symbols is not in conflict with the facts about pictorial competence, so long as pictorial symbol systems are rule-governed. Our mastery of a system of depiction might consist in a grasp of rules that govern it, enabling us to understand novel pictures in the system in a way that adds to our knowledge of their subjects. In this case, any set of marks on a flat surface may depict anything else, given suitable principles of correlation. But if those principles of correlation are regular across all pictures within the system, mastery of the regularities enables viewers to understand and learn from novel pictures.

It will be helpful to summarize this in the following principle, which I call the 'competence constraint'. A theory of depiction should explain how mastery of pictorial systems is possible, where this mastery includes an ability to understand novel symbols and to learn about the appearance of unfamiliar objects through pictures. Competence in a system can be explained as a consequence of either the system's reliance on perceptual processes or learning the rules of the system.

The facts about pictorial competence do not help or hinder the case for the symbol theory. As it happens, though, some of Goodman's statements call into question whether the theory, as he understands it, can explain pictorial competence. Not only does Goodman reject perceptual correlations between pictures and their subjects, but, despite talk of systems as '*principles* of correlation', he also rejects the notion that pictorial systems are rule-based. 'Understanding a picture is', he writes, 'not a matter of bringing to bear universal rules that determine the identification and manipulation of its component symbols.'[27]

In Goodman's view pictorial competence is explained by the possession of background knowledge about a system, knowledge in virtue of which the system is entrenched. Entrenchment provides Goodman with a way to evade both perceptual theories of depiction as well as theories which construe pictures as rule-based and conventional. But placing such a heavy burden on possession of the relevant background knowledge for understanding pictures seems to me to render depiction an opaque, mysterious phenomenon. My inclination is to accept this position only in the last resort.

3.5 Competence and Systems

The strength of Goodman's symbol theory of depiction lies in the way it relativizes picturing to systems. A picture represents something as having certain properties only in the context of a system. This insight promises to explain the diversity of depiction. Unfortunately, one weakness of Goodman's theory is that it also takes this insight as a licence to endorse the radical view that any set of (analogue and relatively replete) picture–object correlations may count as a pictorial system. Another is that it provides no account of how to individuate pictorial systems—of how to tell one system of depiction from another.[28]

If, as I have speculated, pictorial competence is system-relative, then it is possible to use that fact to provide an account of what it is to be a system of picturing. This idea has been developed in detail by Flint Schier in his book *Deeper into Pictures*.[29] According to Schier, there

---

[27] Nelson Goodman and Catherine Elgin, *Reconceptions in Philosophy and Other Arts and Sciences* (London: Routledge and Kegan Paul, 1988), 110; see also Goodman, *Languages of Art*, 23.

[28] The two weaknesses are linked. If pictorial systems are radically different arbitrary alternatives, the boundaries between systems are clear. But if pictorial systems overlap and blur into each other because they share common perceptual foundations, then it is not clear how we can differentiate them.

[29] Schier, *Deeper into Pictures*, 44–8.

are distinct pictorial systems only because competence with some kinds of pictures does not entail competence in others.

However, we should be aware that pictorial systems overlap, and competence in one may produce partial competence in another. Remember that someone competent in a system can interpret any picture in the system provided that its subject is one whose appearance is familiar. But although competence in one system does not guarantee competence in another, it may, and usually does, provide a foothold. For instance, mastery of Albertian depiction is an aid (some would argue a precondition) to interpreting cubist pictures. If you have competence in Albertian picturing, you can probably interpret some cubist pictures, though not all. Partial mastery of a system puts full mastery within relatively easy reach, however. A survey of the diverse range of pictorial systems used by humans suggests, I think, the general rule that competence in any system of depiction entails partial competence in any other.

In this regard pictorial competence is quite unlike competence in a language. We do not as a general rule expect knowledge of one language to provide any basis for understanding even some expressions in other languages, whereas the overlap between systems of depiction, and thus between the abilities constituting mastery of them, may well point to common underlying processes.

Nevertheless, the fact that pictorial competence is fragmented among systems should be taken as a warning for certain perceptual theories of depiction. For example, if pictures depict because we can see their resemblances to their subjects and our ability to see resemblances is innate and automatic, then we would expect pictorial competence to be monolithic, so that being able to interpret any picture should suffice for being able to interpret any other picture whatsoever.

This suggests an addendum to the competence constraint. A theory of depiction should explain how it is possible for a viewer to possess competence in one system and not another. And it should explain how a viewer who has competence in one system can have partial competence in another.

Goodman's views on depiction are conveyed with vigour and a delight in overturning long-established assumptions. For this reason, rightly or wrongly, they serve either as exceptional foundations or foils, as the case may be, for discussions of depiction. In the following chapter I defend thesis (1), arguing that pictures are referential, while in Chapter

5 I dispute thesis (3) by arguing that pictorial reference depends on predicative content. In the end, I hope to have set the stage for a compatibilist account of depiction, one which will make possible a rethinking of the place of perceptual mechanisms in explaining depiction.

4
Symbols and Substitutes

THE core of the symbol theory is the claim that pictures belong to systems which can be described as sets of designs referring to objects, types of objects, and properties. Although Goodman additionally holds that this correlation is an arbitrary one, nothing in the core claim entails arbitrariness. The truth of the symbol theory does not hang on whether pictorial design–object references are perceptual or arbitrary.

This chapter addresses one challenge to the symbol theory that does not rest on the assumption that the symbol theory is incompatible with perceptual explanations of depiction. The crux of this challenge is that pictures are not symbolic, because they are not denotative. The point is not simply that some pictures, being fictional, do not refer to anything; rather, pictures are non-denotative in principle, because they may serve as substitutes for objects.

4.1 Substitutes

The basis for the challenge to the symbol theory is to be found in Gombrich's early essay 'Meditations on a Hobby Horse', the theoretical forerunner to *Art and Illusion*.[1] The principal aim of this essay was to develop the tools needed for an account of the history of systems of depiction, from the early stylizations of our Neanderthal ancestors through the naturalism of Constable and returning to the stylizations of modern primitives, Picasso and his ilk. The key to Gombrich's view of why depiction has a history is a class of pictures which appear to function as substitutes for things, rather than symbols of them.

The paradigm of a substitute is a child's toy, such as a hobby-horse. A broomstick makes an excellent substitute for a horse because it is rideable and, given a little of the imagination which children possess in abundance, button eyes and a straw mane are all that is required to

[1] E. H. Gombrich, 'Meditations on a Hobby Horse, or the Roots of Artistic Form', in *Meditations on a Hobby Horse*, 4th edn. (Chicago: University of Chicago Press, 1984), 1–11.

transform it, imaginatively, into a dashing steed. In other words, substitutes are not bound by the requirements of mimesis: with sufficient imagination, just about anything can stand as a substitute for anything else. Since substitutive pictures need delineate the features of what they stand for in only the most cursory fashion, Gombrich speculates that the stylization and artificiality typical of the 'conceptual' pictures which dominated art's early history are a consequence of their substitutive origins. The rule for the substitutive is an economy of representational means. A few simple brush strokes on a cave wall make a substitute for a horse; stylized inscriptions in an Egyptian tomb suffice to make substitutes for the servants and goods that will be wanted in the afterlife. Indeed, the artificiality of substitutive depiction serves an important purpose. Substitutes must not grow too lifelike lest they actually come to life. A substitute, as Gombrich warns, 'must not become a double under the artist's hands. . . . One false stroke and the rigid mask of the face may assume an evil leer.'[2] Thus conceptual style is a response to what might be called the 'Pygmalion complex'.

According to Gombrich's survey of the history of art, depiction advances by abandoning its substitutive origins. Early art is the product of a desire to create substitutes for things, and is consequently free from the demands of mimesis. In later art, pictures become records of visual experience rather than substitutes, their purpose being to create an illusionistic match with viewers' experiences of their subjects. But matching becomes possible only after it has been understood that pictures may refer to things without being them. Only once pictures cease to serve as substitutes for things and come instead to refer to them does the Pygmalion complex cease to operate as a check on mimesis. In sum, substitution and denotation are at odds with each other, substitution being allied to conceptual art, denotation to illusion or imitation.

Clearly Gombrich's conception of how substitution works is in part a product of the historical role that he wishes to assign to it. He first assumes that early art is conceptual in style and that later art is illusionistic. Then he associates illusionism with reference and the conceptual with substitution—substitution explains the early history of depiction only if conceptual art is substitutive. Having made these two assumptions, Gombrich is then able to characterize the history of art as a progression from substitutive—that is, conceptual—pictures to illusionistic—that is, referential—ones.

---

[2] Gombrich, 'Meditations on a Hobby Horse', 8.

As an explanation of the historical origins of depiction, this account suffers from serious deficiencies. It is not obvious that conceptual art is in fact representationally primitive, and, as recent developments have shown, it is unlikely that the history of art is necessarily a march towards greater illusion. Nor is there any reason to conflate substitution with conceptual styles and imitative pictures with the denotative and non-substitutive. For instance, a stylized image, such as a cigarette in a 'No Smoking' sign, may refer (distributively) to cigarettes. Moreover, the Pygmalion complex is not endemic, so substitutive art may be illusionistic. Indeed, pictorial substitution may have sprung from the lifelikeness of non-substitutive pictures with illusionistic effects. Who cannot confess to touching or addressing words to a photograph of an absent beloved as if he or she were present in the picture? The truth is that we cannot tell a substitutive picture simply by its style of representation. Any picture may be a substitute.

If substitutive pictures are not simply conceptual or stylized ones and any picture may be substitutive, then we must reconsider what it is to be a substitutive picture. One fact which may offer us a clue is that we often speak of pictures in ways that seem to indicate that we take them for substitutes. A child drawing a horse will declare that she is 'making a horse'—and her drawing may show little if any concern for matching (an infant of two or three will happily draw a horse as any kind of squiggle or dot). Similarly, adults, when asked 'What is that?' by someone pointing to a picture, will readily answer 'the Piazza San Marco' or 'Prince Vessantara'. But what we say is no proof that we are making substitutes for, rather than references to, objects: 'That's x' might just be a lazy way of saying 'That's a picture of x.'

A better suggestion is that what makes a picture substitutive is not so much what people say about it as the mental attitude they bear towards it (perhaps as evidenced by what they say). A picture is a substitute only if viewers' mental states can be described as those of taking the image to be what it represents. This mental state may be a belief; in looking at a picture of a horse, I may believe that there is a horse. But I see no reason to suppose that such beliefs necessarily underlie substitution; indeed, there is reason to suppose they cannot. If a child knows that her toy is a stick, how can she also believe that it is a horse? Surely it is putting it too strongly to say that she is engaged in self-deception! It is better to say that although she does not believe that her toy is a horse, she pretends to believe that it is. Unfortunately, it is far from clear what constitutes pretended belief and how pretended belief is related to ordinary belief. A more promising suggestion that I shall soon explore in detail is that the appropriate mental state is one of imagining a horse.

At any rate, having such an attitude may be necessary for an image to function as a substitute, but it is not sufficient. Just as a stick qualifies as a substitute horse in part because it is rideable, a picture qualifies as a substitute for a horse in part because one may act towards it in ways characteristic of being in the presence of a horse. One need not, of course, treat an image just like its subject in order for the image to function as a substitute; nevertheless, substitutes must possess at least some features that will allow us to treat them as what they are substitutes for. This principle has implications for the cognitive stance taken towards substitutes. All other beliefs being equal, there will be a systematic parallel between the contents of thoughts in virtue of which things are taken as substitutes and the contents of thoughts we would have about the objects substituted for, such that both kinds of thoughts lead potentially to similar actions. The child's mental attitude to her hobby-horse will be of a kind typically leading to actions she would be likely to perform in the presence of a real horse.

To see this, it may help to consider an extended example of substitutive imagery. That a picture's status as a substitute is intimately connected with what we do with it is evident in the practices surrounding substitutive pictures, of which Buddha image-consecration ceremonies in northern Thailand provide a superb illustration.[3] Like many of their counterparts in places of worship across the globe, Buddha images are sites of daily devotion, providing the faithful with an opportunity to enact their relationship to the 'divine'.[4] Of course, it by no means follows that Buddha images or other devotional images are substitutes. Praying *before* a statue is not the same as praying *to* a statue. Nevertheless, certain features of the ceremonies conducted by monks to consecrate Buddha images do highlight the images' substitutive status within a ceremonial context.[5]

---

[3] The majority of these images are figurines and amulets, but there is no reason why similar practices might not have developed around pictures.

[4] The scare-quotes indicate that the category of the 'divine' may not apply univocally across all religious traditions. In particular, it may not be the best way to describe the status of the Buddha in Theravada Buddhism.

[5] I am indebted to the detailed description of this ceremony written by Donald K. Swearer, 'Hypostasizing the Buddha: Buddha Image Consecration Ceremonies in Northern Thailand', *History of Religions*, 34 (1995), 263–80. See Richard Gombrich, 'The Consecration of a Buddha Image', *Journal of Asian Studies*, 26 (1966), 23–36, for an account of somewhat different ceremonies in Sri Lanka.

A central component of the consecration ceremony is a recitation of the Buddha's biography (which is why the ceremony is sometimes described as 'training an image'), and important events recounted in the biographical narrative are enacted as part of the ritual. For example, the description of the Buddha's enlightenment is marked by uncovering the image's head and eyes.[6] A second component of the ceremony is a performative utterance whose purpose is to identify the image with the Buddha. The monks chant: 'I pay homage to [the] Buddha. May all his powers be invested in this image. May the Buddha's boundless omniscience be invested in this image until the religion ceases to exist.'[7] Towards the end of the ceremony, the monks fan the newly consecrated image with peacock feathers, while the laity 'feed' it with an auspicious mixture of rice, milk, and honey. The image is now treated as the veritable presence of the historical Buddha.

In sum, what makes the image a substitute is our cognitive stance towards it, as potentially manifest in what we do with it, frequently as this is governed by social practices.

4.2 Pictures as Fictions

Having detached substitution from what Gombrich calls conceptual art and analysed it instead as a particular use of pictures, it is now possible to recount a challenge posed by Kendall Walton to the contention that pictures denote in symbol systems.[8] On the basis of this challenge, Walton proposes that pictures are fictions.

Walton's challenge is not that some pictures are fictions and so do not denote anything. Goodman does not require that every symbol in a system have a referent in order for the system to be denotative. What he does require is that symbols in a system be 'ostensibly provided with denotata. The rule correlating symbols with denotata may result in no

---

[6] In Sri Lanka, the culminating moment of the ceremony occurs when the image's eyes are painted. Richard Gombrich believes that this marks the point at which the image comes to life as the Buddha, and much of the ceremony is directed at averting the dangers of this moment. See Gombrich, 'Consecration of a Buddha Image'.

[7] Quoted in Swearer, 'Hypostasizing the Buddha', 278. It strikes me that in stipulating that the image be the Buddha 'until the religion ceases to exist', the monks recognize that the image's status as a substitute depends on the way it is treated and the regard in which it is held by its users.

[8] Kendall Walton, 'Are Representations Symbols?', *Monist*, 58 (1974), 236–54; and *idem, Mimesis as Make-Believe*, 122–30, 351–2.

assignment of any actual denotata to any symbol, so that the field of reference is null; but elements become representations only in conjunction with some such correlation, actual or in principle.'[9] Compare pictures to language. Pictures of yeti or Dr Strangelove no more disprove the thesis that pictorial systems are generally denotative than expressions like 'Mrs Newsome's ambassador' or 'Gulliver travelled' show that language is not denotative. These expressions belong to linguistic categories (descriptions and names) which, as a rule, have referents— and when they do not, they nevertheless ostensibly refer. By the same token, pictures of fictional objects may also belong to categories— portraits and pictures of kinds—which are normally provided with referents, or else seem to refer (see Ch. 10).

Walton's challenge is that depiction is not denotative because entire pictorial systems may be substitutive and hence non-referential. Imagine a society of people who make piazza-pictures, pigeon-pictures, opera-star-pictures, and the like, but not pictures used to refer to actual piazzas, pigeons, or opera stars. Drawing a pigeon, in this society, is thought of as creating a pigeon substitute, not as symbolizing or referring to an animal already in existence. There is no convention in Waltopia to make pictures referring to actual things. Nor would Waltopians know what it is to refer to anything by depicting it, so they never intend to refer to something by making a picture of it. Depiction, then, is independent of denotation.

Pictures stand in sharp contrast to representations, such as linguistic utterances, that are referential or symbolic. While linguistic expressions may be fictional (e.g. 'Gulliver travelled'), there can be no fictional language without non-fictional language, because the use of fictional expressions is parasitic on the use of serious, non-fictional ones. By contrast, we have just seen that there may be a community all of whose pictures are substitutive and non-denotative. Depiction does not depend on the possibility of pictorial reference. The failure to mark this contrast between pictures and language Walton considers to be the root of much confusion about depiction. He insists that it is a serious mistake to hold, as Goodman does, that pictures are importantly analogous to other symbols, specifically linguistic ones, and he counsels us to reject language or symbol models of picturing.

Before coming to the defence of the symbol theory, I wish to pursue some further implications that Walton draws from the Waltopian

---

[9] Goodman, *Languages of Art*, 228.

thought-experiment. If pictures are not necessarily used to denote, it is unreasonable to expect denotative systems such as language to provide useful models for explaining depiction. Walton suggests as an alternative that pictures be modelled on fictions.

Fiction, though, is not simply what one gets in the absence of denotation. Fictions, according to Walton, depend on imaginings generated within the context of games of make-believe. A game of make-believe consists in a set of rules prescribing what we are to imagine in a defined context, and to play a game of make-believe is to allow one's imaginings to be governed by these rules. It should be noted that the imaginings prescribed by a game are independent of players' actual imaginings, since games prescribe that players imagine things whether or not anybody complies with what the game mandates. A fiction, then, is not any imagining, nor is it any imagining that occurs in the context of a game; it is an imagining mandated by a game of make-believe.

It is obvious that Walton's general theory of fiction takes as its paradigm the phenomenon of substitution. The notion of a game of make-believe foregrounds and formalizes key features of the idea that what makes something a substitute is what we do with it, together with our cognitive stance towards it. The child playing hobby-horses is playing a game of make-believe with relatively simple rules. A broomstick is a horse, because it possesses certain features, and the rules of the game mandate players to imagine that anything with those features is a horse and that standing astride it counts as riding a horse. The game makes it fictionally true that there is a horse and that anyone standing astride it is riding it. A more sophisticated game of make-believe is mud pies, a game whose rules mandate imagining that a pat of mud is a pie, a pebble is a raisin, a box is an oven, and carrying lumps of mud to one's mouth while making masticating movements is eating. These rules generate further fictional truths—for instance, 'This pie's burnt' or 'I'm eating the leftover dough from the pie that's now in the oven.'[10]

Having explained why fictions depend on make-believe, Walton goes on to argue, surprisingly, that representations are fictions. Some games

---

[10] Evans, *Varieties of Reference*, 354–5, formulates two principles that generate fictional truths beyond those stipulated by the rules of the game of make-believe. The 'incorporation principle' permits inclusion in the game of any make-believe truth not inconsistent with the initial rules of the game, and the 'recursive principle' permits inclusion in the game of any make-believe truth entailed by the initial rules of the game. The rules of the game, together with the incorporation principle and the recursive principle, allow for the generation or discovery of make-believe truths not envisaged by the initial rules of the game.

of make-believe, such as hobby-horses and mud pies, involve props. A prop in a game of make-believe is an object that, according to the rules of the game, prompts a particular imagining. The broomstick is a prop in the game of hobby-horses, because the game mandates that it be imagined to be a horse, and the presence nearby of a broomstick makes it fictionally true that there is a horse nearby. Representations, including pictures of all kinds, are objects that have been designed specifically to serve as props in highly specialized, complex games of make-believe. These games consist in rules which direct those who would appreciate them to imagine certain propositions, and that is precisely what we do when we grasp a picture's meaning or enjoy a work of literature.

The games of make-believe for which a work is designed are the games 'authorized' for that work. For example, *Gulliver's Travels* was designed to serve as a prop specifically for use in certain games of make-believe, games in which Swift expected that certain imaginings would be mandated. Reading the book, we are expected to play an authorized game of make-believe which requires us to imagine that there is a place called Lilliput populated by tiny people, that the lilliputians tied up Dr Gulliver, and perhaps that, if well organized, the weak can overcome the mighty. Of course, one might imagine, in reading *Gulliver's Travels*, that it contains in elaborate code the definitive account of a plot to assassinate President Kennedy; but this is an imagining generated by an unauthorized game of make-believe, a game for which the book is not designed as a prop. The fictions generated by a work like *Gulliver's Travels* are not simply truths that we happen to imagine when reading the book, they are truths which an authorized game embedded in social practices requires that we imagine.

Walton radically transforms many of the concepts we standardly use in thinking about representation. Representations are fictions. And fictions are imaginings prescribed by games of make-believe. It follows that pictures are not denotative, because they, too, are fictions—props in pictorial games of make-believe. All that remains is to give an account of *pictorial* games of make-believe.

The kinds of imaginings prescribed for pictures are what set pictorial games of make-believe apart.[11] *Piazza San Marco* is a picture, because it is a prop in a game of make-believe which directs viewers to imagine that they *see* and *visually inspect* the Piazza San Marco before them, with its basilica, stone horses, discoursing loiterers, and the like. It is

---

[11] Walton, *Mimesis as Make-Believe*, 293–6.

true that in reading *Moby Dick*, we might imagine seeing the whale amidships, and indeed the literary fiction game might direct readers to imagine seeing the whale amidships. The difference is that the pictorial game requires that viewers imagine that their act of looking at the designed picture surface is looking at the Piazza San Marco. The literary fiction game does not mandate that readers imagine *of their act of looking* at Kafka's story that they are seeing Gregor Samsa's twitching insect legs. When standing before a picture, we must make-believe that our act of looking at the picture is seeing, visually recognizing, noticing, inspecting its subject.

The Buddhist consecration ceremony described earlier can certainly be considered a pictorial game of make-believe. It is not true that the Buddha is there, nor do the monks fan him; but it is fictionally true that the Buddha is there, because the consecration ceremony mandates imagining that the Buddha is there and that looking at the image is looking at the Buddha. The image is a prop which, in the context of the game of make-believe embedded in the ceremony, mandates certain imaginings and acts, including acts of looking. Of course, the consecration ceremony is unlike other representational games because it is taken seriously by many players, who do not think it fictional that the Buddha is there and that they are looking at the Buddha when they look at the image.

Nevertheless, what is true of Buddha images in northern Thailand, Walton holds to be true of all pictures: all are fictions. Buddha images are fictions, because understanding them requires us to imagine literally false but fictionally true propositions such as 'The Buddha is seated there'. Likewise, pictures are fictions, because they are designed as props in games of make-believe in which players are directed to imagine that looking at the pictures is looking at their subjects. Understanding a picture therefore consists in having the imaginings mandated by the pictorial game in which it is a prop.

4.3 Meaning and Make-Believe

I believe that Walton's willingness to categorize all pictures as fictions rests on two errors. The first is a failure to foreground pictures' information-conveying role—a failure which perhaps reflects a general disregard for the fact that the vast majority of pictures, including many of those which function as substitutes, are demotic pictures rather than art pictures. The second is a failure to distinguish what can be done with symbols, their use, on the one hand, from the part of their meaning that is independent of their use, on the other. Drawing this distinction dispels the disanalogies between pictures and language that appear to surface in the Waltopian thought-experiment.

An important function of representations, linguistic or pictorial, is to communicate information. Pictures have earned a place among the technologies of communication because they are particularly well suited to storing and conveying certain kinds of information. A fixation upon art pictures sometimes obscures this fact. Typically, art pictures are either fictions, which do not refer at all, or else, in the majority of the remaining cases, their reference contributes little to their aesthetic value. It hardly matters, aesthetically, whether we can tell who sat for a portrait by Ingres, for example—I doubt that appreciating *Madame Moitessier* hangs on knowing who it refers to.[12] Yet the vast majority of pictures are what I have called 'demotic pictures', pictures whose purpose is very often to convey information. For confirmation of this point, one need look no further than the family photo album. A portrait, for example, conveys information (or misinformation) by referring to a person and predicating some properties of him, so that we can learn whether he was tall or short, fair or dark, and the like.

Walton acknowledges that pictures can be used to store and convey information, to instruct, and to illustrate, yet, he insists, the serious use of pictures to convey information depends on their being fictions. The use of pictures in make-believe is a precondition for other uses.

This is in contrast to language, where instructing and informing are in the forefront, and proceed without the assistance of make-believe. Walton observes that we read *The Times* to find out what happened in Brussels or Washington, not what happened in the make-believe world of *The Times* (the op-ed pages aside).[13] To be sure, words also find a place in make-believe, but only when they have no referents (when they are fictional in the usual sense). Moreover, linguistic games of make-believe are always parasitic on serious uses of language. There could be no fictional statements or names without the practice of using non-fictional statements containing non-fictional names to convey knowledge of actual states of affairs: telling lies and pretended truths require a practice of telling truths. The serious use of language

---

[12] Appreciating the portrait might, however, depend on imagined knowledge of who its subject is. See Ch. 10.

[13] Walton, *Mimesis as Make-Believe*, 70.

is that of making assertions, and fictional texts depend on the assertoric use of words.

The key to the distinction that Walton wants to draw between words and pictures clearly lies in the nature of assertion. According to Walton, words used seriously perform their assertoric function by providing good reasons for beliefs.[14] Providing a good reason for a belief does not entail prescribing that it be imagined to be true. The statement 'The mayor is a crook' elicits a belief about municipal corruption, because it provides a reason for believing its truth, without prescribing an imagining about the mayor's corruption. Not all linguistic utterances are assertoric, of course. Joyce's statement that snow fell throughout Ireland is not designed to cause readers to have a certain meteorological belief; it merely prescribes that the belief be imagined to be true. Words in fictions are not designed to persuade us to accept beliefs; they simply mandate that the belief be imagined to be true.[15]

Pictures can also be used to give good reasons for accepting beliefs. I can persuade you of the mayor's corruption by telling you that she takes bribes or, perhaps more effectively, by drawing a picture or taking a photograph of her accepting a bribe. Here I am not merely prescribing that you imagine something; I am also providing evidence calculated to secure your acquiescence to a claim. It is also possible to use a picture deceptively, to gain assent to a falsehood or to what is thought to be a falsehood. But although pictures can be used assertorically, to elicit beliefs by providing good reasons for them, Walton holds that they must do so by first prescribing imaginings. My picture of the mayor, if it elicits a belief in you, must do so by first prescribing that you imagine seeing the mayor taking a bribe.

This, then, is the disanalogy that Walton sees between words and pictures. The assertoric use of words does not depend on their use in make-believe; on the contrary, their use in make-believe depends on their serious use. But when pictures are used seriously, they give reasons for accepting a belief by mandating that viewers imagine the belief to be true. Thus the assertoric use of pictures depends on their use in make-believe. And as the Waltopian thought-experiment shows,

---

[14] Ibid. 70–2.
[15] An obvious qualification is needed. We may not be expected to come to believe that the sentences in a fiction are veridical, but imagining them to be true might provide good reasons for readers to accept some further proposition. By reading that the lilliputians captured Dr Gulliver, one may come to believe that the weak can sometimes vanquish the strong.

pictures need not be used seriously at all, because a society can use pictures without referring.

My aim thus far has been merely to clarify what I take to be Walton's view that any use of pictures depends on their use in make-believe and any use of language depends on assertion. The question now arises as to what reason can be given to show that one use of a medium of representation is fundamental.

It is a truism that meaning is a function of use, and this applies as much to pictures as to linguistic expressions. To know the meaning of an expression like 'She took the money and ran' is in part to know the point of the utterance—what is being done with it or can be done with it in a context of use. But there is an additional ingredient of linguistic meaning that is constant across contexts of use and is independent of any particular use—what I call its 'sense'.[16] The sense of an utterance is generally held to be a function of the meanings of the words that make it up. Thus 'She took the money and ran' has a sense that does not vary across the uses to which it can be put, but depends on its constituent parts.

There are a multitude of ways in which a picture can be used to represent. I mentioned that *Piazza San Marco* can be folded up to represent an airplane; similarly, *Wivenhoe Park*, laid on a table, can token the Spanish Armada in a military briefing. David Novitz observes that a suitor can practise a love speech by addressing it to the *Mona Lisa*.[17] The Rockeby Venus can be used to illustrate exploitative images of women. However, in each of these cases, there is a gap between what the picture is used to represent and what it depicts. A theory of pictorial representation is concerned only with how pictures represent *as pictures*.

Of course, there are many uses of pictures as pictures. A single picture of a person, say, can be used to provide instruction in human anatomy, to illustrate sign language, to advertise a product, to warn about the effects of moral dissolution, or to invite the viewer to reverie. The available uses to which a picture can be put *qua* picture are constrained by its sense.[18] I define pictorial sense simply as that part of the

---

[16] My use of 'sense' should be taken as minimalist—I do not wish to endorse a full-blown Fregean theory of sense. However, I am indebted to Dummett's views about the role of accounts of sense and use in a theory of meaning. See Dummett, *Frege*, chs. 5 and 10; and *idem*, 'What Is a Theory of Meaning?', in Samuel Guttenplan (ed.), *Mind and Language* (Oxford: Oxford University Press, 1975), 97–138.

[17] Novitz, 'Picturing', 147.

[18] Discussions of difficulties of pictorial 'interpretation' do not revolve around determining what a picture's reference and content is or how viewers understand its reference and content. They concern how we can decide which of the possible uses to which a picture with a given sense can be put are correct or are intended by the artist. Grasp of a picture's sense underdetermines correct interpretation.

meaning of a picture as a picture that remains constant whether it is used to communicate, to warn, to serve as a substitute, or what have you. We do not yet know what determines a picture's sense, though I have stated my view that it is both symbolic and perceptual.

Translated into these terms, Walton is claiming that the sense of pictures depends on one use, namely a use in make-believe. In Walton's words, 'the use of pictures in visual games is prior to their possession of semantic content. It is nearly always by using pictures in make-believe that we ascertain what "information" they contain, what propositions they pick out.'[19] The assertion that a sentence can be used to make does not depend on make-believe, because its sense does not depend on make-believe. But serious uses of pictures depend on make-believe, because the sense of a picture derives from the imaginings prescribed for it in an authorized game of make-believe. If pictorial meaning derives from one use, Waltopian depiction shows that use must be a use in make-believe, because pictures need not be used to refer.

My view is that sense, linguistic or pictorial, is not dependent on any particular use: no use is fundamental. Furthermore, a theory of depiction will be a theory of pictorial *sense*, not *use*. The Waltopian thought-experiment poses no obstacle to these claims: first, because we can imagine linguistic Waltopias, and second, because we can imagine pictorial anti-Waltopias.

I see no reason to rule out possible societies whose members use a language but never to refer. We know that in some real societies the use of names is taboo because speaking the name puts its referent in the power of the speaker.[20] Perhaps in these societies names are used as substitutes for things (so that the taboo is a response to a linguistic version of the Pygmalion complex). What is to prevent people in an imaginary society from taking all its words as substitutive and limiting their use to ceremonial contexts in which objects and properties are evoked by linguistic means but never described?

Or we can imagine a game of make-believe in which players use an invented language only to express fictional truths prescribed by the game. Although it is never used outside the gaming context, the make-believe language may acquire a sophisticated grammar and lexicon— all the trappings of a full-blown language. For instance, some children

---

[19] Walton, *Mimesis as Make-Believe*, 351. Walton does not explain the qualification 'nearly always'.

[20] See James George Frazer, *The Golden Bough: A Study in Magic and Religion*, abridged edn. (New York: Macmillan, 1963), 284–305.

playing 'cowboys and Indians' may devise what they consider to be a native American language, which they use only to express fictional truths such as 'The fort surrenders' and 'Smiling Wolf will meet you on top of the mesa' (where the 'fort' is in fact a garden shed and the 'mesa' a neighbour's flower-bed). Again, it may be that the children never use their invented language to refer or to express true propositions. It is true that this language *could* be used to refer, but so could the Waltopians' pictures.

Two observations can be made about these scenarios. The first is that since Waltopian languages are not used to refer, the sense of the expressions making them up cannot be parasitic on a referential use. But, second, it would be hasty to conclude either that the serious uses of languages or the senses of linguistic expressions necessarily derive from their use in make-believe. Yet, this is precisely Walton's inference in the case of Waltopian depiction, that it shows pictures to be fictions.

To clinch the point, we can consider a pictorial anti-Waltopia, a society which makes pictures always subject to the provision that they have referents to which they must be used to refer. Artists in such a society might make mistakes, sometimes drawing a picture without a referent, but they would never make pictures designed not to refer. We might go so far as to stipulate that members of this society simply lack a concept of fiction. It has been said that a necessary condition for making and understanding sentences is a conception of truth and falsity. But surely it is not a precondition of making or understanding representations (linguistic or pictorial) to know that they can be used to convey falsehoods that are to be imagined to be true. Waltopian depiction no more shows that pictures are essentially fictional than anti-Waltopian depiction shows them to be essentially denotative.

In challenging the symbol theory, Walton assumes that an account of how pictures represent, of how they accrue meaning, must take as its starting-point what we do with them. He contends that pictures are used centrally in games of make-believe because they need not have a referential use. But all that Waltopian depiction shows is that pictures need not be *used* to refer. It gives us no reason to believe that pictorial sense depends on pictures' uses in games of make-believe.

I have argued, contrary to Walton, that pictorial meaning is independent of any single use to which pictures may be put. To deny that pictorial sense cuts across uses is to say that if a visiting anthropologist were to show Waltopians a symbolic picture, they would be unable to comprehend it, even by construing it as a substitute. But it seems highly implausible, to say the least, that there could be a society which produced bison substitutes but which could not understand a symbolic picture of a bison. There is part of a picture's meaning that transcends the uses to which it can be put.

I am not proposing to dispense with the dictum that meaning depends on use. Pictures do not depict unless they are used to depict. What I do deny is that meaning depends on one specific use. I take it that a theory of depiction must explain how pictures represent across uses (though it should also explain the range of uses to which pictures can and cannot be put, as pictures).[21]

Surely whatever determines what a picture represents in a game of make-believe can determine what it represents in other contexts of use. If the imaginings a picture prescribes are determined by symbolic or perceptual factors or a blend of the two, then those very factors may determine what pictures represent outside games of make-believe. For instance, if a picture's resemblance to one's beloved is part of what determines that one is to imagine seeing him or her, then surely that resemblance can determine what the picture denotes. Likewise, the fact that pictures need not be used to refer is not inconsistent with the possibility that what they represent is in part a matter of their membership in systems in which they are correlated with their subjects. That pictures need not be used to refer does not show they are not denotative at the level of sense.

4.4 *Imagination*

Walton's challenge to the symbol theory rests on the Waltopian thought-experiment, but another challenge might go as follows. Pictures are fictions because understanding what a picture represents is an enterprise that requires the exercise of the visual imagination. After all, when looking at *Peasant Dance*, it certainly *seems as if* there are some festive peasants, and it seems natural to describe this experience as one of imaginatively seeing peasants partying (Fig. 15). We do not really see peasants; we make-believe that we see peasants.

However, the intuitive appeal of construing pictorial seeing as imaginary seeing is undermined from two directions. First, if a perceptual theory of depiction is ultimately correct, then there will be a sense in

[21] See Dummett, 'What Is a Theory of Meaning?', 99.

which we do just see what pictures represent. Perceptual processes will carry some of the burden in explaining pictorial representation and the phenomenology of pictorial experience. There will be no need to talk of imagined seeing. Furthermore, there is something strained in saying that I imagine seeing a model when I look at a magazine ad, or imagine seeing the Queen when I look at a banknote. I, for one, would want to insist that I just see the model when I look at his picture or the Queen when I look at hers. Granted, this is a mere statement of intuition; however, it counters the intuition that pictorial seeing is imagined seeing.

The second consideration undermining the claim that depiction depends on imagination is that there is really quite a gap between our experience of most pictures and paradigm cases of imaginative substitution. Walton has rightly pointed out that some of our mental attitudes and reactions to pictures are similar to our reactions to seeing the objects that the pictures represent. Looking at a picture of the slime that ate Manhattan, we want to flee, just as one would in a genuine encounter with the slime. Of course, it is an additional puzzle that we do not in fact flee the slime substitute but rather enjoy seeing the slime and experiencing the fear it excites. Both the parallels and the divergences between viewers' reactions to pictures of things and the things themselves can be explained if substitutes are props in games of make-believe that mandate certain imaginings and certain actions.[22] However, not all pictures, perhaps very few, elicit imaginings of this richness. Interpreting *Peasant Dance* does not entail having attitudes or performing actions characteristic of seeing peasants partying. Attitudes and reactions to pictures are not necessarily those consistent with calling them substitutes. What appeal the make-believe theory derives from cases of true substitution is unlikely to illuminate the majority of pictures—pictures like postcards, landscape paintings, or architectural elevations.

[22] Kendall Walton, 'Fearing Fictions', *Journal of Philosophy*, 75 (1978), 5–27.

5

Pictorial Reference

WHILE I have argued that pictures belong to denotative symbol systems, I have also urged that this need not be taken to be incompatible with perceptual accounts of depiction. There remains, however, an impediment to a perceptual theory of pictorial reference: namely Goodman's insistence, in his fifth thesis, that a picture's reference in no way depends on its content—the properties it represents its subject as having. I begin by outlining two theories of pictorial reference derived from standard accounts of naming.[1] One, the description theory, is inconsistent with Goodman's independence thesis; the other, the causal or genetic account, is more congenial to Goodman's view of reference. In learning why neither theory of naming adequately models pictorial reference, we shall see why the independence thesis is false. I end by describing a perceptually based theory of reference in language that promises to explain reference in pictures.

5.1 Two Accounts of Pictorial Reference

One source for an account of pictorial reference is the so-called description theory of naming. According to this theory, a name such as 'Aristotle' denotes what an associated description such as 'the pupil of Plato and the teacher of Alexander' uniquely satisfies. (Since different name-users may associate different descriptions with a name, its 'sense' may be a cluster of descriptions.[2]) Along similar lines, we may say that what a picture refers to is whatever has properties uniquely matching the picture's content. *Piazza San Marco* portrays a particular place because it represents something having features uniquely possessed by that place. This is not at odds with the fact that there can be different

---

[1] See also Anthony Savile, 'Nelson Goodman's *Languages of Art*', *British Journal of Aesthetics*, 11 (1971), 3–12; and Jenefer Robinson, 'Two Theories of Representation', *Erkenntnis*, 12 (1978), 37–53.

[2] See John Searle, 'Proper Names', in Peter Strawson (ed.), *Philosophical Logic* (Oxford: Oxford University Press, 1959), 160.

ways of representing the same object, since distinct pictorial contents might be uniquely true of an object. In sum, then, a picture portrays (singularly refers to) an object if and only if, for some description φ, it is a φ-picture, and that object is uniquely φ. A parallel account of pictures that represent kinds of objects would hold that a picture denotes an *F* if and only if it is a φ-picture such that *F*s are uniquely φ.

Confirmation of the description theory is most likely to be found among pictures whose function is specifically to convey accurate information about the world. Maps are clear examples of informative pictures, since their purpose is to give true descriptions of places—the shape of the land, the systems of drainage, and the type of vegetation and human construction to be found there. Looking at a map, we can tell what place it represents, so long as the map is accurate and we are familiar with the geography of the place. Likewise, though some portraits function chiefly as aesthetic objects rather than transmitters of information, many portraits, such as those found in police databases or family photo albums, are informative. As a general rule, identification of a portrait's subject depends on it accurately conveying distinguishing features of a familiar object. A picture representing a stout, white-haired, intuitionist logician will, for instance, be identified, by those who know him, as Michael Dummett.

Conveying true information about people and objects establishes a standard of correctness and usefulness for many pictures, but it is neither a necessary nor a sufficient condition for pictorial reference. The description account requires that pictures' contents match properties of their subjects, but the fact is that pictures may, and often do, misrepresent their subjects.

To begin with, pictures that are metaphorically true of their subjects raise questions about the notion of 'truth' upon which the description view relies. When a picture depicts an object metaphorically, it denotes it, and has a content that is metaphorically true of it. Picasso's portrait of Françoise Gilot represents her as a flower, perhaps because she possesses a flowery disposition; nevertheless, it is not literally true that she is a flower (Fig. 17). Granted, this picture's content might strictly match Gilot in a sufficient number of respects to pick her out as its unique subject; still, there are clear-cut cases of pictures not literally true of their subjects in any way at all. In the Van Eyck brothers' altarpiece at St Bavo's in Ghent, for instance, the centre of attention in the depicted scene is a lamb standing on an altar. Of course, the picture

Fig. 17. Pablo Picasso, *Françoise Gilot, 'Femme Fleur'*, 1946

represents Christ, whose innocence is being compared to a lamb's, yet none of the properties it ascribes to him is literally true of him.

The difficulties posed by metaphorical pictures are symptomatic of our ignorance of the relation of metaphorical truth to literal truth in metaphors of all kinds. Happily, we need not pursue a general theory of metaphor, for pictures can ascribe properties to their subjects that they possess neither literally nor metaphorically. Maps may misrepresent their subjects for the most prosaic of reasons: terrain changes, and buildings crumble. In portraiture, the practice of idealizing the appearance of sitters is so commonplace that Cromwell found it necessary to make a point of being painted 'warts and all'. We must conclude that pictures need not embody descriptive information uniquely true of their subjects in order for viewers to grasp what they denote. Nor does the fact that a picture happens to represent an object accurately guarantee that it refers to that object. No matter how accurately a picture visually describes two indiscernible objects, it may nevertheless depict one and not the other. A picture might, for example, refer to only one of a pair of identical twins, though it matches both equally.

Goodman's insistence that pictorial reference does not depend on accurate matches between pictures' contents and properties of their subjects appears justified. The existence of pictures which deliberately misrepresent their subjects shows that while pictorial content may sometimes determine what a picture refers to, it need not. Pictures denote when they do not accurately describe their referents; and if a picture is uniquely true of something, that thing need not be its referent.

In recent years philosophers inspired by Saul Kripke's *Naming and Necessity* have taken up a theory of reference for certain linguistic terms which eschews the description paradigm. They argue that the reference of proper names, in particular, is not determined by associated descriptions, but depends instead on the history of a name's production and subsequent use. Thus, if pictures do not refer descriptively, then perhaps they refer 'directly', as do names.

Kripke's attack on the description account of naming has two prongs, one concerning how identity statements containing proper names can be necessary, the other centring on the observation that 'very often we use a name on the basis of considerable misinformation'.[3] The latter echoes precisely what is wrong with the description theory of pictorial reference. The description theory predicts that a name refers to whatever

---

[3] Saul Kripke, *Naming and Necessity*, rev. edn. (Oxford: Basil Blackwell, 1980), 83–4.

satisfies a description associated with the name. But suppose the description we associate with 'Gödel' is 'the person who discovered the incompleteness of mathematics', and suppose that, unbeknownst to us, it was not Gödel but a man named Schmidt who really proved the incompleteness of mathematics. Kripke notes that, on the description view, 'Gödel' refers to Schmidt, which is absurd.

Kripke supplies the outlines of an alternative to the descriptive account of naming: a name's reference depends upon the history of its production and use. At an early stage in a name-using practice, the meaning of the name is fixed for those who are acquainted with the object named. This takes place in the context of what Kripke calls a 'baptism', a possibly very informal ritual in which the name is given to an object picked out by ostension or by an identifying description. The notion of a baptism, however, is really a metaphor for the idea that a name refers to an object that played a specific role in the genesis of the name-using practice. After the initial baptism, the name is passed from link to link in a chain of communication, and is successfully communicated along the chain as long as each speaker intends to use the name with the same reference as previous speakers. It is not required that later speakers fix the reference of the name in the same way as earlier speakers; later speakers may in fact have no acquaintance with the name's referent and know no uniquely identifying description for it. Consequently, a name may be used in conjunction with any amount of misinformation.

This description-free account of reference may illuminate how pictures refer independently of their content. Consider a portrait of one of two indiscernible objects. If the portrait portrays one twin and not the other, then the two kinds of depiction, reference and predication, are independent. Pictorial content does not determine denotation descriptively, for any picture whose content is true of one twin is also true of the other. Rather, the picture portrays one twin and not the other because that twin played the appropriate part in the genesis of the picture. And just as a name may denote an object about which we harbour tremendous misinformation, flattering portraits and outdated maps denote just those objects that figure in their production.

What, then, are the genetic factors that determine a picture's reference? The role of a picture's referent in its production may vary, as there are many acceptable ways of making pictures. In the case of photographs and other mechanically produced pictures, the referent might be the object that reflected light on to a photo-sensitive surface to form an image. In the case of images made by hand, the object a picture denotes might be the object that served as a model, guiding the artist in the production of the picture. In either case, a picture's reference would be determined not by its content, but by the history of its production.

Difficulties for the genetic theory of pictorial reference do arise, however, particularly in connection with whether genetic facts are sufficient to determine a picture's denotation. Suppose that I am such an inept draughtsman that, assigned the task of painting Baroness Thatcher, what comes off my easel is a tangle of lines, apparently representing nothing (I overlook the possibility that I have created a wire-wool-picture that is metaphorically true of the iron lady). Surely we would want to say that, even though she played the required role of sitter in its production, my work does not portray Thatcher. The reason is that my scrawl simply does not represent her as having any visual properties—properties she may be seen to have.

This conclusion is at odds with Goodman's insistence on the independence of reference and predication. Goodman writes:

> If I tell you I have a picture of a certain black horse, and then I produce a snapshot in which he has come out a light speck in the distance, you can hardly convict me of lying; but you may well feel that I misled you. You understandably took me to mean a picture of the black horse as such; and you therefore expected the picture not only to denote the horse in question but to be a black-horse-picture.[4]

Presumably Goodman is maintaining that his snapshot was caused by a black horse and denotes one, even though it is not a black-quadruped-suitable-for-riding-picture. The rule that, in this case, a picture of a black horse represent a black horse *as* a black horse is a matter of convenience, not a prerequisite for reference.

None the less, Goodman's snapshot fails as a counter-instance to the proposition that a picture refers to an object only if it represents the object as having *some* property. After all, Goodman's snapshot *is* a black-horse-picture. It does not represent a black horse as a black horse in the informative way we might normally expect, which is indeed a matter of convenience, but it does represent it as having some properties. It represents the black horse as having just the sort of visual features that a black horse would be seen to have from a distance.

Recall the distinction I drew in the Introduction between figurative

[4] Goodman, *Languages of Art*, 29.

and abstract pictures. The pure abstraction of Mondrian's later years, for which he is famous, developed out of an earlier figurative painting, and certain transitional pictures began as figure studies and ended as abstractions. But despite its causal connection with a waterfront scene, one such picture, *Pier and Ocean*, does not depict a waterfront. My botched portrait of Thatcher falls in the same class as Mondrian's abstractions (though without its aesthetic pretensions). It is a picture, but not a figurative picture, because it does not represent its subject as having at least some visual properties.

Unless we abandon the distinction between figuration and abstraction, we must accept the principle that pictures represent objects only in so far as they represent them as having some visual properties. A Saenredam church interior may represent its subject in intricate detail, satisfying a large number of properties, whereas a far-away-horse-picture, no doubt inconveniently, represents its subject as satisfying few properties. My portrait of Baroness Thatcher does not depict her because it does not represent her as having any properties she may be seen to have. Genetic facts do not suffice to secure pictorial reference.

Of course, it is incumbent on a theory of pictorial reference accepting the principle that reference depends on content to specify what kinds of properties pictures must represent their subjects as having. If, as seems likely, they are visual properties, we need to know what counts as a visual property. For the moment, though, I simply rely on the intuitive distinction between abstract and representational pictures.

Neither the description nor the genetic theory of pictorial reference is adequate. On the one hand, pictures may misrepresent their subjects, so their content need not match what they denote. On the other, pictures must represent their subjects as having some properties—the independence thesis is false.

There is an important parallel between perceptual experiences and pictures: what both represent depends on a combination of their content and their genesis. To perceive Nessie is in part to have an experience with a particular content, but it is also to be in causal contact with a certain beast. Characterizing the percept–object relation solely in terms of the percept's content distorts an account of misperception—you see a square tower even if you see it *as* round—just as characterizing the picture–object relation solely in terms of pictorial content distorts an account of misrepresentation. But causal connections are not enough. A picture must have some content about its subject—content, moreover, that discloses its subject.

5.2 Hybrids and Puzzles

According to hybrid theories of pictorial reference, a picture denotes the object which played a suitable role in its production, as model or sitter, but only if it also represents its model or sitter as having some properties. The challenge for such accounts is to say how a picture's content contributes to its reference, if not descriptively. In this section I profile a hybrid account of pictorial reference proposed by David Kaplan.[5] Kaplan's hybrid is, I think, a step in the right direction, though I argue that it proves unable to accommodate a number of puzzle cases. The reason is that it fails to characterize adequately the relationship between pictorial content and reference.

Kaplan distinguishes between what he calls the 'descriptive content' and the 'genetic character' of a picture. The former comprises 'features of a picture, in virtue of which we say it resembles or is a likeness of a particular'.[6] Although this definition makes use of the concept of resemblance, it does not prejudice Kaplan's arguments to construe descriptive content as the properties that a picture represents its subject as having, whether or not resemblance is involved.[7] Now, Kaplan does not require that a picture's descriptive content *match* its subject, but only that it be 'vivid'. Vividness is in part a matter of how many properties a picture represents its subject as satisfying—a picture of Central Park in the dark is less vivid than a passport photograph (though it may be as accurate). But vividness additionally depends on the interests and concerns of viewers. As Kaplan puts it, 'to the clothier, nude portraits may be lacking in detail, while to the foot fetishist a picture showing only the left big toe may leap from the canvas'.[8]

Genetic character, on the other hand, reflects features of the causal chain culminating in the picture's production. If a picture denotes an individual or a kind, that object or some object of that kind must have served in some way in the production of the picture. Kaplan says that the picture is 'of' the object which figured appropriately in its production. Genetic character is independent of descriptive content, because a picture does not make visible its genetic history.

---

[5] David Kaplan, 'Quantifying In', in Donald Davidson and Jaako Hintikka (eds.), *Words and Objections*, rev. edn. (Dordrecht: Reidel, 1975), sect. 10.

[6] Ibid. 225.

[7] I also disregard Kaplan's simplifying limitation of his theory to portraits of persons.

[8] Kaplan, 'Quantifying In', 229. Kaplan's conception of vividness parallels some definitions of pictorial realism. See Lopes, 'Pictorial Realism'.

For Kaplan, 'there are no necessary connections between how vivid a picture is and whether it is *of* anyone'.[9] The trouble with this is that it allows a gap to open up between a picture's aetiology and its content. What a picture is 'of' and what its content represents it as of may not coincide, leaving us with a puzzle about what it denotes.

For example, I once again try my hand at portraiture, setting out to portray Queen Victoria; but this time not only is my picture botched, it happens to be botched in such a way that its content uniquely identifies Divine, the famous drag queen. According to the hybrid view, the picture represents Queen Victoria. After all, she figured in the picture's production, and it has some content relating to her, albeit not content enabling viewers to identify the picture as of her. But this seems wrong. It implies that the difference between a Divine-picture and a Victoria-picture 'of' the Queen has no representational significance.

Dilemmas also arise whenever an artist uses one thing as a model to depict another. For instance, on a number of occasions Rembrandt used his mistress, Hendrickje Stoffels, as a model for paintings of Bathsheba. It is fair to assume that the contents of these pictures are true of both Hendrickje and Bathsheba, because a particular model is chosen for its similarity to what it models. By the genetic standard, Rembrandt's picture refers only to Hendrickje, who features in the required way in its genesis. Nevertheless, some would deny that the picture portrays Hendrickje at all, and everybody would agree that it portrays Bathsheba.

Of course, there comes a point where reference is indeterminate, but I doubt that these cases have reached that point. Rather, Kaplan's hybrid is unable to provide coherent, intuitive predictions of pictorial reference in complex cases because it too loosely associates genetic character with descriptive content. I suggest that we seek a stronger link between a picture's genesis and its content, so that differences in origin generate differences in content, and content shows the way to origin.

5.3 Reference, Perception, and Thought

Description and naming do not supply adequate models for pictorial reference. In this section I look for an alternative model among the class of linguistic symbols whose most familiar denizens include demonstrative

---

[9] Kaplan, 'Quantifying In', 227–8.

expressions like 'this such-and-such' and 'that so-and-so'. Unlike descriptions and names, these expressions are intimately tied to the exercise of perceptual capacities. To understand an utterance such as 'That man sings opera' requires being in perceptual contact with the man the speaker is perceiving.

For an account of reference of such terms capable of providing a suitable model for pictorial reference and its links to pictorial content and perception, I turn to Gareth Evans's book *The Varieties of Reference*. Evans devises what is in effect a hybrid theory of linguistic reference. Certain expressions require language-users to think of their referents by identifying them on the basis of information derived from them. Information-based identification has both genetic and content-sensitive elements.

The information system. According to Evans, certain expressions refer by calling on speakers to entertain thoughts about their referents that are grounded in the workings of what he calls the 'information system'.[10] Evans sees humans as 'gatherers, storers and transmitters of information'.[11] Perception, memory, and communication are all components of the information system: perception is the source of much new information, while memory stores information, as do media of communication, linguistic, pictorial, or otherwise. But these are truisms; Evans's notion of information is a technical one with a precise meaning.

In the first place, informational states have a distinctive place in human cognition. Unlike beliefs, information states are typically explained at the sub-personal level of brains, neural processes, and psychological mechanisms. (This is not to say that they are inaccessible to consciousness—perceptual states, for example, are informational and often conscious.) Moreover, information states are 'belief-independent', because their contents are inalterable in the face of beliefs and desires.[12] In Ponzo's illusion the top line appears longer than the bottom line, and this appearance is not affected by knowledge that the lines are equal in length (Fig. 18). Finally, information states are typically 'non-conceptual'—their content need not consist of properties of which the

---

[10] This section draws on Evans, *Varieties of Reference*, esp. 89–92, 100–5, 121–35.

[11] Evans, *Varieties of Reference*, 122.

[12] Belief-independence is roughly equivalent to Fodor's notion of 'cognitive impenetrability', the inalterability of a representation's content in response to changes in the representer's beliefs: Jerry A. Fodor, *The Modularity of Mind* (Cambridge, Mass.: MIT Press, 1983), 66–7.

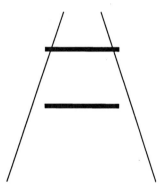

Fig. 18. Ponzo's illusion

subject possesses concepts.[13] In order to see and respond to a spectrum of colour, one need not have a concept of every visible colour. Thus perceptual states can represent the world as having properties which the perceiver may experience and to which her behaviour may be responsive, although they are not part of her conceptual repertoire. Evans defines information states as states of information systems, mechanisms for information transmission and storage. A piece of information is 'of' whatever object was the 'source' of the information, the input to the information system. To the extent that the system is reliable, a state's content will match properties of its source; but nothing prevents unreliable information transmission, in which the content of a state is a garbled version of the properties of its source. Furthermore, two states may be 'of' the same source though they do not have the same content, and identical contents may have different sources. Information is 'of' its source, whether or not its content matches its source.

The paradigm of an information system is a mechanism such as a camera. A piece of information is 'of' its object in the way that a photograph is 'of' whatever reflected light on to the film, no matter what the resulting image looks like. However, information systems need not be strictly causal mechanisms, and Evans emphasizes the importance of what he calls social information systems, systems in

---

[13] See Evans, *Varieties of Reference*, 226–7; Christopher Peacocke, 'Perceptual Content', in J. Almog, J. Perry, and H. K. Wettstein (eds.), *Themes from Kaplan* (New York: Oxford University Press, 1989), esp. 297–323; and Adrian Cussins, 'The Connectionist Construction of Concepts', in Margaret Boden (ed.), *The Philosophy of Artificial Intelligence* (Oxford: Oxford University Press, 1990), 380–4.

which pieces of information are stored in human memory and transmitted linguistically, pictorially, or by other means from person to person. As we know, such systems can be unreliable; but although the pieces of information they transmit are easily garbled, they remain 'of' their sources.

Information-based identification. Someone in possession of a piece of information can think of its source in two ways. Most simply, he can think of its source simply as 'whatever was the source of this information'. This method of identification does not depend on the content of the information or the reliability of the system. Thus, when a piece of information is garbled, we are apt to identify its source by tracing its causal history—this may be how Goodman targeted a certain horse as the subject of his black-speck-photograph. The drawback of this method is that singling out the source of a piece of information *as its source* requires a sophisticated conception of the information system and of what counts as a source.

Provided a system maintains sufficiently reliable correlations between the properties of sources and the contents of outputs, it is possible to identify the source of some information in a second way, on the basis of its content. Thus one may identify the source of some information by means of a 'mode of identification' appropriate to a state with a particular kind of content. One familiar mode of identification is descriptive, but the bulk of *The Varieties of Reference* is devoted to describing alternative modes of identification that are tied up with perceptual skills and that underlie the functioning of a variety of referring expressions. Shortly I shall outline Evans's account of demonstratives and their basis in a demonstrative mode of identification. Another mode that Evans describes, recognition-based identification, will play a key role in the theory of depiction I present below.

For now, it is important to note the following difference between the two methods for identifying sources of information. Since success in employing a mode of identification to target the source of some information depends on the system's reliability, these identifications are defeasible in a way that identifications of the first kind are not. An identification of the source of some information as whatever was its source, cannot but succeed in hitting its target (if it has one). By contrast, an identification on the basis of a state's content is 'well-grounded' only if it picks out the very object from which the information was in fact derived. An identification of the alleged source of a piece of information is 'ill-grounded' if the object identified is not the source, if nothing is identified as the source, or if the information in fact has no source.

Constraints on thought. So far, we have described the information system and the possibility that objects can be identified as the sources of pieces of information. As Evans insists, the information system and its attendant processes of identification operate at a sub-personal level. However, much of the importance (for our purposes) of information-based modes of identifying objects lies in their making available certain ways of thinking about and hence referring to them. Evans calls thoughts about objects which identify them as the sources of information with certain contents 'information-based thoughts'. One way to think of an object, for instance, is by being in perceptual contact with it. Such a thought is information-based, because its content stems from the deliverances of the perceptual information system.

Having distinguished the sub-personal information system from the personal level of thoughts, intentions, and desires, it is incumbent upon Evans to explain what more is required of an information-based thought than simply possessing a piece of information. Information-based thoughts, like all thoughts, are subject to two constraints.

First, to think of an object, one must have a concept of it that distinguishes it from all other objects. Evans calls this 'Russell's principle'. The second constraint, the generality constraint, is an elaboration of Russell's principle. Evans observes that our concepts of objects and properties reflect the structure of our cognitive capacities. In order to grasp the thought that 'a is F', for example, one must have a concept of a that enables one to understand the thoughts that 'a is G' and 'a is H', carrying on for every property of which one has a concept. Similarly, being able to entertain the thought that 'a is F' requires a concept of F that enables one to understand the thoughts 'b is F', 'c is F', and so on for every object one can think of.[14] In other words, the ability to think of John is structured by the fact that there is something common to understanding the thoughts 'John is happy', 'John is sad', and all other thoughts about John. The ability to think of things in different ways is integral to possessing concepts of them.

---

[14] Having a concept of a and F means knowing what it would be for the thought 'a is F' to be true, but it does not follow that it is easy to understand 'a is F'. On this point and for a defence of the generality constraint, see Christopher Peacocke, *A Study of Concepts* (Cambridge, Mass.: MIT Press, 1992), 42–51.

A way of identifying an object on the basis of information derived from it enables one to think of the object only if it meets these two conditions. Note that identifying an object just as the source of a piece of information derived from it meets neither condition. We must therefore consider what modes of identification provide us with adequate ways of thinking of the sources of information.

Perceptual demonstratives. Having outlined his conception of the information system, introduced modes of identification, and established constraints on information-based thought, Evans proposes that understanding certain categories of referring expressions consists in thinking of their referents on the basis of information derived from them. Different kinds of expressions require thinkers to identify their referents using different modes of identification, some of them perceptual. The paradigm case is that of demonstrative reference, which I shall outline in only the roughest way.[15]

According to Evans, understanding an expression like 'that horse on the horizon' depends on having a thought about that horse based on a demonstrative mode of identifying the horse. Demonstrative identification requires that the perceiver maintain a perceptual connection with an object which provides information about it over a period of time.

How does demonstrative identification satisfy the constraints on thought? Consider a voice heard over the radio which elicits the utterance 'That woman is astute'. Surely in this case an information link with the woman does not distinguish her from other objects. One possibility is that the thought about that woman must incorporate a conception of the informational situation, so that we think of her as the input to a radio-cum-auditory information-transmission system. Evans argues, however, that since such cases of mediated demonstration are unusual, it makes little sense to generalize the awareness of informational situations that they might be thought to require to all instances of demonstrative identification. As an alternative, Evans suggests that demonstrative identification generally provides discriminating knowledge because it confers an ability to locate the object perceived.

In sum, demonstrative identification enables a perceiver to think of an object as occupying a unique path in space and time. To understand a demonstrative expression is to think of its referent on the basis of an ongoing perceptual link with it that meets Evans's two constraints on thought.

    [15] Evans, *Varieties of Reference*, ch. 6, esp. 143–51.

5.4 Subject and Content

In my view, Evans's conception of reference and its connection to information-based thought provides a suitable model for a perceptual account of how pictures refer. On this model, pictures are part of an information system, individual pictures conveying perceptual information from their subjects. A picture represents an object only if it conveys information from it on the basis of which it can be identified. To understand pictures, viewers must employ a specifically pictorial mode (or modes) of identification which single out, on the basis of their contents, the pictures' sources.

This proposal bears the marks of a hybrid theory. An object or kind of object is a picture's subject only if it served as the source of the information contained in the picture. But a picture's content plays an ineliminable role in its representing its subject, for it is on the basis of its content that we identify its subject. These two factors are balanced in the requirement that identifications be well grounded. Of course, it remains to be seen how this version of the hybrid theory resolves the puzzles posed by the use of artists' models and by pictures like my botched painting of Queen Victoria.

The more pressing task, however, is to ascertain what kind of information pictures embody and what mode or modes of perceptual identification viewers employ in identifying their subjects. We know that there is little reason to assume that we identify pictures' subjects descriptively. And whatever mode or modes of identification turn out to be appropriate for identifying pictures' sources, we must not forget that they must provide viewers with conceptions of pictures' subjects which meet Evans's two constraints. It is only with an understanding of pictorial modes of identification that we will see how a picture's content contributes to its reference and how its content is constrained by its reference.

It should be obvious by now that the claim that pictures belong to denotative symbol systems in no way diminishes the viability of perceptual explanations of depiction. Goodman's insight that pictures can fruitfully be modelled on other kinds of representation was handicapped by an austere and somewhat idiosyncratic view of linguistic reference. But there is no reason to be bound by Goodman's conception of reference. The ties between reference and perception are richer than we might at first have imagined. If pictures are symbols, they may be symbols whose reference depends on the exercise of perceptual skills.

PART THREE
Aspect Recognition

6

Pictorial Content

PARTS One and Two introduced two models for explaining depiction, one focusing on pictures' perceptual characteristics, the other on their symbolic ones. I have argued that these models are not incompatible. What pictures symbolize may depend in crucial respects on the perceptual skills of their interpreters. Unfortunately, none of the perceptual theories of depiction surveyed in Part One proved adequate. The following four chapters lay out what I dub the 'aspect-recognition theory' of depiction. This theory connects depiction to perceptual processes in a way that accommodates pictures' symbolic structure and meets the diversity, phenomenology, and twofoldness constraints. This chapter and the next develop the theme that pictures present recognizable aspects of objects; Chapter 8 contributes a supplementary account of non-recognitional pictorial modes of identification; and Chapter 9 seeks to explain the phenomenology and twofoldness of pictorial experience.

This chapter lays the groundwork for the aspect-recognition theory by taking up two themes. The first is the distinctive nature of pictorial content. Interestingly, perceptual and symbol theorists alike are frequently beguiled by a myth that pictorial content is essentially determinate or specific. A notable exception is Gombrich, whose insistence in *Art and Illusion* that pictures are by necessity selective in how they represent their subjects has been neglected, unduly, I think.[1] I refine Gombrich's insight about pictures' selectivity, and develop from it a way of describing and individuating the 'aspects' that pictures select.

This leads to the second theme: how pictorial systems differ from each other as well as from other representational systems. I believe that this question cannot be adequately answered without an account of pictorial content as aspectually structured. By examining the aspectual differences between pictorial systems, we take the first step towards explaining their diversity.

---

[1] Schier, in *Deeper into Pictures*, 162–5, also discusses selectivity, but without recognizing its significance for explaining depiction.

6.1 Myths of Specificity

According to most perceptual theories, as well as Goodman's formalist version of the symbol theory, a distinctive feature of pictures' contents, and by implication their designs, is their specificity. This specificity has been described in numerous ways, all echoing the platitude that a picture is worth a thousand words.

One manifestation of the myth of pictorial specificity is the attribution to pictures of the formal properties of analogicity and relative repleteness. As we saw in Section 3.2, Goodman argues that pictures are analogue in the sense that any difference, no matter how small, in a picture's design potentially makes for a different character with a different content or reference. In this respect pictures are quite unlike language, which is made up of a limited number of differentiated elements.

It is not an objection to Goodman's use of analogicity that some pictures are fashioned of a limited, differentiated array of elements, as, for example, are the halftone reproductions in this book, which are composed of a matrix of fairly regular black ink dots that we can imagine to be syntactically disjoint and differentiated. In Goodman's view, analogicity is not a property of individual symbols but rather of systems of symbols. Although a halftone picture might not be analogue, it belongs to a system which is. Any slight difference in the matrix— a misalignment of one dot—would in principle render it a different symbol in the system.

Must all pictorial systems be analogue, though? Goodman gives no argument to show that they must. On the contrary, as Kent Bach has pointed out, nothing rules out a system of pictures comprised of a restricted repertoire of dots of differentiated sizes and colours—imagine a system made up of pictures composed of Ben Day dots in colours straight from the tube, à la Lichtenstein.[2] Such a system would not be analogue if the rules for reading it were to demand that we overlook small variations in dot size, shape, and colouring, in the way that readers of this book are to overlook variations in leading or a missing serif as not relevant to determining what characters are inscribed. Surprisingly, Goodman admits that a notational, or non-analogue, picture system could arise through 'custom' or 'express stipulation'.[3] Analogue specificity is not essential to depiction.

---

[2] Bach, 'Part of What a Picture Is', 126.   [3] Goodman, *Languages of Art*, 193.

As analogicity never sufficed to distinguish picturing from other kinds of representation, Goodman added that pictures also belong to relatively replete systems. One system is replete relative to a second if the design properties with representational relevance in the second are included among those with relevance in the first. Thickness and intensity of line are representationally significant in *Piazza San Marco* but not in an EEG read-out, so the former is replete compared to the latter. Repleteness is also a kind of specificity: pictures are more specific in the sense that more of their design properties are representationally significant.

I mentioned that one of the themes of this chapter is what distinguishes pictorial systems from each other as well as from non-pictorial systems. Goodman gives the impression that it is possible to individuate pictorial systems in a neat, unequivocal manner, but he nowhere explains what criteria are to be used for distinguishing systems, and I believe this omission to be one root of the undefended claim that anything can depict anything else. However, it might be thought that relative repleteness may serve to individuate pictorial systems. One system of depiction differs from another if and only if one possesses some representationally relevant property that the other does not. Colour photography is a different system from charcoal drawing, because colour is representationally significant in the former but not in the latter.

The trouble is that a design property may correlate with different contents in different systems. In Albertian depiction, size on the picture plane represents spatial location, whereas in Byzantine icon painting, it represents the relative importance of the figure represented. Surely Albertian naturalism and Byzantine iconography are different systems, even if they share the same design properties.

More troubling still, if relative repleteness is a matter of degree, then to claim it as the mark of the pictorial is to imply that some pictures are more pictorial than others.[4] Are paintings more pictorial than drawings because they possess more representationally relevant design properties than drawings? Or imagine a system of pictures that are 'life-size'. Life-size pictures have a representationally salient property not possessed by other pictures, so they are more replete than undersize or oversize pictures. Are they more pictorial too? Clearly the number of representationally relevant properties that a system possesses relative to other systems is not what makes it pictorial.

---

[4] Strangely, Goodman sees that repleteness is a matter of degree, and accepts the counter-intuitive conclusion that the pictorial is also a matter of degree. See Goodman, *Languages of Art*, 230.

Fred Dretske, in his book *Knowledge and the Flow of Information*, employs a notion of 'analog' representation distinct from Goodman's (I preserve Dretske's orthography to signal the distinction).[5] Dretske introduces his notion of analogicity in order to characterize the specificity of perceptual as well as pictorial content.

The apparatus needed to construct Dretske's notion of analog content is as involved as that needed to describe Goodman's. To begin with, an informational or representational state representing its source as F can carry additional information about its source (Dretske is not using 'information' in Evans's special sense). Often this additional information is *nested* in its representing its source as F. The information that something is G may be nested in information that it is F when Fs are Gs by definition, when all Fs are Gs, or when there is a natural law to the effect that whatever is F is G.

If a representation carries the information that its source is F and carries no more specific information, the F-information is 'digital'. On the other hand, a state that carries the information that its source is F and also carries additional, *more specific* information *not nested* in its being F, then the F-information is 'analog'.

For instance, the remark that 'The cup has coffee in it' carries the information that the cup has coffee in it in digital form. This is because it carries plenty of other nested information, such as that the cup contains a drink brewed from the seeds of the shrub *Coffea arabica*; but it carries no more specific information not already nested in the information that the cup contains coffee. By contrast, a picture of a cup of coffee conveys the information that the cup has coffee in it in analog form. This is because, in carrying the information that the cup has coffee in it, the picture also carries more specific information, about the approximate amount of coffee in the cup, whether it contains milk, what the cup's shape and colour is, and so on.

Dretske claims that most information a picture carries is 'by necessity' analog. The information that a man is blowing a bubble is carried by Chardin's picture in analog form, because the picture carries additional, more specific information not nested in the information that a man is blowing a bubble (see Fig. 13). The picture specifies the size of the bubble, the instrument with which it is blown, and the unusual

---

[5] Fred Dretske, *Knowledge and the Flow of Information* (Oxford: Basil Blackwell, 1981), esp. 135–41.

coiffure of the bubble-blower. The digital information that this picture carries is all that we can learn by looking at it, and to put this information in verbal form would require an enormously detailed description. Dretske reflects that, 'to say a picture is worth a thousand words is merely to acknowledge that, for most pictures at least, the sentence needed to express all the information contained in the picture would have to be very complex indeed. Most pictures have a wealth of detail, and a degree of specificity, that makes [this] all but impossible.'[6] Dretske proceeds to argue that perceptual experience, like pictures, is analog, or highly specific, unlike cognition, which is digital.

However, Peacocke has pointed out that Dretske's notion of analog does not capture what is special about perceptual content.[7] His objection is that an utterance that 'John is a bachelor' carries the information that John is a man in analog form, because the utterance also carries the more specific, non-nested information that John is an unmarried man. If both an utterance and a perceptual experience carry the information that John is a man in analog form, then analogicity does not distinguish them. A parallel argument shows that analogicity does not distinguish the content of a picture from that of an utterance. Both a picture of John and the statement that 'John is a bachelor' carry the information that John is a man in analog form.

A further problem with Dretske's distinction is that every representational state carries in digital form that information which is given in an exhaustive description of its content. It may be that the content of a picture or an experience cannot be specified verbally, but it does not follow that pictures and experiences have no digital content. What does follow is merely that a complete specification of the content of either a picture or a perceptual experience is essentially pictorial or essentially perceptual. At any rate, there are some very simple pictures whose contents can be given complete verbal expression. Relative specificity therefore fails to single out what is distinctive about the content of either pictures or perception.

The most widespread and virulent form of the myth of pictorial specificity is the belief that pictorial content is determinate for some properties. It is thought that there are certain properties that all pictures must represent their subjects either as having or not having. A classic instance of this myth is Daniel Dennett's *Content and Consciousness*,

---

[6] Ibid. 138.   [7] Peacocke, 'Perceptual Content', 314–15.

where pictorial specificity plays a pivotal role in an argument against construing mental images as pictorial.[8]

Some take evidence that the time needed to perform certain mental tasks such as rotating and matching imagined shapes to show that we employ mental images whose contents are similar to the contents both of pictures and visual experiences.[9] Dennett rejects this alleged similarity. Form a mental image of a person. Does your image represent him (her?) as wearing a hat or not wearing a hat? Obviously, a mental image of a person, like a description, need not go into the matter of headgear (or gender). By contrast, Dennett claims that a picture of a person, like a visual experience of a person, must represent him or her as either hatted or bareheaded (unless something occludes the figure so that we cannot tell). Likewise, I can imagine a striped tiger without imagining it as having a particular number of stripes; but if I draw a tiger, my drawing must represent the tiger as having some particular number of stripes, or else avoid the issue by obscuring the tiger (as oversize leaves might obscure the stripes in a tiger painted by Henri Rousseau). Whereas mental images and descriptions need only go into features of objects that are of interest to the imaginer or the describer, pictures, like visual experiences, are determinate with regard to certain properties.

As with Goodman's and Dretske's versions of pictorial specificity, the claim that pictures must be determinate in the way Dennett suggests turns out to be a myth.[10] A stick figure need not represent a man as either hatted or bareheaded. A cartoon may represent writing without going into the number of letters, words, or lines represented—or indeed, what they say (Fig. 19). Like descriptions, pictures can simply refuse to go into such matters. As I insisted in Chapter 5, pictures must represent their subjects as having or not having some of the properties that an ordinary visual experience could represent them as having, but they need not go into all their subjects' visual properties. Pictures need not be determinately specific.

[8] Daniel Dennett, *Content and Consciousness*, 2nd edn. (London: Routledge and Kegan Paul, 1986), 132–7. See also Zenon Pylyshyn, 'The Imagery Debate: Analog Media Versus Tacit Knowledge', in Ned Block (ed.), *Imagery* (Cambridge, Mass.: MIT Press, 1981), 151–206.
[9] See Roger Brown and Richard J. Herrnstein, 'Icons and Images', in Block (ed.), *Imagery*, 18–49.
[10] See Fodor, *Language of Thought*, 187–91; Ned Block, 'The Photographic Fallacy in the Debate about Mental Imagery', *Noûs*, 17 (1983), 651–61; and Robert Schwartz, 'Imagery—There's More to it than Meets the Eye', in Block (ed.), *Imagery*, 124.

Fig. 19. Man reading newspaper

6.2 Selective Aspects

In place of specificity, I want to establish selectivity as the distinguishing mark of pictorial content. However, there are two ways in which pictures may be selective about their contents, and it is the second type of selectivity that is distinctively pictorial.

One of the themes of Gombrich's *Art and Illusion* is that few pictures can approach true determinacy.[11] The 'copy theory' assumes an ideal of depiction in which nature can be captured in its infinite detail, but 'the amount of information reaching us from the visual world is incalculably large, and the artist's medium is inevitably restricted and granular'.[12] Lewis Carroll mocked the ideal of determinacy by pointing out that a perfectly determinate map of Britain would need to occupy a space the size of Great Britain itself. Gombrich concludes that artists must make some selection of properties that they will represent things as having or not having, remaining non-committal about the rest. Moreover, what selection an artist makes is highly variable. Different traditions of picturing employ different visual vocabularies or 'schemata' of motifs for which pictures select.[13]

---

[11] See esp. Gombrich, *Art and Illusion*, 85–7, 219–20, 314–15. See also Schier, *Deeper into Pictures*, 162–73.

[12] Gombrich, *Art and Illusion*, 219.

[13] A knowledge of the selections characteristic of a tradition informs viewers' expectations about how to interpret pictures, and when the actual selection corresponds with the expected selection, the result is illusion. That is, when we see represented those properties of things that we expect to see represented, we do not see what is left out.

This conception of pictorial selectivity is an antidote to overly high expectations regarding pictures' information-handling capacities. Unfortunately, it is also a form of selectivity that pictures share with other representations. I can portray a face without going into whether it is freckled or not, just as I can describe the face without either asserting or denying that it is freckled. Descriptions are usually indeterminate in this way for the same reason that pictures are. It is beyond the practical capacity of a description to take into account every feature that an object may or may not possess and state whether it does or does not possess that property. Only an object with very few properties can be drawn or described in perfect detail.

The second form of selectivity derives not from the impracticability of determinacy, but from structural features of depiction. While Dennett overlooked the possibility that pictures can refuse to go into certain features of their subjects, he did allow that, because they represent scenes from particular points of view, pictures are precluded from representing their subjects as having or not having certain properties. There are four possibilities. It is one thing to draw a person in a hat, another to draw her bareheaded, and a third to draw her without going into the matter of hattedness. The fourth possibility is to draw her as observed in conditions which make it impossible to tell. The figure's head might, for example, be obscured by some object. It is the selectivity represented by this fourth possibility that I wish to focus on.

Some terminology borrowed from Ned Block is helpful in keeping track of the four options.[14] A representation (of any kind) is 'committal' with respect to a property F provided that it represents its subject as either F or not-F. If it does not go into the matter of F-ness, it is 'inexplicitly non-committal' with respect to F. Finally, a representation is 'explicitly non-committal' with regard to F when it represents its subject as having some property (or properties) that preclude it from being committal with regard to F.[15]

A picture is inexplicitly non-committal about the number of stripes a tiger sports if it simply refuses to go into the matter, as a stick figure does not go into the matter of headgear. Rousseau's picture of a tiger

[14] Block, 'Photographic Fallacy', 654.
[15] I have slightly revised Block's definition of explicit non-commitment. According to Block, a picture is explicitly non-committal with regard to F if it represents its subject as having properties which preclude its representing its subject as F. This is incomplete, since representing a person as hatted precludes representing her not only as red-haired but also as not red-haired.

is explicitly non-committal about the tiger's stripes because it represents the tiger as obscured by leaves, and this precludes it from representing all the tiger's stripes. A picture that represents a man as hatted may for that reason be explicitly non-committal about whether he is bald.

Descriptions are never explicitly non-committal in this way. It is true that a description may proclaim that it will not go into whether or not what it describes has a given property, but such a proclamation does not entail that it be non-committal regarding that property. Saying 'I have no comment about allegations of the mayor's corruption' does not preclude me from adding, 'except to say she's an extortionist'. Describing something as having one property puts no limitations on what other properties it may be described as having or not having.

The totality of a picture's commitments and non-commitments comprise what I shall call the 'aspect' it presents of its subject. Pictures present different aspects of the very same object when they are committal, inexplicitly non-committal, or explicitly non-committal regarding different properties. More precisely, two pictures embody distinct 'aspects' of an object if and only if there is at least one property with regard to which one is committal and the other is not, or one is explicitly non-committal and the other is inexplicitly non-committal.

6.3 Diverse Pictorial Aspects

I think of a pictorial aspect as a pattern of visual salience, a pattern as much of what a picture leaves out as of what it includes. Clearly, certain patterns of commitments and non-commitments are characteristic of pictures. What are they? What is it for a picture to present an aspect of its subject?

It is tempting to follow Dennett and others in attributing the explicit non-commitments that pictures make to the 'rule for images in general' that they must represent objects seen from a single point of view.[16] According to this line of thought, the set of properties with regard to which a picture of an object is committal and explicitly non-committal consists simply of those properties with regard to which a visual experience of the object itself is committal and explicitly non-committal, when seen from a single viewpoint. It is the fact that they represent from

---

[16] Dennett, *Content and Consciousness*, 135–6.

visual viewpoints that determines the particular aspects characteristic of pictures, as well as mental images and visual experiences.

As Gombrich puts it, we 'see only one aspect of an object' because of 'a simple and incontrovertible fact of experience, the fact that we cannot look round a corner'.[17] What Gombrich calls the 'eye-witness principle' translates the viewpointed nature of vision into a precept for the artist, who 'must not include in his image anything the eye-witness could not have seen from a particular point at a particular moment'.[18] Representing something as having properties visible from one point of view precludes representing other properties only visible from a different point of view.

That this conception of the viewpointed structure of pictorial content tacitly endorses a resemblance theory of depiction is made plain in John Searle's discussion of pictures as embodiments of perceptual viewpoints.[19] Searle holds that 'all vision is from the point of view of one's body in space and time relative to the object being perceived. The aspect under which the object is perceived is altered if one alters one's point of view.'[20] Because vision is viewpointed and pictures mimic vision, depiction, too, is viewpointed.

The truth of the matter is that pictures need not be viewpointed in the way that Dennett, Gombrich, and Searle suggest. As we have seen at length, reducing pictorial aspects to visual aspects falsely assumes that depiction mimics vision and that all pictures are Albertian. We need hardly be reminded that depiction is not constrained by a rule that it represent things as seen from a single viewpoint.

The split-style picture in Figure 2 does not represent a bird seen from a single perceptual viewpoint, but rather endeavours to represent features visible from a set of standard viewpoints. It is often suggested that pictures like Picasso's cubist *Vollard* represent objects from multiple viewpoints; at any rate, this is the stated intention behind David Hockney's neo-cubist paintings and photographs.[21] Some pictures represent objects as seen from indeterminate viewpoints, making commitments and explicit non-commitments consistent with those made by visual experiences of objects seen from any number of viewpoints. A

[17] Gombrich, *Art and Illusion*, 250.

[18] E. H. Gombrich, 'Standards of Truth: The Arrested Image and the Moving Eye', in *The Image and the Eye*, 253.

[19] John Searle, '*Las Meninas* and the Paradoxes of Pictorial Representation', in W. J. T. Mitchell (ed.), *The Language of Images* (Chicago: University of Chicago Press, 1980), 250–3.   [20] Ibid. 251.

[21] David Hockney, *On Photography* (New York: André Emmerich Gallery, 1983).

familiar example is the squatting figure in the lower right of the *Demoiselles d'Avignon* which is represented as if seen either from the front or from the back.

Furthermore, some pictorial aspects are *essentially pictorial*: a picture may make a combination of commitments and explicit non-commitments that cannot be made by any visual experience. Pictures in reversed perspective, as in the Japanese scroll reproduced in Figure 20, and curvilinear perspective, as in Hockney's *A Walk around the Hotel Courtyard Acatlan* (Fig. 21), are explicitly non-committal in some respects because of the commitments they make; but the particular kinds of commitments and explicit non-commitments they make are not those that could be made by viewpointed visual experience. The kinds of commitments and explicit non-commitments that 'X-ray' pictures make are not those made by viewpointed visual experience or the Albertian picture (see Fig. 9). These pictures are committal regarding animals' internal features, though this means that they are explicitly non-committal about their surface features. Yet one of the axioms of Albertian depiction is the principle of occlusion: light does not pass through solid objects.

Impossible or paradoxical pictures also undermine the hope of reducing pictorial to visual aspects. Such pictures often represent objects as having combinations of properties that no ordinary (non-pictorial) experience could represent them as having. This is not true of all picture paradoxes—for example, enterprising psychologists have constructed a three-dimensional model that when viewed from the right point replicates the appearance of the Penrose triangle.[22] Even so, neither simple illusions like the two-pronged trident (Fig. 10) nor the more elaborate ones found in Hogarth's *False Perspective* or Escher's *Waterfall* could be so modelled in three dimensions as to enable us to experience them as presenting the aspects they do.

Aspects should not be regarded as purely spatial. Commitments to texture and colour properties can impose explicit non-commitments. To take a simple example, one way to represent objects as distant is to lighten their colour, but aerial perspective precludes representing objects as having the colours they have under standard viewing conditions. For a more interesting example, we might look to Michael Podro's observations about colour selectivity in Poussin's *Worship of the Golden Calf*.[23] Different commitments and explicit non-commitments

[22] Richard Gregory, 'The Confounded Eye', in Gregory and Gombrich (eds.), *Illusion in Nature and Art*, 87–8.
[23] Podro, 'Depiction and the Golden Calf', 165–70.

Fig. 20. *Scenes from the Life of Gensei Shohin*, Kamakura period

Fig. 21. David Hockney, *A Walk around the Hotel Courtyard Acatlan*, 1985

are associated with different techniques of representing gold objects as gold. Gold foil has the advantage of representing a gold object as shiny, though gradations in colour representing nuances of modelling, shading, and texture are forfeit. Poussin's use of ochre and umber paint to represent gold forfeits a commitment to shininess as the price of commitments to modelling and shading properties. Podro comments that 'the degree of completeness with which any factor or feature can be represented is constrained by what other features you want to represent . . . you have to make an interlocking set of sacrifices'.[24]

It is clear that pictures are committal and explicitly non-committal in a multiplicity of ways, regarding a variety of different kinds of properties. The diversity of the aspects that pictures can present belies the Albertian rule that images should present objects as having properties they could be seen to have from some point of view. Indeed, the signs of internalizing content are unmistakable. The fact that vision makes certain commitments and explicit non-commitments is taken to show that visual experience has a viewpointed structure. Then it is claimed that pictures are also viewpointed, so that the sharing of this feature may explain how pictures' contents mirror those of visual experience. But the truth of the matter is that the aspects presented by pictures expand on those presented in ordinary visual experience. Pictures can represent objects as having combinations of properties that they could not normally be seen to have.

6.4 Essentially Aspectual Contents

Pictorial content is aspectually structured. No picture's content consists solely in the properties it represents its subject as having or not having. Pictures may be inexplicitly non-committal, so that a specification of their content will also include the commitments they abstain from making. More important, since pictures are always explicitly non-committal, their content also encompasses the commitments they are prevented from making as a result of the commitments they make. Two pictures representing the same object as having the same properties may nevertheless differ in content if one is explicitly non-committal regarding properties about which the other is not.

Pictures, I maintain, are essentially selective, because every picture

²⁴ Podro, 'Depiction and the Golden Calf', 166.

is *explicitly non-committal* in some respect. That is, every picture represents its subject as having some property that precludes it from making commitments about some other property. Not all commitments impose explicit non-commitments, of course, but certain commitments do. There is a class of commitments, having to do with spatial properties, that all pictures must make and that impose explicit non-commitments. I shall henceforth understand a *pictorial* aspect to be one which necessarily imposes explicit non-commitments.

This is part of what distinguishes depiction from other forms of representation. Pictures are not merely selective because they neglect to make commitments about some properties. Pictures are selective because, in order to represent some spatial features of their subjects, they are precluded from representing others. The reason is simply that not all spatial relations between objects in three-dimensional space can be represented on a two-dimensional surface. Selecting to represent some spatial relations makes other relations unrepresentable.

If this hypothesis is correct and pictures are representations embodying aspects of their subjects that always include explicit non-commitments, then we should expect that pictures may be individuated according to the aspects they present.

Figure 22 shows a lecture room seen both from the perspective of someone looking down from the ceiling and from the perspective of someone looking towards the lectern. One might wonder whether this is one picture or two.[25] As a matter of fact, the same question can be raised about many more familiar pictures. It is possible, for example, to explain a cubist picture such as Picasso's portrait of Vollard as a mosaic composed of fragments of Albertian pictures each showing a part of the art dealer seen from a different viewpoint (see Fig. 8). This implies that *Vollard* is not one but many pictures. After all, it would be a mistake to stipulate that pictures are made up of single designed surfaces. A postcard divided into four quadrants each representing a different view of London is four pictures, not one. Obviously what individuates pictures is a matter of their content rather than their physical substratum. Thus we will want to know what it is about the content of *Vollard* in virtue of which it is one picture, and what it is about the postcard that makes it four. Only then can we decide in a principled way whether Figure 22 is one picture or two.

---

[25] I thank Brian Dutra for raising this question and for suggesting the lecture-hall illustration of it.

Fig. 22. Room from two viewpoints

I suggest that a picture is a representation whose content presents a 'spatially unified' aspect of its subject. By this I mean that every part of the scene that a picture shows must be represented as standing in certain spatial relations to every other part. What these relations are is not absolute or fixed for every picture alike.[26] Pictures present a variety of different kinds of spatially unified aspects, depending on what relations are selected and what are precluded. There is no reason why the spatially unified aspects that pictures embody must be those definitive of Albertian pictures, for instance.

In the cubist *Vollard*, each part of the art dealer and his surroundings is represented as spatially related to every other part. These relationships are not ones that conform to Albertian canons; they are spatial relationships to which cubist pictures are characteristically committed. By contrast, each quadrant of the postcard represents a different sight of London, but they do not represent each sight as spatially related to the others in a way that counts as pictorial. It is true that the sights are

---

[26] Nor need the spatial relations constituting the aspect that a picture presents be precisely determinable. It may be ambiguous in a picture of an angel over a landscape whether the angel hovers over this copse or that patch of grass.

represented as being in London, but neither 'being in London' nor 'being in the same place' are spatial relations a commitment to which suffices for being a picture. According to this line of thought, then, Figure 22 is one picture, provided the objects represented in each half are represented as spatially related to each other in ways that are constitutive of depiction. It appears that this condition is met, since the objects in each half of the picture stand in such relations as 'is next to', 'is in front of', and 'is facing in the direction of' objects in the other half.

Precisely what kinds of spatially unified aspects pictures can present, given the limitations of the two-dimensional medium for representing three-dimensional space, is a matter for empirical study. A philosophical account of picturing must be content with the following. Pictures are representations that present spatially unified aspects of objects, presenting objects and parts of objects as related to each other spatially. Of course, a description may do the same (e.g. 'The knee bone's connected to the leg bone'). What makes pictorial content distinctive is that pictures are essentially selective. Since a picture cannot be committal regarding all its subject's spatial properties, commitments it makes to some spatial properties entail explicit non-commitment about others. It is the potential for making different commitments, resulting in different kinds of spatial aspects, that I shall suggest accounts for the diversity of systems of depiction.

6.5 Systems of Depiction

There are, as I noted at the outset, two questions about pictorial systems that we must answer. First, what distinguishes pictorial systems from other systems of representation? Then, what distinguishes pictorial systems from each other? None of the standard theories, symbolic or perceptual, begins to answer the second question, for the features that these theories claim distinguish depiction from other representational systems—resemblance, analogicity, and the like—are unvarying features of all pictorial systems. I have argued that depiction differs from other forms of representation in that pictorial content is aspectually structured, and different pictures present different kinds of aspects. I now propose that systems of depiction differ from each other in the kinds of aspects they typically present.

Although many theorists recognize the need to classify pictures into what have variously been called systems, styles, or modes of representation, Goodman is to be credited with introducing the conception of a system of depiction modelled upon the logician's conception of a language. In the abstract, a language is a representation of all the propositions that can be constructed with a particular set of linguistic building blocks. This abstract model of language can be contrasted with a conception of a language as consisting of actual utterances. Similarly, a system of depiction, in the abstract, is the set of all pictures that could be made by combining pictorial referents with pictorial predicates. We can imagine a very simple system in which pictures can portray only two objects, *a* and *b*, as having any combination of three properties, *F*, *G*, and *H*. Abstractly conceived, this system contains twenty-one pictures, though none of them need actually be made. I employ the abstract notion of a pictorial system as the set of all possible pictures in the system.

It might seem that pictorial systems, abstractly conceived, have boundless representational potential, since there is an indefinite number of things that they may refer to, using an indefinite number of predicates combinable in a complex variety of ways. Linguistic systems certainly are boundless for these reasons. However, I have maintained that pictorial content is aspectual, and this imposes a constraint on allowable combinations of predicates. That is, some commitments that pictures make entail explicit non-commitments, so that representing an object as satisfying some available properties precludes representing it as satisfying others. This is obvious if selectivity is added to the simple system just described. Suppose a picture that is committal about its subject being *F* cannot be committal about whether its subject is *G*. The system then consists of only fifteen possible pictures.

The key to differences among systems of depiction is, I suggest, that they present different types of aspects of objects. They are committal and non-committal regarding different types of properties. The most important differences among systems will be differences in those commitments that impose explicit non-commitments. Consider some examples.

The defining characteristic of Albertian depiction is the use of perspective projection. Albertian pictures belong to a system or family of closely related systems made up of pictures which are committal regarding properties that their subjects could be seen to have from a single viewpoint and are thus explicitly non-committal regarding properties invisible from that viewpoint. For this reason, the Albertian system may be said to capture an optical aspect of represented objects.

Pictures in curvilinear perspective represent all sides of objects but their backs, producing a strong sense of three-dimensionality (e.g. Fig. 21). Proponents of curvilinearism point out that this system conveys properties that objects can be seen to have by an eye that, unlike the fixed eye posited by Albertian depiction, can pan and scan its environment. The costs of curvilinearism include the imposition of explicit non-commitments about degree of curvature of represented edges and the relative size of represented objects.

By contrast, axonometric systems are those in which parallels are represented as parallel. One advantage of such systems is that they allow pictures to be stretched in any direction while maintaining constancy of represented shape and size. This is a particularly important consideration when scenes are to be pictured on long scrolls (Fig. 20).[27] The price is an explicit non-commitment regarding depth.

In each of these cases, systemic differences can be traced to different rules of projection, which determine how three-dimensional objects are to be transferred on to a two-dimensional medium.[28] There are systems, including split-style depiction, caricature, and cubism, not based on consistent geometrical formulae. But these systems are also characterized by the types of commitments that the pictures comprising them make. In caricature the representation of proportionality of features is relinquished for the sake of representing character traits associated with overemphasized enormous noses, tiny chins, and floppy ears. A cubist might insist on representing a table as four-legged at the price of representing its orientation in space.

Split-style pictures represent animals as having all the important anatomical details, and the bilateral symmetry of animal anatomy is preserved. This commitment is at the cost of an explicit non-commitment about overall shape. In the context of north-west coast First Nation art, this explicit non-commitment is turned to advantage, though. The overall shape of a figure can be ignored when fitting it to a triangular house front, a canoe paddle, or, as a tattoo, to a man's back.

Although I have not attempted an exhaustive enumeration of the commitments and non-commitments characteristic of every system of picturing, it is clear that the distinctiveness of each of the systems to

[27] John Willats, 'The Draughtsman's Contract: How an Artist Creates an Image', in Barlow *et al.* (eds.), *Images and Understanding*, 238.

[28] For a detailed discussion of systems of depiction based on different systems of projection on to flat planes, see Margaret A. Hagen, *Varieties of Realism: Geometries of Representational Art* (Cambridge: Cambridge University Press, 1986).

which these examples belong can be captured by specifying the types of aspects they characteristically present. Each pictorial system is selective in its own way, making commitments and explicit non-commitments regarding combinations of types of properties not made by pictures in other systems. We may therefore delineate what is distinctive about a system through a description of the types of properties with regard to which pictures in that system are committal and the types of properties with regard to which they are inexplicitly and explicitly non-committal. Note that *systems* differ in the *types* of properties about which they make commitments and non-commitments. That is, they differ not by making different commitments regarding properties like being red or having six sides, but rather by making commitments about types of properties such as having atmospheric colour or having straight edges.

The apparatus of aspects individuated by commitments provides the basis for a taxonomy of systems of representation. Let me reiterate, however, that this is a taxonomy of systems of depiction in the abstract sense. It is probable that the identity conditions for abstract systems do not correspond exactly to those for actual systems.

For instance, it is sometimes ambiguous what commitments a picture makes and does not make. This is in effect an ambiguity of scope: there may be nothing to distinguish a picture that represents its subject as not-F from one that does not represent it as F. Do pictures of Madonna represent her as not having pimples, or do they merely refrain from going into the matter of her pimples? (Of course, the manipulative use of images in advertising trades on this ambiguity.) Further ambiguities surface if we individuate systems by inexplicit as well as explicit non-commitments. Strictly speaking, drawings and paintings that follow Alberti's rules belong to different systems, because paintings are committal about colour and drawings are inexplicitly non-committal about colour. Albertian depiction may break down into a family of closely related systems.

If they turn out to be more ambiguous than the apparatus of commitments predicts, it may be necessary to define actual systems as families of systems individuated in the precise way I advocate. It is not surprising that any attempt to state full identity conditions for actual systems will have to wrestle with the fuzziness symptomatic of the products of human culture. This much we can say, though: if two pictures are committal and non-committal regarding all the same types of properties, then they belong to the same system, and pictures belong to different systems only if they are committal and non-committal regarding some different types of properties.

A final note about my account of pictorial systems. We have seen that those who endorse traditional perceptual theories of depiction are often tempted to argue that certain kinds of aspects, and by implication, certain systems of depiction, are more accurate, or more truthful, versions of the visual world. Peacocke, by internalizing the Albertian system as explanatory of visual experience, implies that Albertian depiction accurately replicates visual experience. Gombrich similarly insists that Albertian depiction mirrors visual appearance and that other systems are 'conceptual' rather than 'visual'. My account of systems of depiction takes a neutral position. An understanding of what distinguishes depiction from other forms of representation and what differentiates pictorial systems from each other does not depend on judgements about what is 'visual' and what is 'conceptual', what is 'real' and what 'constructed'.

6.6 Why Pictorial Systems Are Not Conventional

Two points have come to light that amount to a refinement of the phenomenon, first pointed out in Chapter 1, of the diversity of pictures. One is that pictures in different pictorial systems present aspects that are characteristic of their systems. The second is that the aspects presented by pictures in different systems are not circumscribed by the rules either of optics or of perspective projection, as we see them enshrined in Alberti's principles. Pictorial diversity reflects the fact that there are as many ways to depict as there are aspects of the world for which pictures may select.

In Chapter 3 I noted one way to accommodate the diversity of depiction. Goodman claims in his fifth thesis that there are many systems of depiction, none of which is constrained by perceptual mechanisms, so that anything may represent anything else. Pictures are like languages, because one language will do as well as any other to represent the world.

But I also noted that Goodman's adherence to thesis (5) is tendentious. The quite separate insight that pictures are system-relative accommodates the fact that there can be different ways of depicting, while remaining open to the possibility that perceptual mechanisms explain this diversity. The additional claim that pictorial systems are arbitrary with respect to perceptual facts and that anything may stand for anything else is not necessary to explain diversity. Nor does Goodman provide any further argument for it. He does not even refer to a system as radically different from the systems with which we are familiar as would illustrate anti-perceptualism. Goodman's radical conception of pictorial diversity simply neglects the actual differences between pictorial systems.

Nevertheless, some of those inspired by Goodman have sought support for the view that anything may depict anything else by arguing that what a picture represents is a matter of convention. In the parlance of one adherent of the convention theory of depiction, the existence of 'consensual regularities' embedded in 'social formations' is what explains pictorial representation.[29] In this section I argue that conventionalism is incompatible with the aspectual structure of pictorial systems.

The convention theory of depiction has a natural affinity with Goodman's anti-perceptualism because, as David Lewis observed in his classic studies of convention, conventions arise when choices are to be made arbitrarily among equally good alternatives, and one implication of Goodman's theory is that any system of depiction is as good as any other.

Lewis's analysis of 'convention' is roughly this.[30] At the highest level of generality, a convention is a regularity in the actions of members of a group. A textbook example of a conventional regularity is driving on the left side of the road in Britain. Conventional regularities conform to five conditions. A regularity R in the action of members of a community C is a convention if and only if: (1) everyone in C conforms to R; (2) everyone in C expects and believes that everyone else in C conforms to R; (3) the expectation and belief that others in C conform to R gives everyone a good reason to conform to R; (4) everyone prefers full conformity to R over conformity by all but one; (5) there is an alternative regularity R', not identical to R, which could meet conditions (3) and (4); and (6) conditions (1)–(5) are (or are potentially) common knowledge.

Condition (5) enunciates a crucial feature of conventions: a regularity without an alternative is not a conventional regularity, because conventions arise only when choices are arbitrary rather than strategic. That is, conventions arise as solutions to co-ordination problems: provided that

---

[29] Bryson, *Vision and Painting*, 51. Goodman himself rejects convention theories because they imply that systems are rule-governed. See Sect. 3.4.

[30] David Lewis, 'Languages and Language', in Keith Gunderson (ed.), *Language, Mind, and Knowledge*, Minnesota Studies in the Philosophy of Science, 7 (Minneapolis: University of Minnesota Press, 1975), 5–10; and *idem, Convention*.

R and *R'* are equally good alternatives but it is preferable for members of *C* to agree to do the same thing, a convention may arise in *C* to do either *R* or *R'*. If it is preferable to do *R* rather than *R'*, that is sufficient reason to do *R*, and conventions are superfluous. Driving on the left side of the road is a conventional regularity in Britain, because everyone there drives on the left and expects everyone else to, this expectation is a good reason to drive on the left there, and full conformity to the regularity is preferable to partial conformity. Finally, driving on the left has an equally good alternative—driving on the right.

Language is conventional because there are many alternative languages which are equally good ways of conveying truths, but it is preferable that members of a community agree to speak the same language. Similarly, one might think that depiction is conventional because there are many alternative systems of depiction that are equally good ways of representing objects as having visual features, but it is preferable that members of picture-using communities agree to use the same system. According to one system, *Wivenhoe Park* represents Wivenhoe Park; according to another, it represents a pink elephant. Most adhere to conventions which sustain use of the former system, though perhaps some readers of *Languages of Art* adhere to conventions sustaining the latter. For them, *Wivenhoe Park* depicts a pink elephant.

If systems are conventional, then, by definition, choices among them are arbitrary. When alternative systems are equally good candidates for a picture-using community, and it does not matter which system is used so long as all community members use the same one, then the solution is a convention to adopt one rather than another. If there were any independent reason to prefer one over the other (e.g. one is easier to learn), then the preferable system would be the one adopted, and conventions would be superfluous. As long as use of one system is conventional in a community, it follows that it has an alternative, and that the *only* reason the entrenched system, not its alternative, is used by any member of the community is that all the other members use it, and all prefer to use whatever system the others use. The convention theory implies that there is no reason why the Kwakiutl should use one system and the seventeenth-century Dutch another, apart from the fact that those are the systems that each group has agreed to adopt.

The convention theory is therefore committed to the claim that pictorial systems are true alternatives, as Lewis's fifth condition requires. However, I have argued at length that systems of depiction differ from each other in the kinds of aspects they present, and so in the kinds of properties they can represent objects as satisfying. It only remains to decide whether differences in the aspect systems present make some preferable over others, at least in particular contexts. If some are preferable to others in some contexts, then that explains why they are adopted in that context—they are not conventional. This does not mean that systems are never conventional. They may be conventional, provided that aspectual differences do not matter; but they cannot be conventional when aspectual differences determine preferability.

Clearly, aspectual differences generally do matter. They sometimes matter for 'compositional' reasons, when preference is given to certain kinds of marks, shapes, patterns, colours, or textures on the picture surface. Thus a taste for compositional symmetry and the need to fit pictures on to surfaces of predetermined shapes might have made the split-style preferable to the Kwakiutl. Similarly, axonometric projection seems to be the appropriate choice for scroll painting, for it allows a scene to be extended indefinitely in either a horizontal or a vertical direction without distortion. A choice of system may be largely stylistic, drawing attention to pictures' formal, expressive, or technical properties or manifesting the means by which they are made.

Aspectual differences may also matter for representational reasons, because pictures are frequently made precisely in order to make explicit certain aspects of the world. In technical drawing, for instance, pictures serve to convey information useful for building things. Thus a system of axonometric perspective is used which represents receding edges as 'true lengths'. In Albertian painting the aim is to replicate a set of properties, defined by the rules of perspective projection, which record versions of occurrent visual experience. By contrast, Alberti's Byzantine predecessors aimed not to represent the sort of occurrent visual experiences criticized by the Platonist philosophers, but to represent an ideal version of reality.[31] Their system conveys information about the relative theological importance of the figures depicted, whose size corresponds not to location in a projected space but to location in a divine hierarchy. According to one expert, the thought behind Australian X-ray painting is that 'there is more to man, or to an animal, than his (its) outward appearance. The artist in this case is not satisfied with an outline sketch: he wants to show what makes his subject live.'[32]

---

[31] Leo Steinberg, 'The Eye Is a Part of the Mind', in *Other Criteria* (London: Oxford University Press, 1972), 297–9.
[32] Ronald M. Berndt, *Australian Aboriginal Art* (New York: Macmillan, 1964), 6.

There has been some debate among anthropologists about split-style depiction among the north-west coast First Nations. Franz Boas argued that the style originates in purely formal concerns, specifically the need to adapt the shapes of represented figures to the various shapes of the objects on which they were painted (or carved).[33] Claude Lévi-Strauss speculated that the split style reflects the cultural psychology of 'mask societies' in which there is a deep rift between private life and public roles.[34] The premiss implicit in Boas and Lévi-Strauss, that the split style serves no representational purpose, is expressed explicitly by Jan Deregowski: 'some societies have developed the split-style to a high artistic level. This development occurs if the drawings are not regarded as a means of communication about objects.'[35] But while I do not dispute that the choice of the split style may reflect formal and possibly psychological factors, I do not think it need therefore be seen as a turning away from communication. It is, rather, a different kind of communication—communication of different aspects of objects.

It would be a mistake to think that all pictures are made for the same purpose, to achieve the same compositional effects, or to make explicit the same properties, as those who privilege Albertian picturing suppose. On the contrary, the diversity of systems demonstrates that pictures are made for a great variety of purposes, in accordance with many compositional norms, emphasizing many different aspects of the visual world.

The convention theory of depiction assumes that pictorial systems are equally good alternatives. I have argued that in fact different pictorial systems present different characteristic aspects of objects, so that some systems are preferable to others in given contexts of use. Choices among systems are not always, or usually, arbitrary. A better theory of depiction must take into account the aspectual structure of depiction and explain how it is that different systems of depiction can present different aspects of reality.

[33] Franz Boas, *Primitive Art* (New York: Dover, 1955), *passim.*
[34] Claude Lévi-Strauss, *The Way of the Masks*, trans. Sylvia Modelski (Seattle: University of Washington Press, 1982), *passim.*
[35] Jan Deregowski, 'Pictorial Perception and Culture', in Richard Held (ed.), *Image, Object and Illusion* (San Francisco: W. H. Freeman, 1974), 85.

7

Pictorial Recognition

THIS chapter introduces a perceptual mechanism that I believe explains pictures' diversity and system-relativity. The idea that depiction is diverse has undergone considerable refinement. Not only do pictures' designs map on to their contents in a variety of ways, but there is also a wide latitude in the kinds of contents they have. Consequently, a theory of depiction must explain why pictorial content is aspectual. Moreover, while I have argued that pictorial systems are individuated by the kinds of aspects they characteristically present, it is also a fact that pictorial competence is always competence in a system. We want to know why an ability to understand a picture entails an ability to interpret pictures presenting the same kind of aspects, but not an ability to interpret those embodying different kinds of aspects.

The first three sections of this chapter describe the main features of perceptual recognition, and in the rest of the chapter I argue that recognition plays a fundamental role in identifying what pictures represent. A picture represents by conveying aspectual information from its subject, on the basis of which viewers can recognize its source. Recognition is, I contend, a mode of identification which explains pictures' diversity and aspectual structure, as well as the system-relativity of pictorial competence. It should be kept in mind throughout that I develop my account of recognition-based pictorial identification within the Evansian framework outlined in Chapter 5.

7.1 Perceptual Recognition

For many creatures, identifying an object currently perceived as one previously encountered depends entirely on an ability to track objects with which they maintain continuous perceptual contact. A frog, for instance, may be able to re-identify a fly as one it was looking at a moment ago because it has kept a vigilant eye on it. But objects disappear from view only to be encountered again, often after significant passages of time, and the ability to recognize objects with which we have lost contact *as* objects previously encountered can be an invaluable one. Recognition skills gain importance in proportion to the mobility of objects in space, together with the usefulness of information about whether they are dangerous, friendly, good to eat, and the like. A creature possesses a recognition ability when, on the basis of perceptual encounters with objects, it assembles dossiers of information enabling it to identify those objects as ones previously encountered.[1]

One of the distinguishing characteristics of recognition in humans is its phenomenology, which reflects the kind of information it evokes. Almost everyone has had the experience of meeting an acquaintance not seen for many years, perhaps not since childhood. At first, we experience something familiar in the sight of his face, but only after a moment do we recognize him, seeing more or less clearly how his current features echo his earlier appearance. The ability to visually recognize objects involves and makes available a rich store of visual information acquired in earlier encounters with them. And while it is true that when an object is recognized, we often recall certain facts about it—its name, salient features, and past doings—what is typical of recognition is the way it forges links with information from past encounters that remains in occurrent perceptual form. Recognition depends on what has come to be called 'episodic memory'.[2] When I recognize a former acquaintance, I may remember her name and that I met her in 1988, but often I will also be able to conjure up visual memories of past episodes—visiting a certain tea-stall in Madurai with her, where we discussed Coates and Clarks looms. This is not to say that recognition requires rich information from past episodes. It may, at a minimum, consist in nothing more than a disposition to identify an object currently perceived as one encountered in the past, together with a feeling of familiarity with it.

Recognition takes three forms: we recognize features, individual objects, and kinds of objects. Although I shall concentrate on recognition of individuals, what I say goes for all forms of recognition. Feature-recognition and kind-recognition can exist without particular-recognition—our frog can probably recognize flies when presented with them, but may not be able to recognize individual flies as ones previously

---

[1] My account of recognition is inspired by Evans's in *Varieties of Reference*, ch. 8. See also J. O. Urmson, 'Recognition', *Proceedings of the Aristotelian Society*, 56 (1955), 259–80; Noel Fleming, 'Recognizing and Seeing As', *Philosophical Review*, 66 (1957), 161–79; and H. H. Price, *Thinking and Experience* (Cambridge: Cambridge University Press, 1962), ch. 2.

[2] See Endel Tulving, *Elements of Episodic Memory* (Oxford: Oxford University Press, 1983), 302.

encountered.[3] The ability to recognize individuals no doubt accompanies the formation of social structures that depend on being able to re-identify those objects with which we have had dealings. Face-recognition is probably the most sensitive recognition ability that humans possess. Most people can recognize hundreds, perhaps thousands of faces, often associating them with copious information from past encounters. Psychologists describe recognition abilities of a certain sophistication as 'dynamic'. Rudimentary, non-dynamic recognition abilities are those which require overwhelming similarity between incoming information and information stored from the past. But objects change in countless ways, and dynamic recognition abilities are those that link currently perceived objects with objects perceived in the past despite what may amount to radical changes in appearance.

It is possible to recognize things as they change positions in space, as they are seen from different points of view, as they are seen under distorting conditions—through heat hazes, in trick mirrors, and so forth. Face-recognition is exceptionally dynamic. We can recognize faces though their features are contorted by laughter, grimaces, and other expressions, and we can recognize them changed over time—often, as we are wont to exclaim, to the point of being beyond recognition. Indeed, some psychologists *define* face-recognition as an ability to recognize faces changed in these ways.[4]

To say that recognition is dynamic is to say that features, objects, and kinds of objects can be recognized, in the terminology of Chapter 6, under different aspects. That is, recognition is dynamic when an object once seen as having one set of visual properties can be recognized at a later time under another set of properties. If recognition is dynamic over differences in viewpoint, then an object seen in profile, for example, can be recognized on the basis of stored information about its visual appearance when seen frontally.[5]

A perceiver endowed with a sophisticated recognition ability can gather information from an object so as to be able to recognize it when confronted with it under many different aspects, but the dynamism of recognition is not without limits. First, an object may have changed in

---

[3] It is arguable that a concept of an individual is always a concept of it as a kind of object. If so, there may be no individual-recognition without the application of a kind-concept.

[4] e.g. Vicki Bruce, 'Changing Faces: Visual and Non-Visual Coding Processes in Face Recognition', *British Journal of Psychology*, 73 (1982), 105.

[5] I am simplifying here, because most recognition depends on, and invokes information derived from, multiple earlier encounters with an object seen under multiple aspects.

ways that overstretch a dynamic recognition ability. Although one may be able to recognize faces as they change with age, a particular face may age literally beyond recognition. To be able to recognize faces despite ageing does not imply an ability to recognize faces despite any amount of ageing. Similarly, an ability to recognize objects in fun-fair mirrors may not extend to recognizing objects seen in extremely distorting conditions. Even when dynamic, recognition is not boundlessly elastic.

The second limitation on recognitional dynamism derives from the fact that recognition abilities are always dynamic relative to kinds of aspects. An ability to recognize objects in distorting mirrors does not entail an ability to recognize objects from different viewpoints or as they age. When the information available from a familiar object marks a change over which recognition is not dynamic, recognition fails. This is seen at a pathological level in some forms of visual agnosia, whose symptoms include losses in abilities to recognize everyday objects seen from unusual viewpoints or to recognize faces when their expressions change.[6]

An ability to recognize objects seen from different spatial locations is dynamic over one kind of aspect; an ability to recognize aged faces is dynamic over another. I call the kinds of aspects with respect to which objects can vary but remain recognizable 'dimensions of variation'. Recognition may thus be reckoned more or less dynamic in proportion to the number of dimensions over which it is preserved, and it may be said to have reached a limit when one is unable to recognize objects across a new dimension of variation.

The boundaries of recognitional dimensions of variation are evident not only in their aspectual structure. The amount, as well as the type, of information required for recognition differs from one dimension of variation to another. Whereas a great deal of information, gathered over several encounters, may be required to recognize a face that has aged, one glance at an object may suffice to be able to recognize it when it is seen from a slightly different angle.

The fact that recognitional dynamism is relative to dimensions of variation is what explains its generativity. Generativity is a crucial feature of any useful recognition ability: being able to recognize an object under a new kind of aspect must suffice for being able to recognize

---

[6] See Martha J. Farah, *Visual Agnosia: Disorders of Object Recognition and What They Tell Us about Normal Vision* (Cambridge, Mass.: MIT Press, 1990).

other objects under the same kind of aspect. Thus recognition is generative over changes in viewpoint when being able to recognize one object seen from a novel viewpoint suffices for being able to recognize other objects transformed in similar ways. Being able to recognize one face after ageing is generative if it suffices for being able to recognize other faces after ageing. Of course, generativity is subject to the first limitation on recognition—it is not boundlessly elastic within a dimension of variation. However, aspects are generative only within dimensions of variation.

7.2 Recognition and Thought

Recognition is one perceptual skill that enables us to think of objects, and so potentially to refer to them. Since I have endorsed Evans's strictures on thought, it is necessary to consider briefly whether recognition-based thoughts meet the requirements encapsulated in Russell's principle and the generality constraint.

As Russell's principle requires, recognition provides discriminating knowledge: recognizing an object, kind of object, or property means being able to distinguish it from all other objects, kinds of object, or properties. I cannot recognize my friend if I cannot distinguish him from other people; nor can I recognize maples if I cannot tell them from sycamores, or teal if I cannot tell it from aquamarine. We may predict that recognition-based thoughts satisfy Russell's principle if it is true that recognition evolved in response to perceivers' needs for fine-grained discriminations among the inhabitants of their environment.

The dynamism and generativity of recognition ensure that recognition-based thoughts also satisfy the generality constraint. Imagine a simple dimension of variation comprised of upside-down aspects of objects (monkeys are particularly good at recognizing objects seen thus). If recognition is generative within this dimension, a thinker able to judge a thought that an object recognized upside-down has some property is able to judge thoughts about other objects seen upside-down. And to say that recognition is dynamic is to say that one who can entertain a thought about an object seen under one aspect can entertain a thought about the object recognized under a different aspect. For example, someone who has a relatively dynamic recognition ability for Peter Sellars can judge a thought about him recognized as Clouzeau, as Dr Strangelove, and indeed under any of the disguises that her recognition ability sees through. A master of a recognition-based concept can think of an object as having as many different appearances as her recognition abilities encompass.

Dynamic and generative recognition abilities endow their possessors with concepts of objects, kinds, and properties. It does not follow, though, that concepts of the *aspects* under which they are recognized must (though they may) figure in thinkers' conceptual repertoires. To recognize an object under a range of aspects is to have a concept of the object, but not necessarily to have a concept of those aspects of it. In other words, the aspectual information on which recognition is based is non-conceptual. Features of objects' appearances to which recognition is sensitive need not be features of which perceivers possess concepts. For instance, there is evidence that face-recognition depends on a perceptual sensitivity to such properties as the proportional distances between facial features, but these are not properties of which perceivers need have or, indeed, usually have concepts.[7]

David Marr's theory of recognition illustrates the non-conceptuality of recognition nicely, and is also interesting because it is developed with an eye to dynamism.[8] An axiom of Marr's account of vision is that different cognitive abilities depend on mental representations with different kinds of contents. Consequently, the mental representations on which recognition operates must possess a kind of content which serves to explain its dynamism. He reasons that the underlying mechanism for recognition is a 'stable shape description that depends little, if at all, on viewpoint . . . . the pieces and articulation of a shape need to be described not relative to the viewer but relative to a frame of reference based on the shape itself'.[9] The stable shape description is meant to possess properties that account for all aspects under which an object may be recognized.

Perceivers obviously need not have concepts of stable shape descriptions in order to recognize objects. The contents of mental representations

[7] See Susan Carey and Rhea Diamond, 'From Piecemeal to Configurational Representation of Faces', *Science*, 195 (1977), 312–14; and Hadyn D. Ellis, John W. Shepherd, and Graham M. Davies, 'Identification of Familiar and Unfamiliar Faces from Internal and External Features: Some Implications for Theories of Face Recognition', *Perception*, 8 (1979), 431–9.

[8] David Marr, *Vision* (New York: W. H. Freeman, 1982), 295. See also Vicki Bruce, 'Recognizing Faces', *Philosophical Transactions of the Royal Society of London*, B302 (1983), 424–5; and John G. Seamon, 'Dynamic Facial Recognition: Examination of a Natural Phenomenon', *American Journal of Psychology*, 95 (1982), 379.

[9] Marr, *Vision*, 295–6.

underlying recognition, whether they are templates, feature-detectors, or stable shape descriptions, are non-conceptual. Their workings are explained at the sub-personal level—the level of neural organization and psychological architecture—rather than the personal level of sensations, beliefs, thoughts, and intentions.[10]

7.3 The Autonomy of Recognition

This picture of recognition, its place in thought, and the type of information on which it is based is at odds with the view of recognition that dominates the philosophical literature. This view is that there is little to say about recognition, because recognition is reducible to descriptive identification. For example, H. H. Price writes that 'recognition of individuals itself depends on recognition of characteristics . . . . To recognize an individual person or object I must first recognize a characteristic characterising a present particular', and subsequently '*remember* an earlier particular . . . which was an instance of that same characteristic.'[11] If Price is right, then recognition is neither non-conceptual nor an autonomous mode of identification. However, this assimilation of recognition to description is mistaken.

In the first place, descriptive identification, as Price acknowledges, requires recall of an object's identifying features. But, as I have suggested, recognition and recall draw upon and evoke different kinds of information.[12] Whereas recognition involves an awareness of an earlier encounter with the object recognized, recall always produces a belief that the item remembered had some property. Evans vividly illustrates the distinction between recognition and recall:

> If asked to describe a route on which I frequently travel, I may be able to recall only a certain number of features or properties, but when I actually travel the route, many things will strike me as familiar which I was unable, even after extended reflection, to recall. . . . there may be a derelict house at one point, and upon coming across it I may say 'Yes, I had forgotten that'. By this I mean that I now remember it—I am quite sure that it was there when I last travelled the route, and has not become derelict only recently; but it was not something I was able to recall.[13]

[10] Dennett, *Content and Consciousness*, 93–4.

[11] Price, *Thinking and Experience*, 39; emphasis original. See also Urmson, 'Recognition'; and Schier, *Deeper into Pictures*, 103–5.

[12] I follow Evans, *Varieties of Reference*, 284–96, in distinguishing between recognition and recall.   [13] Ibid. 286.

In minimal cases of recognition one may feel familiar with an object and identify it as something encountered before, yet be unable to recall anything about its past appearance.

Not only is it possible to recognize an object without being able to recall its features, it is also possible to recognize something when recall is actually erroneous. I might recognize somebody as someone I met in Paris; but when I discover that we really met in Vienna, I need not conclude that I failed to recognize my acquaintance. Recognition is defeasible of course—I can misrecognize someone—but successful recognition is insulated from failures of recall. It is not necessary to know that something is the such-and-such in order to be able to recognize it as an object encountered before.

Nor, indeed, does recall suffice for recognition. Although the such-and-such is before you and you know that a is the such-and-such, you may still be unable to recognize a—unable, that is, to establish a link with occurrent perceptual information derived from past encounters. It is disconcerting, but not uncommon, to know the identity of someone met on a particular occasion, to know where and when you met him and what he was doing at the time, yet to fail recognize him. There is no recognition without the evocation of some occurrent information from past encounters accompanying the sense of familiarity with the object recognized.

That knowledge of an object's identifying features is insufficient for recognition is obvious in the case of perceivers who have lost the ability to recognize objects. One patient whose visual agnosia deprived him of the ability to recognize individual objects but not features of objects was left with descriptive matching only, and this clearly represented a serious deficit:

> When confronted with portraits [of celebrities] he would proceed deductively, analysing one feature after another, searching for the 'critical detail' which would yield the answer. In human faces, this was rarely forthcoming. There was somewhat less difficulty with animal faces. A goat was eventually recognized by its ears and beard, a giraffe by its neck, a crocodile by its dentition, and a cat by its whiskers.[14]

Identifying things by recognizing them is not a matter of recalling features they possessed in the past and descriptively matching them with features they are currently perceived to have. This conclusion is

[14] C. A. Pallis, 'Impaired Identification of Faces and Places with Agnosia for Colors', *Journal of Neurology, Neurosurgery and Psychiatry*, 18 (1955), 220.

important for two reasons. It secures an autonomous place for recognition within human cognition. More important for present purposes, though, it sustains the hope that recognition might be the underlying perceptual mechanism that explains depiction—for depiction, as we have seen, is not descriptive.

7.4 Pictorial Recognition

I propose that identifying what a picture represents exploits perceptual recognition skills. In particular, viewers interpret pictures by recognizing their subjects in the aspects they present.[15] The thrust of this is not simply that pictorial representation makes use of recognition abilities for objects, kinds, and properties. Rather, the ability to recognize pictures' subjects is an extension of the dynamism of recognition. Pictures are visual prostheses; they extend the informational system by gathering, storing, and transmitting visual information about their subjects in ways that depend upon and also augment our ability to identify things by their appearance.

As evidence in support of this proposal, it is worth mentioning that the methods of the psychological sciences treat the ability to recognize an object in a picture as proof of an ability to recognize the object itself. Tests of object recognition are almost always tests of depicted-object recognition. Arthur Danto has observed that psychologists who investigated recognition capacities in sheep by showing them pictures unwittingly discovered that sheep can interpret pictures—unwittingly because 'the scientists were so used to referring to pictures by what they were pictures *of* that it never occurred to them that their subjects were responding to pictures'.[16] As it happens, there is evidence that humans recognize things in pictures, especially stylized line-drawings, more quickly than they recognize the things themselves.[17]

It would be a mistake to suppose, however, that pictorial recognition

---

[15] See also Mark Roskill, 'Recognition and Identification', *Critical Inquiry*, 3 (1977), 709–23; Neander, 'Pictorial Representation', 220–2; and Schier, *Deeper into Pictures*, 99–102.

[16] Arthur Danto, 'Animals as Art Historians: Reflections on the Innocent Eye', in *Beyond the Brillo Box: The Visual Arts in Post-Historical Perspective* (New York: Farrar, Straus and Giroux, 1992), 23.

[17] Paul Fraisse and Edwin H. Elkin, 'Étude génétique de l'influence des modes de présentation sur le seuil de reconnaissance d'objets familiers', *L'Année psychologique*, 63 (1963), 1–22.

is identical with ordinary visual recognition. Unlike ordinary recognition, pictorial recognition operates at two levels. A picture is first of all a flat surface covered with marks, colours, and textures, and the primary purpose of a theory of depiction is to explain how this design, as I have called it, comes to represent scenes and objects as having properties. We have seen that it is unlikely that pictures' designs resemble their contents in any uniform way. I propose instead that pictures' designs present recognizable aspects of things. If you reflect upon your experience of trying to grasp Picasso's cubist *Vollard* or the Kwakiutl bird, you encounter this kind of recognition at work. Pictorial recognition at this level may be called 'content-recognition', since it consists in recognizing a design as the features making up an aspect of its subject.

At the second level, viewers recognize pictures' contents as of their subjects. The victory-signing-man-with-hooked-nose-and-drooping-jowls-picture is recognized as an aspect of Nixon—this is 'subject-recognition'. Subject-recognition may fail when a viewer sees a picture as representing a figure as having such-and-such properties but is unable to identify the picture's subject because she cannot recognize what such-and-such is an aspect of. Somebody who has never seen Nixon (even in a picture) may not be able to recognize a picture as of him, though she can recognize what kind of man it represents.

Content-recognition and subject-recognition are not entirely insulated from each other. It goes without saying that a picture's subject is never recognized *tout court*; as we saw in Chapter 5, it is always recognized as having some properties. More interestingly, though, subject-recognition frequently has a bearing on what properties a picture is seen to represent its subject as having. Ambiguous figures illustrate this phenomenon. Seeing the duck–rabbit figure as a duck foregrounds one set of properties—it is a billed-creature-picture—while seeing it as a rabbit foregrounds others—it becomes a big-eared-creature-picture (see Fig. 12). Moreover, what design features have representational relevance may depend on what subject is recognized. The dimple on the right-hand side of the duck–rabbit figure takes on significance (as a mouth) only when the figure is identified as of a rabbit. Thus I want to reject an over-simple picture of the relationship between content-recognition and subject-recognition according to which we first recognize a picture's content, then, on that basis, recognize its subject by matching content to subject. Content-recognition can be informed by simultaneous subject-recognition.

Having acknowledged this complexity, it nevertheless remains the case that recognizing a picture's subject in its content and its content in its design are different skills. Each is exercised within different dimensions of variation, and competence in one does not entail competence in the other. One may possess a robust ability to recognize objects and features changed across many dimensions of variation, yet lack the ability to recognize objects and features when they are shown in pictures (though doubtless this ability is easily acquired).[18] And being able to recognize what kinds of objects pictures represent does not imply being able to recognize the objects themselves.

This makes sense of the fact that there are two ways to fail to grasp a picture. You can fail to grasp a picture's content—it just looks like a jumble of shapes and colours—even though you know it represents a familiar object. Or you can tell what kind of object is represented, yet fail to grasp that the object is *that* familiar object.

I now turn to how the hypothesis that recognition plays a role in identifying what pictures represent accommodates the diversity and competence constraints.

Diversity. In Chapter 1 I argued that depiction is diverse in the sense that a wide range of marks on pictures' surfaces are representational, and in Chapter 6 I added that pictures in different systems of representation depict their subjects under different aspects—as having different combinations of properties. It is the dynamism of content-recognition that explains the first kind of diversity and the dynamism of subject-recognition that explains the second.

Pictorial recognition operates over some of the same dimensions of variation as does ordinary perceptual recognition. Pictures can represent their subjects as having the very sets of properties that their subjects might be seen to have in the flesh. In such cases we can recognize objects as represented in pictures because we can recognize those objects under the same aspects in ordinary vision. The ability to recognize a victory-signing-politician aspect of Nixon in a picture may be the same ability as is exercised by those capable of recognizing Nixon himself under such an aspect. Likewise, content-recognition skills sometimes overlap with skills exercised in ordinary perception, as pictorial dimensions of variation overlap with aspects presented in mirrors, silhouettes,

---

[18] See J. Hochberg and V. Brooks, 'Pictorial Recognition as an Unlearned Ability: A Study of One Child's Performance', *American Journal of Psychology*, 75 (1962), 624–8.

imaginary interposed glass planes, and the like. When the dimensions of variation over which pictorial recognition is dynamic are the same as those over which ordinary recognition is dynamic, we may conclude that the recognitional processes by means of which pictures represent are similar to ordinary visual processes.

But not all pictorial aspects are aspects that could be presented in ordinary visual experience. Resemblance theories wrongly restrict the range of recognizable aspects that pictures may present to those that could be presented in ordinary perception. For example, Peacocke argues that only those shapes on the picture surface similar to those which trace the shape of an object seen through an interposed glass plane are recognizable as aspects of that object. And this privileging of Albertian depiction lends itself to imposing certain false limitations on pictorial content. Pictures must represent their subjects as having only those combinations of properties that they may possess when seen from some viewpoint; they cannot represent their subjects as having combinations of properties not seen in ordinary visual perception.

But there is no reason why pictorial designs must be projections on to an imaginary interposed plane, or why pictures must represent their subjects as having combinations of properties that they could be seen to have from some viewpoint. That is to say, there is no reason why the dimensions of variation over which pictures' contents and subjects are recognizable should be circumscribed by the rules of optics. On the contrary, if recognition is a dynamic ability to re-identify objects in a world in which things undergo radical changes in appearance, confining pictorial recognition to an ability to re-identify objects only over optical dimensions of variation severely reduces its effectiveness.

The dimensions of variation across which pictorial recognition is dynamic go far beyond those across which ordinary recognition is dynamic. Pictures can be recognized when they represent their subjects as having combinations of properties quite unlike those their subjects could be seen to have. Pictures' subjects can be recognized when skewed and bent out of shape (Figs. 6 and 7), when shown in reversed or curvilinear perspective (Figs. 20 and 21), and when shown inside out or rearranged, as in X-ray and split-style pictures (Figs. 2 and 9). Finally, the ability to recognize faces distorted by the satirist's pen seems hardly surprising when considered an extension of our ability to recognize faces changed by growth and age.

The main advantage of explaining depiction as an ability to recognize pictures' subjects over pictorial aspects is that the dynamism of recognition accounts for the diversity of depiction. The particular dimensions of variation, including essentially pictorial ones, over which recognition is dynamic determine the variety of ways that pictures can depict. They alone set the limits on the pictorial imagination.

Competence. Pictorial competence is system-relative because recognition is generative within pictorial dimensions of variation. I argued in Chapter 6 that the kinds of aspects that pictures present can be organized into systems of depiction: pictures in a system make commitments, explicit non-commitments, and inexplicit non-commitments about the same kinds of properties. Thus Albertian picturing is committal about the kinds of properties that objects are seen to possess from one point of view, and is non-committal about others; whereas, say, curvilinear picturing makes commitments about properties of what might be called ambient space, and so makes explicit non-commitments about properties of 'Cyclopian' space. But I have also suggested that recognition is preserved despite variations in certain kinds of properties. It seems plausible to infer that pictorial systems are those that present aspects belonging to the same dimensions of variation.

In support of this inference, there is empirical evidence that pictorial recognition abilities vary in speed and accuracy with system of representation.[19] Kinds of objects are recognized most effectively in simplified, stylized cartoons, then in photographs and shaded drawings, and least effectively in line-drawings. Individuals are best recognized in certain kinds of photographs. (Surprisingly, detailed drawings of objects are recognized faster than the objects themselves!) These data suggest that recognition abilities vary with systems of depiction.

The ability to recognize things in pictures is generative only within, not between, systems, because recognition is generative only within dimensions of variation. Being able to recognize something presented under a pictorial aspect typical of one system does not suffice for being able to recognize anything presented under an aspect typical of another system. Competence in Albertian depiction does not guarantee competence in the split-style system, or vice versa. But once a viewer has gained the ability to recognize some objects with which she is

---

[19] See T. A. Ryan and Carol B. Schwartz, 'Speed of Perception as a Function of Mode of Representation', *American Journal of Psychology*, 79 (1956), 60–9; Fraisse and Elkin, 'Étude génétique'; and Graham Davies, Hadyn Ellis, and John Shepherd, 'Face Recognition Accuracy as a Function of Mode of Representation', *Journal of Applied Psychology*, 63 (1978), 180–7.

acquainted when they are presented in split-style aspects, she is then, in principle, able to recognize any object with which she is acquainted under split-style kinds of aspects.[20] Competence in depiction is gained a system at a time, rather than a picture at a time.

Pictorial competence is manifest not only through generativity, but also through transference. Whereas generativity is the ability to interpret novel pictures of familiar objects, transference is the ability to identify an unfamiliar object through a picture of it. But if recognition is an ability to identify familiar objects, how can it explain transference? One answer to this question is that pictures of unfamiliar objects are usually recognized as objects having familiar properties. Thus transference depends on the generativity of content-recognition, not subject-recognition. A second answer is that a picture may convey information about the properties of an unfamiliar object so as to endow a viewer with a recognition ability for that object. Pictures, as well as visual experiences, can convey information sufficient to initiate recognition abilities. We can recognize the movie star walking down Hollywood Boulevard as someone seen in *People* magazine.

The claim that interpreting pictures depends on the exercise of aspect-relative recognition abilities explains not only why pictorial systems are individuated by the aspects they present, but also why pictorial competence is tied to systems. Pictorial competence is system-relative because recognition is relative to dimensions of variation; systems can be individuated by the kinds of aspects they present because we are able to recognize objects with dimensions of variation defined by those aspects.

My suggestion is, in sum, that pictures embody information enabling viewers to recognize their contents and their subjects. The recognition skills we bring to pictures depend on and extend the dynamic recognition skills exercised in ordinary perception. I have argued that recognition is not reducible to description, that it is dynamic, aspectual, and systematic, and that this explains the diversity and generativity of depiction. The task for philosophy ends at identifying these structural and logical properties of recognition and their implications for thought and reference.

What I am offering may be described as a naturalized account of

---

[20] Generativity does not, of course, guarantee that any novel picture can be recognized. The first limitation on recognition remains in effect: any recognition ability can be overstretched.

pictorial reference. One of Evans's most important insights was that an account of reference, or certain varieties of reference, must draw upon an understanding of certain psychological mechanisms. If my proposal that depiction depends on recognition is correct, then it will need to be supplemented by psychological studies of pictorial recognition.

Such studies will need to survey the different dimensions of variation over which human recognition abilities may be dynamic, the kinds of aspects constituting them, and the relations among them. Some of the psychological studies of speed and ease of recognition across systems of representation begin to fill this need. Their weakness is an almost exclusive concentration on subspecies of Albertian picturing.[21] A psychology of picture perception that does justice to its diversity will need to explore the dependence of every available system of depiction on underlying perceptual processes.

The acquisition of pictorial recognition abilities amounts to a significant enhancement of our visual concepts. These abilities enable their possessors to think of objects that are presented as having a wide variety of appearances, including appearances that might only be visible in pictures. The value of this should not be underestimated. By presenting recognizable aspects of their subjects, some of which are beyond the capacity of ordinary visual experience, pictures provide us with an assortment of representational tools that can add to our knowledge of the visual world.

7.5 Recognition and Resemblance

Pictures resemble their subjects. This is hardly surprising, since just about everything resembles everything else in some respect. What I have taken great pains to deny, especially in Chapter 1, is that viewers discover what pictures represent as a result of noticing certain representation-independent resemblances between their designs and their subjects. The fact is that pictures' resemblances to their subjects are highly variable from one system to the next, and noticing these resemblances, while integral to our experience of pictures, depends in part on the processes by which we interpret pictures. In other words, pictorial resemblances are representation-dependent.

This claim can now be given a little more precision. What design

---

[21] A notable exception is Hagen, *Varieties of Realism*.

properties we experience as similar to properties that objects might be seen to have depends on the recognitional processes by which we interpret them. Thus picture–subject similarities are aspect and system-relative. Pictures in different systems present different aspects of objects recognizable in different dimensions of variation. For example, depending on the kind of aspect presented, similarities among sizes on the picture plane may correspond to similarities among real sizes, among distances, or, in icon painting, among positions of persons represented in the celestial hierarchy.

Ambiguous pictures nicely illustrate the recognition-dependence of pictorial similarities. In recognizing the duck–rabbit either as a duck on the one hand or a rabbit on the other, we come to notice different similarities between the shape of the figure and a silhouette of an animal (see Fig. 12). Indeed, in this case, what similarities we notice are determined rather precisely by which animal we recognize. The large protruding shape on the left of the figure that looks like the blades of a pair of scissors (now that I mention it to you!) looks like a bill if you recognize the figure as a duck or a pair of ears if you recognize it as a rabbit. What is most surprising is that when the picture is recognized as of one object, the other resemblances disappear.

What resemblances we notice are at least in part a matter of the processes of recognition in virtue of which we recognize the picture's content and subject. Moreover, these recognition-dependent resemblances vary with systems of depiction. Any design can depict any object provided it is recognizable as of that object, and the kinds of designs in which we can recognize things may vary with the dimensions of variation across which recognition is dynamic.

7.6 Basic Picturing

A picture is a representation that embodies information on the basis of which its source can be identified by a suitably equipped perceiver. To be sure, not all pictures' subjects can be identified through recognition alone, and the next chapter lists alternative modes that can be employed to identify pictures' sources; but recognition is basic to all pictures. In this section I set out the two forms of basic picturing—basic portrayal and basic depiction.

A picture 'basically portrays' an object or scene if and only if it embodies aspectual information from it on the basis of which a suitable perceiver is able to recognize it. ('Portrayal', as I use it, is the depiction of any single object, whether human or not.) Though it would be expected to do so, I do not require that a basic portrait actually trigger someone's ability to recognize its source. A picture can present a recognizable aspect of Mr and Mrs Andrews or the Piazza San Marco without ever being recognized as of the Andrews or the Piazza. Moreover, it is not required of a basic portrait that all viewers possess the ability to recognize its source when presented with it—not all viewers are 'suitable perceivers' of a picture.

While not all pictures are portraits, we have seen that all represent their subjects as having some properties, and this goes also for portraits of individuals who cannot be recognized. A picture 'basically depicts' a property or kind of object F if and only if it embodies aspectual information derived from Fs on the basis of which a suitable perceiver is able to recognize it as an F. The *Pioneer* spacecraft portrays nothing, but it basically depicts two specimens of *Homo sapiens*; Canaletto's painting basically depicts some Venetians, horses, and the like. Again, an F-picture need not trigger recognition in all those who view it, not even those who view the picture and are able to recognize Fs.

Of course, basic portrayal and depiction are by no means infallible. Ambiguous pictures may be recognizable as of multiple objects or kinds of objects, and some pictures may not be recognizable as of their subjects by any suitable perceivers. Chapter 8 describes some alternative pictorial modes of identification that are useful when recognition meets its limits, though it also explains why recognition is basic to all pictures.

For the remainder of this chapter I want to qualify and defend my claim that basic pictures need be recognizable only by 'suitable perceivers'. The implication is that a picture can be beyond the recognition skills of some viewers but nevertheless basically picture its subject. But then who are 'suitable perceivers', and why are they the benchmark for depiction? In particular, what sort of skills must one possess to qualify as a suitable perceiver?

I suggest that a suitable perceiver for a given picture is one who possesses a *suitably dynamic* recognition ability. We have seen that there are two levels of recognition. A suitable perceiver must have certain competencies at each level.

To begin with, suitable perceivers must be adept at interpreting pictures—they must be able to recognize pictures' contents. This is the general requirement. A more specific one is that suitable perceivers *of a given picture* must additionally have recognition abilities for pictures in the same system. A suitable perceiver for Picasso's *Vollard* must be able to recognize cubist design–content correlations. Somebody who can recognize Vollard but cannot interpret cubist pictures is not a suitable perceiver of such a picture. We may say that a suitable perceiver of a picture must have a competence in its system. But not everybody with competence in a picture's system can thereby recognize its subject. Its subject must also be familiar. Not everybody who can recognize flower-aspects of people can recognize one of Françoise Gilot, and not everybody who can interpret split-style pictures can recognize the sisiutl (a mythic serpent). Suitable perceivers of a given picture are those who possess a recognition capacity for its subject.

To sum up, then, a picture basically portrays an object x under pictorial aspect A if and only if it embodies information from x on the basis of which someone who has a recognition capacity for x and who is able to recognize pictures under the dimensions of variation to which A belongs is able to recognize x. A picture basically depicts an F under pictorial aspect A if and only if it embodies information from some F on the basis of which someone who has a recognition capacity for Fs and who is able to recognize pictures under the dimensions of variation to which A belongs is able to recognize an F.

Note that I do not require that a suitable perceiver of an x-as-A-picture or an F-as-A-picture be able to recognize x or F under A—that would render my accounts of basic portrayal and depiction circular. For example, a suitable perceiver of a split-style portrait of Peter Sellars must be able both to recognize Peter Sellars under a dynamic range of aspects and to recognize objects under split-style aspects. Being able to recognize Peter Sellars under a split-style aspect is *not* a precondition for being a suitable perceiver of this picture—that would be circular.

There are two possible objections to this proposal. On the one hand, it seems to set too exacting a standard, because many pictures represent objects and people with whom we have lost contact and whom nobody can recognize. On the other hand, it seems to set too permissive a standard, since any scribble that somebody somewhere can recognize as of its subject counts as a basic picture. Let me answer these objections in turn.

Unlike verbal utterances, pictures often remain in existence for long periods of time. As a result, it is true that as time passes their viewers are less likely to be acquainted with their subjects. The *Mona Lisa* is perhaps the most famous portrait of a figure with whom we have long lost acquaintance, though art museums are full of pictures whose sitters we do not know. Suitable viewers possessing recognition capacities for the subjects of these pictures no longer exist. That this is so is a not wholly unexpected or undesirable implication for my theory of depiction. Pictures like the *Mona Lisa* have suitable viewers, albeit they do not have suitable viewers *now*. And it would be absurd to claim that a picture's subject must be recognizable by viewers in every time and place. Furthermore, the requirement that suitable perceivers be able to recognize a picture's subject explains the difference between the understanding enjoyed by Leonardo's contemporaries, who were acquainted with whoever sat for the *Mona Lisa*, and that enjoyed by modern viewers, who are not acquainted with her.

In any case, the argument that many pictures have no suitable perceivers is overstated. It wrongly assumes that a recognition ability for an object depends on an acquaintance with it. In fact, recognition abilities need not derive from personal acquaintance with things. Information endowing perceivers with recognition abilities may be, and often is, put into circulation by those who are directly acquainted with an object, for the benefit of those not acquainted with it. Often this information is distributed in the form of verbal testimony, but the role that pictures play in circulating information that can prompt recognition is not insignificant.

We must remember that pictures are not infrequently our initial perceptual contact with objects, and enable us to re-identify them in the future. Pictures, in other words, can endow us with recognition abilities. And although somebody who gains a recognition capacity for Wellington from a £5 note will assuredly never exercise it to identify Wellington himself, she might exercise it to identify Wellington as the source of other pictures. Thus recognition might come into play when seeing an aspect of an unfamiliar object in a picture provides a basis for recognizing the same object if ever confronted with it under other aspects. Basic depiction can depend on an extant recognition ability or the provision of a new one.

Finally, pictures of unrecognizable objects may be treated in somewhat the same way as we treat fictions. Although viewers may know that a picture had a source and was intended to depict it, identifying that source may have become impossible. But when appreciation of a picture, particularly a portrait, calls upon us to entertain thoughts about the character and doings of its subject, we may pretend to have recognized it, as a way of having the sort of thoughts required for aesthetic appreciation. This is comparable to the way in which readers of chronicles of distant times and places can appreciate the stories they contain by treating them as fictions (see Ch. 10).

The second line of protest to requiring that basic pictures be recognizable to suitable perceivers is that it is too permissive, conferring the status of a basic picture on anything that might trigger the cultivated recognition capacities of any small class of viewers. If certain Parisians belonging to an *ante bellum* avant-garde can recognize art dealers under cubist aspects, then cubist picturing is basic. However, we should not lose sight of the crucial fact, which is the *sine qua non* of depiction, that our repertoire of recognition skills can be enlarged. Recognition is generative in new dimensions of variation, new systems. Once we understand how the Kwakiutl depict ravens, we are usually able to interpret their pictures of whales, bears, and beavers as well.

I grant, however, that there is a limit to what counts as a suitably dynamic recognition capacity. It is necessary to rule out pictures which trigger highly idiosyncratic recognition abilities. The artist Henri Michaux produced abstract frottages and water-colours of objects as they appeared to him under the influence of mescaline. If Michaux's pictures accurately represent, as well they may, what their subjects look like to somebody in a drug-induced state, then we may suppose that anybody in such a state would be able to recognize them. Yet it seems wrong to say that Michaux's pictures are basic pictures just because they trigger *some* perceiver's recognition skills. For a less *outré* example, consider Josef Karsh's photograph of Pablo Casals, shown from the back, playing the cello. It seems wrong to say that the photograph basically represents Casals just because a few close acquaintances can recognize him from the back. It seems equally strained to insist that a child's 'drawing' represents its mother because the child (and its mother, no doubt) can idiosyncratically recognize its subject.

The notion of a 'suitable perceiver' is in some measure a normative one. A suitable perceiver of a picture is one who possesses recognition abilities that a normal person would possess. It is in part because depiction has built into it a normative conception of what skills should be required for interpreting pictures that our ideals of pictorial representation have a history, changing from time to time and place to place. Albertian depiction embodies an ideal of pictorial recognition as requiring only those recognition skills that are employed in quite restricted perceptual conditions. Cubism challenges the Albertian ideal, requiring suitable perceivers to possess radically different recognition skills.

It strikes me as not at all implausible that, since the invention of photography, our ideal of picturing has been liberated from its Albertian constraints, and the history of recent art is a history of experimentation with the limits of pictorial recognition. Perhaps, then, our normative concept of the pictorial has become an essentially contested one, so that what counts as a suitable way of engaging viewers' perceptual talents is not only variable and sensitive to context, but also a matter of dispute.[22]

[22] See W. B. Gallie, 'Essentially Contested Concepts', *Proceedings of the Aristotelian Society*, 56 (1955), 167–98.

8

Pictorial Meaning

PICTURES represent by basically depicting or basically portraying their subjects—by presenting information on the basis of which their subjects can be recognized. This thesis needs to be elaborated and qualified. It will be necessary to consider artists' intentions and their implications for the aspect-recognition theory. We must also return to the puzzles introduced in Chapter 5 and show how they can be accommodated within the apparatus of basic picturing. Finally, since recognition is not the sole route to depiction, I describe what other modes of pictorial identification are available and how recognition is basic to all.

8.1 Picture Meaning, Artist's Meaning, and Intentions

It is commonplace in discussions of depiction to assert either that the meaning of a picture depends on its maker's intentions or that understanding its meaning depends on recognizing its maker's intentions. I believe neither assertion to be warranted. But before I set out my position, I want to acknowledge a distinction that has been at work, clandestinely, in my argument from the outset.

I have from the beginning tried to explain how pictures represent by considering how viewers come to understand what they represent. An account of one is, I believe, impossible without an account of the other. This is obviously axiomatic for any perceptual theory of depiction. The resemblance theory, for instance, openly analyses pictorial representation in terms of how viewers learn what pictures represent: namely, by noticing resemblances. In the same vein, the aspect-recognition theory is cast as an account of the perceptual skills that make it possible for viewers to grasp what pictures represent. Pictures, I have argued, are representations that embody information derived from scenes or objects, on the basis of which they can be visually recognized as of those scenes or objects. By extension, viewers understand what pictures represent when they actually put their recognitional abilities to work and thereby identify their subjects. To understand a picture is, in basic cases, to entertain a thought which links the visual information presented by the picture with a body of stored information from its subject. There are, as I noted in Chapter 4, many ways in which pictures can be used to represent, not all of which count as *pictorial* representation. *Piazza San Marco* folded up a certain way might represent an airplane, but it does not depict one. Since a theory of depiction is not properly concerned with such cases, I proposed that what a picture represents as a picture can be thought of as constrained by what I called its pictorial sense, and a theory of depiction is a theory of pictorial sense. I am now in a position to add that one form of pictorial meaning or sense is captured in the definition of basic picturing (some others are described in Section 8.5). If I make a doodle and declare it to be a picture of Parfit, I may have created a representation of Parfit, but I have not created one that represents pictorially. A pictorial representation of Parfit will be one that represents him by presenting visual information on the basis of which he can be identified by appropriate means.

Just as pictures can be put to many representational uses, so they can be understood in many ways. For example, I can come to know what a picture represents by reading its title or by being told what it represents. I can also, as Evans points out, identify its subject as whatever happened to be its source. Clearly, knowing what a picture represents in one of these ways does not amount to understanding it *as a picture*. Wittgenstein expresses the point succinctly: 'If you see the drawing as such-and-such an animal, what I expect from you will be pretty different from what I expect when you merely know what it is meant to be.'[1] Not any way in which a viewer comes to know what a picture represents constitutes understanding it as a picture.

To understand a picture *qua* picture, a viewer must not only identify its subject, she must do so by grasping its meaning as a picture, its pictorial sense. To grasp a picture's meaning as a picture, viewers must learn what its subject is by employing an appropriate mode of identification, usually one that depends on the exercise of recognition skills. Recognition is by no means the only way to grasp a picture's meaning— Section 8.4 enumerates two further modes of understanding pictures *qua* pictures, and there may be more. Moreover, I do not mean to overlook the fact that we might find ourselves unable to understand a picture by retracing the way it secures its reference. What I do want to suggest is that there is a crucial difference between knowing what a

---

[1] Wittgenstein, *Philosophical Investigations*, 205.

picture represents by tracing its genesis as a picture and knowing what it represents by alternative means.[2]

The informational model that I have endorsed suggests the following additional observation about understanding pictures. A viewer understands a picture *qua* picture only if her attempt at identifying its source is well grounded—if what she identifies as its source is in fact its source. An identification is ill-grounded if what is identified as the source of a picture is not in fact its source, if nothing is identified as its source, if something is identified as its source and it has no source, or if nothing is identified as its source and indeed it has no source.

Having clarified the relationship between what pictures represent and viewers' understanding of what pictures represent, we can now turn to what role artists' intentions might play in each. To permit artists' intentions some role in understanding pictures appears to take cognizance of the fact that pictures are media by which one person may communicate with another. By looking at a picture, viewers want to learn what the artist hoped to accomplish by making it. And this imposes a demand on the artist that, by making the picture, she enable viewers to know what it is she is trying to do. We are led quite naturally to the conclusion that the meaning of pictures depends on what artists intend by making them, and that understanding pictures involves recognizing these intentions.

The difficulty with this conclusion is that what a picture means is not always what the artist intends by making it. I might intend to depict Thatcher at Charing Cross, yet make a picture embodying information from and recognizable as Thatcher at Piccadilly. Here a gap opens up between what I intend to depict and what I in fact depicted, and the existence of this gap is the only way to explain the expected response to my picture: namely, that I have not succeeded in doing what I intended to do. Intending to depict an object is not necessary or sufficient for depicting it; nor is knowing what the artist intended to depict necessary or sufficient for understanding her picture.

My view is that artists' intentions are relevant to what *artists* mean and to understanding what they mean, not to what their *works* mean or to understanding their works. What a picture means is what the artist means by making it only when her intention is *manifest* in an appropriate way—that is, through a picture that successfully implements her

---

[2] It should be pointed out that non-pictorial forms of understanding can lead to understanding a picture as a picture. I might come to recognize a picture's subject once I learn its title. But knowing a picture's title or its maker's intentions cannot be necessary for pictorial recognition if basic picturing is to be representation-independent (see Sect. 1.1).

intentions. And in understanding a picture, one is above all required to exercise one's perceptual skills to single out its actual source, intended or not. This is not to say that artists' intentions are to be ignored, for it remains true that pictures are used to communicate, and it is often important for viewers to learn what the artist means by making a picture. When she succeeds in her endeavours, this will be revealed by her picture's meaning, but when there is a gap between what a picture means and what its maker meant, knowing the artist's intention can convey important information.

When we are interested in artists' intentions, we must be careful to distinguish intentions of two kinds.[3] The first is a specific intention to produce a picture—a work embodying information which will enable a suitable viewer to identify something by means of a pictorial mode of identification. The second is a general intention just to represent something by one's actions. For obvious reasons, we may call the intention to produce a work pictorially identifiable as of its subject a 'pictorial' intention. The general intention to represent something, I call a 'communicative' intention. As we shall see, it is possible for one intention to succeed where the other fails.

In sum, I distinguish what a picture means from what it is intended to mean, and understanding a picture—which only requires identifying its source by appropriate means—from understanding what the artist means by making it—which requires recognition of her communicative intentions. Artists' intentions are relevant to fixing what artists mean, not what their works mean.

This is, admittedly, a fairly strict anti-intentionalism. The principal reason for rejecting intentionalism comes in response to the need to make sense of our intuitive judgements about certain puzzle cases.

8.2 *Puzzles Revisited*

It is time to return to the puzzles raised in Chapter 5, and to add a new one. All are the consequence either of failures in recognition or of twists in the paths along which information is transmitted in pictures. The new puzzle arises out of pictures' dependence on recognition

---

[3] Cf. Kripke's distinction between 'general' and 'specific' intentions governing descriptive utterances, in Saul Kripke, 'Speaker's Reference and Semantic Reference', in Peter A. French, Theodore E. Uehling, Jr., and Howard K. Wettstein (eds.), *Contemporary Perspectives in the Philosophy of Language* (Minneapolis: University of Minnesota Press, 1979), 15.

capacities. Recognition is supposed to enable us to distinguish some objects from others. But what about indiscernible objects, such as identical twins or, more exotically, doppelgängers and Twin Earth counterparts?[4] If a person is indistinguishable from his twin, there can be no recognition ability for either twin that distinguishes him from all other objects. Hence no picture can basically portray him. Similarly, inhabitants of a Twin Earth, far from our Earth, which contains a substance which they call 'water', which is just like water except that its chemical composition is XYZ rather than H_2O, will be disposed to identify Vermeer's *View of Delft* as representing, among other things, Twin Earth water.[5] If neither we nor Twin Earthers possess adequate recognition capacities for water—capacities that distinguish H_2O from XYZ —then no picture can basically depict water.

Since no recognition capacity can distinguish among indiscernible objects and since basic picturing depends on recognition capacities, my account of basic picturing implies that it is impossible to make basic pictures of indiscernible objects. But this conclusion seems absurd: we surely can depict things even when they are not distinguishable from others.

A second sort of puzzle is attributable to malfunctions in the information system. Some pictures present aspects of their subjects that are so unusual as to be unrecognizable by normal perceivers, and perhaps by anybody. From an information-systemic point of view, such pictures convey garbled information; from a common-sense point of view, they are the products of poor artistic technique. I doubt whether anybody would deny that in most cases these are not pictures at all (see Sect. 5.1). But what should we say about the more puzzling possibility of pictures which are recognizable not as of their subjects but as of entirely different objects instead? The example I gave in Chapter 5 was of a fortuitously botched picture whose source was Queen Victoria although it was recognizable as of Divine.

It would be wrong to assume that these puzzles are invariably outlandish and exceptional. When artists use models, they bring about a deliberate mismatch between source and recognizable subject. We know that Hendrickje Stoffels served as Rembrandt's model for Bathsheba. Although *Bathsheba* is recognizable as of, and contains information

---

[4] Evans discusses the problems that duplicates pose for recognition-based identification in *Varieties of Reference*, 278–84, 299–300.

[5] Hilary Putnam, 'The Meaning of "Meaning" ', in *Mind, Language and Reality* (Cambridge: Cambridge University Press, 1975), 223–7.

originating with, Hendrickje, it is not only, or even primarily, a picture of her. Meanwhile, if, as is surely the case, the picture depicts Bathsheba, it does so in spite of the fact that Bathsheba did not sit as its model and so is not the source of the information it conveys. These last two puzzles were introduced in order to demonstrate a weakness in Kaplan's hybrid theory of pictorial reference. According to that theory, a picture depicts its source provided it has some content about it, but this implies, unacceptably, that my Divine-picture represents Victoria and Rembrandt's *Bathsheba* represents only Hendrickje. The lesson I drew from this is that there should be some connection between a picture's source and its content, and the account I subsequently gave of basic depiction was intended to make good on this. The viability of the aspect-recognition theory therefore depends on its adequately accommodating these puzzles. Any good theory of depiction will support our intuitive judgements about puzzle cases, predicting ambiguity when our judgements about them are ambiguous, and clarity when our judgements about them are clear.

8.3 Intentionalism

It has been argued that to solve these puzzles (or similar ones) we must accept that a picture's meaning depends on what it was intended to represent. Wollheim, for instance, gives recognition of intentions a prominent place in his account of pictorial representation. The seeing appropriate to depiction is for Wollheim an instance of the more general visual phenomenon of seeing-in. We see dragons' heads in clouds and faces in tree trunks as much as we see Last Suppers in frescos by Leonardo and umbrellas in pictures by Renoir. What distinguishes seeing in pictures from generic seeing-in is that only pictures are made with an intention that their subjects be seen in them (this is what I have called a pictorial intention). Thus a picture depicts an object only if the object is intended to be seen in it.[6] Clouds and Rorschach ink-blots do not depict horses' heads, butterflies, or whatever else we see in them, because they were not made with the intention that we see horses' heads or butterflies in them.

Wollheim's argument for assigning such weight to artists' intentions is that some pictures are ambiguous because we can see many different

---

[6] Wollheim, 'Seeing-as, Seeing-in', 205–6.

things in them, and the intentions of the artist set the standard for correct interpretation. Nevertheless, I am sceptical of the claim that artists' intentions serve to disambiguate these pictures. I argue instead that informational factors determine what a picture represents. I also allow, however, that we may legitimately take intentions into consideration when, in certain cases, it becomes necessary to determine the artist's meaning.

According to Wollheim, intentions are necessary to disambiguate pictures. If a picture triggers a recognition capacity for two (perhaps indistinguishable) objects, it depicts the one that is intended to be seen in it. Wollheim thinks of pictures using models as illustrating this ambiguity. He writes that '*A*'s twin brother could serve as a model for *A*'s portrait . . . and if the portrait comes off, *A*, not his brother, is the person correctly seen there'.[7] Thus, when an artist uses one object as a model for another, her intentions determine which object is to be seen in the picture, and consequently which it represents.

There are two problems with the claim that intentions disambiguate such pictures. First, this claim is usually coupled with a distinction between photographs and hand-made pictures that I believe to be insupportable. Wollheim holds that whereas the standard of correctness for most pictures is intentional, the standard of correctness for photographs is causal: a photograph depicts whatever object or scene reflected light, so causing a pattern of exposure on a photographic film. Photographs do differ from other pictures in numerous ways, but not, I submit, in being subject to different standards of interpretation. For one thing, photographs can be made with models. Does a photograph represent Hamlet, or does it represent Mel Gibson, its causal object?[8] Wollheim answers that both standards apply. Seen as a photograph, the picture represents Mel Gibson; seen as a representation, it depicts Hamlet, because 'intention cancels out the deliverances of the causal process'.[9]

This dualism of standards of correct interpretation is not supported by the aspect-recognition theory. All pictures, if they are information-transmitting devices, are causally linked to their sources. The causal component in drawing is simply, and understandably, more circuitous than that involved in photography. Moreover, the same kinds of recognition skills are involved in identifying the subjects of pictures and photographs, and experiences of both have similar phenomenologies

---

[7] Ibid. 208.   [8] I thank Eve Lopes for this example.
[9] Wollheim 'Seeing-as, Seeing-in', 209.

(see Chapter 9). That there is a conflict between Wollheim's view of the relationship between photographs and hand-drawn pictures and mine does not immediately impeach Wollheim's, of course. It does, however, underscore the need for an account of ambiguous pictures that does more than paste on reference to artists' intentions.

A more damaging problem with the intentionalist account of pictures made using models is that in fact both Bathsheba and Hendrickje Stoffels meet Wollheim's two conditions for depiction. Hendrickje was a source for and is recognizable in *Bathsheba*, and the fact is that Rembrandt intended that at least some of its viewers come to know that Hendrickje modelled for *Bathsheba*, and that they come to know this by recognizing the picture as of Hendrickje.[10] Rembrandt's intentions evidently cannot explain the primary identification of Rembrandt's picture as of Bathsheba rather than Hendrickje.

I suggest that we turn to the apparatus of pictorial information transmission to discover why this picture primarily depicts Bathsheba. A picture's source is the object, information from which guided the artist in making a picture which (in successful depiction) capable observers can identify as of that object. Now, it would be a mistake to lapse into a monolithic conception of how we obtain information from objects. It is likely that Rembrandt possessed information, no doubt largely testimonial, which originated with Bathsheba and which guided his actions in making a picture identifiable as of her. Hendrickje's role was as an aid to the transmission of this Bathsheba-information. She was chosen as Rembrandt's model precisely because of features which qualified her as an appropriate vehicle for transmitting that information.

I suggest that we classify pictures' sources as either primary or secondary. An object or kind of object is a picture's primary source if its serving in the picture's production did not depend on the nature of information from any other source that the picture may have had. An object is a picture's secondary source if that object's serving in the picture's production depended on the nature of information derived from the picture's primary source or sources.

Bathsheba is primarily of Bathsheba and secondarily of Hendrickje, because Hendrickje's serving as a model depended on a resemblance to Bathsheba that made her a suitable conduit for information from Bathsheba. Likewise, Mel Gibson is a secondary source of a publicity

---

[10] For some of the reasons behind this intention, see Svetlana Alpers, *Rembrandt's Enterprise: The Studio and the Market* (Chicago: University of Chicago Press, 1988), 65–7, 75.

photograph for the film version of *Hamlet*, for he was cast as Hamlet because of his suitability for transmitting information from Hamlet, the picture's (perhaps fictive) primary source. The workings of the information system, rather than the intentions of the artist, are all that is required for a unified account of both pictures and photographs that use models.

The second set of puzzle pictures suggests that artistic intentions should be allied with artist's meaning rather than picture meaning. Some denizens of this set fail to present aspects that are recognizable as of anything at all—they are just botches—and it is not hard to dismiss them as pictures. Others present recognizable aspects, but only of objects other than their sources. I agree with Wollheim that these pictures, like plain botches, *depict* neither their sources nor whatever objects viewers might be inclined to recognize in them. After all, nobody maintains that intentions suffice to confer meaning on a picture. Yet I do think that there is a sense, however indirect, in which these pictures can function communicatively, for we can still find out what their makers meant by them, and this is why they strike us as puzzling.

This concession is permissible only if artistic intentions go towards fixing not picture meaning but artist's meaning. If one holds that a picture represents what viewers are intended to identify when they look at it, then botched pictures, in which the intended object cannot be identified, are utterly meaningless. Thus Wollheim writes that 'if, through the incompetence, ignorance, or bad luck of the artist, the possible perceptions of a given representation do not include one that matches the artist's intention, there is . . . nothing or no-one represented'.[11] But if one holds that what a picture means is a matter of what viewers can successfully identify and what an artist means depends on her communicative intention, then a failure in pictorial meaning need not provoke a failure in artist's meaning. Evidence for what the artist means can be found outside the picture, so we can understand the artist's communicative intention despite the failure of her pictorial intention.

Let us begin with complete botches. Imagine a young child who draws a squiggle, not recognizable as anything, which he intends to represent his mother. Perhaps he has not yet mastered the concept of a picture, with the consequence that in making his squiggle he does not intend to produce an object embodying visual information from his mother which may trigger the recognition capacity of some suitable

---

[11] Wollheim, 'Seeing-as, Seeing-in', 206.

viewer. Let us disregard this possibility, stipulating that the child does intend to portray his mother and merely lacks the skills required to carry out his intention successfully. Let us also stipulate that the squiggle does not trigger any idiosyncratic child's-perspective recognition ability for its mother—presented with an identical squiggle made by someone else, the child would not be disposed to recognize its mother.

Since it does not meet the conditions of basic portrayal, the squiggle does not pictorially represent the child's mother. But this does not mean that we cannot understand what the child is up to, what he means by the picture. After all, the child does have a communicative intention to represent his mother. In successful depiction, a communicative intention is manifest by making a basic picture, but there are other ways, some highly context-dependent, for a representer to manifest a communicative intention. A viewer who recognizes the artist's communicative intention on the basis of such evidence may be said to understand what the artist meant. Children's pictures are often meaningless failures, though we often know what they are meant to represent. But only in a parent's mind is successful communicative intention sufficient for depiction.

In cases such as this, a gap opens up between what the picture depicts, if anything, and what the artist intends it to represent—and so between understanding the picture's meaning and understanding what the artist means by it. This is exactly what we would expect. It is possible for an artist's pictorial intention to fail, even if he succeeds in communicating what object he means to refer to.

A gap appears also when pictures present their subjects under aspects which would not trigger the recognition capacities of suitable perceivers. If a picture such as Karsh's photograph of Casals from the back presents him from a point of view which fails to trigger recognition in suitable perceivers, we may nevertheless understand Karsh's intent on the basis of the artist's manifest communicative intentions, as evidenced, say, in the photograph's caption.

However, there is an important difference between the child's squiggle and Karsh's photograph of Casals, for the latter basically pictures something—if not Casals, then a cellist and a man. A picture which represents its subject under an unusual aspect still has content concerning it, and so has meaning as a picture. Once, by whatever means, the subject of such a picture is identified, this information can be connected to information about the subject already in one's possession—one might acquire an ability to recognize Casals as seen from the back.

Finally, adequately manifest communicative intentions can shed light on our judgements about pictures which prompt recognitions of objects that are not their sources. Since my Divine-picture of Queen Victoria cannot invoke a visual recognition capacity for Victoria, and Divine is not its source, my picture basically portrays neither. But I would guess that the picture strikes most viewers as ambiguously representing both. The explanation of the temptation to say that it represents Victoria is that the artist revealed his communicative intention to represent Victoria, so that viewers know what he meant by it.

How can the intuition that the picture also represents Divine be accommodated? A special feature of the recognitional mode of identification is that it is, as Peacocke puts it, 'image-dependent'.[12] That is, a recognitional identification which is ill-grounded because it identifies something which did not serve as the picture's source is nevertheless grounded in a recognition ability, and this gives the picture a vicarious or purportive content. The picture has a content concerning, but not 'of', Divine because a viewer is disposed, though mistakenly, to recognize Divine in it.

A similar case illustrates the distinction between pictorial and communicative intentions. Imagine that an artist intends to represent *a* and, believing *a* is *b*, makes a picture embodying information only from and recognizable only as of *b*. While the resulting picture successfully realizes the artist's pictorial intention with regard to *b*, it fails to manifest and successfully realize his communicative intention to represent *a*. Does it depict *a* or *b*? On the present account, there is a genuine ambiguity between what it depicts and what its maker meant it to represent.[13]

8.4 Beyond Recognition

Basic picturing is the core of pictorial representation. It takes as paradigmatic pictures of familiar objects which we are able to recognize— pictures like those found in a family photo album. These pictures do not simply trigger recognition abilities. By conveying information about the appearance of objects in various guises, they help to preserve and extend the dynamism of viewers' recognition abilities. But although it

---

[12] Peacocke, *Sense and Content*, 144–5.

[13] This parallels the ambiguity that Kripke considers to result from the distinction he draws between a descriptive expression's 'semantic referent', governed by 'general' intentions, and its 'speaker's referent', governed by 'specific' intentions: Kripke, 'Speaker's Reference and Semantic Reference', 13–15.

is at work in some way in every representational picture, basic depiction is only one among many varieties of depiction. In this section I describe two additional pictorial modes of identification. One is information-based, the other conventional.

As we saw in Chapter 5, some pictures, having contents that match their subjects, depict in the manner of identifying descriptions. A descriptive picture that represents its subject as such-and-such represents the object or kind of object that is such-and-such. However, few pictures depict *whatever* happens to match their contents, and in the face of misrepresentation it seemed futile to treat all pictures as descriptive.

The apparatus of information-based depiction permits some rehabilitation of pictorial description. We may distinguish purely descriptive pictures, whose subjects are whatever objects their contents match, from pictures that represent by embodying descriptive information from their subjects. Such a picture may represent by embodying information from an object or scene that can be matched with independent information from that object or scene in the possession of suitable viewers. There are two points of difference between information-based and purely descriptive pictures. Neither the information contained in the former nor that with which they are matched need be accurate. And whereas purely descriptive pictures represent whatever they happen to match, information-based pictures provide for well-grounded identifications only if what is identified as the picture's source is in fact its source. Well-groundedness, rather than accuracy of match, is key to information-based pictorial description.

Pictures of objects that we are unable to recognize, but from which we possess some information, perhaps transmitted by verbal testimony, are frequently depicted in this way. Pictures representing historical figures or places are good candidates for descriptive depiction. Literature and verbal testimony having provided information about an individual, pictures invoking this body of information enable viewers to identify the figure or place, even if the information is mistaken. Consider, for example, this verbal description, by his son, of Christopher Columbus. He was 'a well-built man of more than average stature, the face long, the cheeks somewhat high, his body neither fat nor lean. He had an aquiline nose and light-coloured eyes; his complexion, too, was light and tending to bright red.'[14] Possession of this dossier of testimonial information

---

[14] Quoted in Ponce de Léon, *The Columbus Gallery* (New York: Ponce de Léon, 1893), 3.

enables viewers to identify pictures based on it as of Columbus. This is so even if Columbus was in reality dark, scrawny, and pug-nosed. Many pictures that at first glance seem to function as pure descriptions turn out on closer scrutiny to be information-based. For instance, maps are usually documents that embody information about places from which information is available. Although a map's content is a description of a landscape, it does not represent whatever landscape it happens to match; indeed, a map can represent a place despite great inaccuracies. Those who are familiar with a place might identify a map of it even when the place has changed and the map is no longer accurate.

Descriptive pictures are one way to represent objects that we can no longer recognize; iconographic pictures are another. The contents of iconographic pictures are associated in a special way with their subjects: they are the exception to the rule that pictures' contents advert to their subjects' appearance. Instead, the contents of iconographic pictures allude to all kinds of facts about the doings of their bearers. St Jerome, for example, is standardly represented as old, a priest, a cardinal, a monk writing, a penitent in the desert, with a lion nearby, a model of a church, snakes and scorpions, a stone in his hand, a skull nearby. Note the identifying presence of books, a cardinal's hat, a lion, and (to seventeenth-century Dutch eyes) the wilderness in Rembrandt's etching (Fig. 23). These 'emblems', as I shall call them, allude to Jerome's position as a Doctor of the Church, to his desert hermitage, to his work as translator of the Bible into Latin, and to the story of his friendship with a lion from whose paw he removed a thorn.[15] The saint is represented by the presence of a sufficient number of these emblems.

It is tempting to classify iconographic pictures as a special case of pictorial description. If you want to depict Jerome, all you need do is to draw an old monk in the desert accompanied by a lion; and if you fail to put in at least some of the typical marks of Jerome, it is arguable that you have failed to draw a picture of him. However, this temptation should be resisted. Iconographic pictures can misrepresent their subjects—Rembrandt's etching notwithstanding, Jerome did not have the features of a northern European. Nor do iconographic pictures standardly match information relayed from their subjects. Pictures of a desert penitent with a lion companion portray Jerome despite the fact that it

---

[15] My usage should not be confused with the use of 'emblems' to refer to those pictures common until the eighteenth century showing abstract objects described in accompanying mottoes.

Fig. 23. Rembrandt, *Saint Jerome in a Hilly Landscape*, *c.*1653

is likely that the story of his friendship with a lion does not transmit information originating with him. Thus iconography is neither pure nor information-based description.

Rather, iconographic pictures have their basis in conventions prevalent in a community of picture-users which associate certain emblems with certain figures. Thus a picture of an old monk in the desert accompanied by a lion produced by someone in a society ignorant of the conventions of Christian iconography would not count in his society as an iconographic picture of Jerome (it might indeed be a picture of some local guru). By contrast, somebody conversant with the tradition would know that by drawing a picture containing the emblems appropriate to Jerome, they would thereby be drawing Jerome. A representation depicts an object iconographically in a community of picture-users if it has a content φ and there is a convention such that φ-pictures represent that object. Although nothing seems to rule out conventional pictures of kinds of things, examples are hard to imagine—iconographic picturing is probably a relatively inefficient way to represent what can easily be recognized.

The conventionality of iconographic depiction explains the prevalence of some rather esoteric, abstract emblems. Early Buddhist artists complied with a prohibition against representations of the Buddha as a human being by representing him indirectly, as a footprint, as the bodhi tree beneath which he meditated, as the wheel which figures as a metaphor in his teaching, as a stupa, or just as empty space. Reliability in iconographic depiction depends not on how well emblems characterize their possessors, but on the stability of the relevant conventions. One historian of Indian art remarks that the animal 'vehicles' (such as Śiva's bull) uniquely associated with Hindu deities are sometimes our 'sole clues to the identity of the gods depicted: not a few of the more common attitudes, gestures, and weapons are shared by a number of Indian deities, but the vehicles are never changed'.[16]

While iconography is conventional, it is probably not wholly unconnected to description and the workings of the informational system. We can sometimes observe the formation of iconographic emblems in progress, as descriptive information associated with individuals solidifies as conventional emblems. Once descriptive of Napoleon, the curled forelock and hand-in-tunic posture may by now be emblematic of him. Moreover, iconographic conventions may be responsive to discoveries that particular emblems are inappropriate for marking an individual. The discovery that an emblem has an apocryphal origin and is neither true of nor causally linked to its bearer may cause the emblem to drop from use.[17]

---

[16] Heinrich Zimmer, *The Art of Indian Asia* (Princeton: Princeton University Press, 1955), 45.
[17] The sensitivity of iconographic pictures seems to be less than the immediate responsiveness of pure descriptions and greater than the relative conservatism of linguistic proper names.

8.5 Why Recognition is Basic

We may now enumerate four varieties of depiction. Basic pictures embody information which enables their subjects to be recognized by suitable perceivers. Pictures which depict in the manner of pure descriptions represent whatever matches their contents. Other pictures appeal to descriptive information retained by viewers from their subjects. And iconographic pictures depict by reproducing the conventional emblems of their subjects. Since there are four ways in which pictures can refer, there are four varieties of pictorial sense, and understanding a picture as the kind of picture it is means tracing its reference to its subject in the appropriate way.

Despite the variety of modes of identification of which pictures may take advantage, one warrants the epithet 'basic'. Recognition is not the sole mode of pictorial identification, but it plays some role in all cases. From the fact that a picture represents an *F*, it does not follow that it basically depicts *F*, but if it does not, then it basically depicts some *G* partly in virtue of which it depicts *F*.

Descriptive and iconographic pictures represent their subjects through contents that describe them or are emblems for them, and that they have the contents they do is a consequence of basic depiction. Rembrandt's *Jerome* depicts the saint because it can be recognized by suitable perceivers as of an old man, a cardinal, a scholar, a lion, and a wilderness setting, and these are the conventional marks of Jerome—the picture depicts Jerome iconographically by basically depicting his emblems. Likewise, descriptive pictures represent their subjects because they basically depict key descriptive elements. No doubt, matters can attain some complexity: a picture may iconographically depict Jerome by descriptively depicting a cardinal, and it may descriptively depict a cardinal by basically depicting a broad-brimmed hat.

Since non-basic pictures always involve basic depiction at some level, they can take advantage of the dynamism of pictorial recognition. A cubist portrait of Jerome might basically depict his emblems under cubist aspects. But the generativity of pictorial recognition is not shared by descriptive and iconographic depiction. While learning the emblems of Jerome generates an ability to identify other iconographic pictures of Jerome, which may well differ extensively from each other, it does not generate abilities to identify either non-iconographic pictures of Jerome or other pictures of other subjects in the same iconographic tradition. The relations between emblems in a tradition are not intrinsic, as are relations between aspects along a dimension of variation. Descriptive identification is like emblematic identification in this regard.

Recognition is involved in all pictorial representation; it is what distinguishes the meaning of pictures from that of other kinds of representation. Description and iconography, after all, translate well into other media. Furthermore, only recognition is aspectual, and so capable of explaining the essentially aspectual structure of pictorial content. To understand any picture as a picture, then, is to recognize it as presenting an aspect of at least part of what it represents.

9

Pictorial Experience

OF the four constraints to be heeded by an adequate theory of depiction, I have so far concentrated on two, the diversity and competence constraints. The remaining two concern pictorial experience, its phenomenology and twofoldness. Pictures, as Wollheim puts it, allow us to have visual experiences of 'things that are not present to the senses'.[1] Other media, such as words, do not. So how is it that when we look at a picture we typically have a visual experience as of its subject? And how can this experience occur alongside an experience of the picture's designed surface?

9.1 Explaining Experience

In answering these questions, the aspect-recognition theory tests its mettle against its hardiest rivals: the experienced similarity, illusion, and seeing-in theories. What these theories have in common is that each endorses a conception of pictorial experience which it then makes central to explaining pictorial representation.

According to the illusion theory, for instance, a viewer grasps a picture's subject because she has a visual experience of a kind that could, in the right circumstances, cause her to believe that the picture's subject is actually there. The resemblance view holds that pictures represent because experiences of pictures are similar to experiences of their subjects. Finally, the seeing-in theory holds that a picture represents something only if its subject can be seen in it, where seeing-in is a kind of visual experience whose distinguishing feature is its twofoldness. For Gombrich, Peacocke, and Wollheim an explanation of depiction depends on some conception of pictorial experience.

The methodological assumption that a theory of depiction should build upon the fact of pictorial experience is not without some appeal. Pictures do make for vivid experiences as of their subjects. But as I

---

[1] Wollheim, 'Seeing-as, Seeing-in', 217.

argued in the Introduction, explaining depiction in terms of pictorial experience threatens to degenerate into a mere appeal to intuition. Our experiencing pictures as of what they represent is at least in part a consequence of our grasp of their contents. Rather than explaining depiction, pictorial experience needs to be explained by it.

Unlike other perceptual theories of depiction, the aspect-recognition theory makes no mention of pictorial experience. I have been arguing that to understand a picture, a viewer need only identify it as of its subject on the basis of information it contains. This requires only that pictures present aspects of their subjects that their viewers can identify, not that their viewers enjoy certain experiences. There are, as I see it, several advantages to a theory of depiction that is agnostic about the nature of pictorial experience.

First, by not casting a theory of depiction as a theory of pictorial experience, there is little temptation to construe pictorial experience as like ordinary visual experience. This makes room for diverse forms of pictorial experience, not all of which resemble ordinary visual experience. A theory of pictorial experience must explain not only how a standard Albertian picture is experienced as of its subject, but also how a solarized Man Ray photograph is experienced as of a face, how Picasso's cubist *Vollard* is experienced as of a man, and how the Kwakiutl drawing is experienced as of a bird. The diversity of pictorial experience mirrors the diversity of depiction.

Most theories assimilate the experience of seeing something in a picture to the experience of seeing that thing in real life, and this wrongly limits the true character of pictorial experience. Thus we find Wollheim arguing against the convention theory by asserting that we cannot see a landscape in a colour-reversed painting (in which every object is represented by the complementary of its actual colour).[2] But this is just plain false. Of course, our experience of such a picture is not *just like* our experience of its subject—but so what? The fact is that we often do experience such images as of their subjects. The experience that the colour-reversed picture elicits is not of the sort that one might have before its subject in the flesh, but pictorial experience need not replicate ordinary experience.

A second advantage of the aspect-recognition theory is that it allows that pictorial experiences reflect the aspectual nature of depiction. If, in looking at a Kwakiutl picture of a bird, I do have an experience, my

[2] Wollheim, 'On Drawing an Object', in *On Art and the Mind*, 24–5.

experience is better described as an experience of a pictorial aspect of a bird than as an experience of a bird *tout court*. With the notable exception of *trompe-l'œil*, pictorial experience normally represents to the viewer that the aspect of the subject presented is a pictorial one, perhaps one that can be seen only in a picture. But most perceptual theories do not acknowledge that pictorial experiences are aspectual. Finally, standard theories have trouble accommodating what I called in Chapter 2 the spectrum of twofoldness. Having defined pictorial experience as the kind of experience that might in the right circumstances cause one to believe that the picture's subject is there, Gombrich is compelled to deny that experiences of pictures are ever twofold. An experience of a picture as of Parfit outside the Palazzo Ducale, which is also an experience of a flat painted surface, is not the kind of experience likely to dispose one to believe that one is looking at Parfit and the Doge's Palace. Wollheim, by contrast, makes twofoldness a necessary feature of pictorial experience. What distinguishes pictorial from non-pictorial experience is the former's twofoldness: only pictorial experiences are also experiences of flat marked surfaces. The seeing-in theory must reject the possibility that experience of any picture might not be twofold.

In truth, experiences of pictures may or may not be twofold. They can be arranged along a spectrum, with twofoldness at one pole and illusionism at the other. Experience of what I called 'painterly' pictures is twofold, whereas in *trompe-l'œil* images experience of design properties is typically precluded. An adequate account of pictorial experience should entail neither illusionism nor a commitment to twofoldness. Since the aspect-recognition theory assumes no particular conception of pictorial experience, it is compatible with the full spectrum of pictorial experiences, from the 'painterly' to the 'illusionistic'. Of course, if we are to explain pictorial experience, rather than taking it for granted, then our explanation must make clear how the full spectrum of experiences is possible.

Before I attempt such an explanation, I must indulge in a brief aside, the importance of which will be evident at the end of this chapter. I said that the aspect-recognition theory makes no mention of pictorial experience in explaining depiction. Does this mean that pictorial experience is not an essential feature of depiction? The answer depends on what we mean by 'experience'.

For most viewers, to look at and understand a picture of Vollard, say, is to enjoy a visual experience with a recognition-based content as of the art dealer. This much is obvious. But we can imagine viewers who are able to recognize Vollard in a picture without enjoying any conscious visual experience as of him. Some apparently blind humans are said to have 'blindsight', because although they can discriminate visually some features of their environment, they are not aware that they are 'seeing' and indeed insist that they cannot see. Likewise, some prosopagnosics are able to recognize faces without being aware that they do so.[3] Standing before Picasso's drawing of Vollard, a 'pictorially blindsighted' viewer might be able to identify the picture as a man, protesting all the while that his identification is 'a guess' and that he sees—visually experiences—nothing.

Whether these possibilities show that pictorial experience is not necessary for depiction depends on the meaning, ordinary and theoretical, of 'experience'. Somebody who is capable of discriminations as fine-grained as those made by normal perceivers but who nevertheless denies having experiences might best be described as having experiences inaccessible to consciousness. An ability to look at, or in the direction of, *American Gothic* and to describe it as representing, in a flattened naïve style, a red-faced man, a chinless woman in a print dress, and a four-pronged pitchfork with an ash handle is strong evidence for pictorial experience. Ultimately, the plausibility of this position depends on a more mature conception of the role of experience in explanations of perception, belief, and action.

In sum, we require an account of pictorial experience, one that shows how pictorial experience may accompany or preclude design experience. We need not assume that pictorial experience is conscious, though in the vast majority of cases it will be.

9.2 The Objects of Perception

It is no mystery that when we look at a picture we see its design, its marked, coloured, and textured surface. Pictorial design properties are among those properties of all medium-sized physical objects that it is vision's purpose to detect. What stands in need of explanation is how

---

[3] Lawrence Weiskrantz *et al.*, 'Visual Capacity in the Hemaniopic Field Following a Restricted Occipital Ablation', *Brain*, 97 (1974), 709–28; Lawrence Weiskrantz, *Blindsight: A Case Study and Implications* (Oxford: Oxford University Press, 1986); and D. Travel and A. R. Damasio, 'Knowledge without Awareness: An Autonomic Index of Facial Recognition by Prosopagnosics', *Science*, 228 (1985), 453–5.

it comes to be that in looking at a small, flat, decorated surface we enjoy a visual experience as of the Piazza San Marco, Ambroise Vollard, or St Jerome.

Answers to this question are among the most muddled of any pertaining to depiction. It is easy to confuse accounts of the contents of our experiences of pictures with accounts of pictures' contents and the experienced similarities between pictures and their subjects. Rather than treating the problem of pictorial experience as *sui generis*, my strategy is to treat it as a special case of the more general problem of the objects of perception. We can make progress toward an understanding of pictorial experience by considering the nature of visual experience.

I consider some version of the causal theory of perception to be correct. In its most watered-down formulation, this theory holds that one sees an object only if one has experiences that are caused by it. But among the many causes of experiences, only one, for the most part, is the object we perceive. I experience a tomato on a table. The causes of my experience include turbines turning to generate electricity to make a bulb emit light, light-waves bouncing off the fruit to my eyes, the plant that grew the tomato, the table supporting it in my field of vision, my contact lenses, the complex and only partly understood psychophysics and neurophysiology of vision, and, not least, the tomato. Of these and other causes I see only one, the tomato. This, then, is the problem of perceptual objects: what explains which object, of all those that cause my perception, is the one I see?

A very rough solution to this problem is to be found in the following line of thought. The purpose of perception is the acquisition of knowledge about our surroundings, particularly knowledge that enables us to manœuvre among and manipulate them.[4] It is important, therefore, that perception be reliable. That is, it should not only tend to be veridical, it should also be responsive to the states of affairs about which it carries information. Differences in what we perceive should be reflected, to a useful degree, in differences in the world as we perceive it. (Perceptual acuity being limited, not every difference in a scene need cause a different experience.) These are platitudes, but they provide background for the widely endorsed principle that the objects of perception are those that stand in a pattern of counterfactual dependence on our experiences. In the case of vision, one sees a scene only if the scene caused

---

[4] This does not entail that the contents of experiences are to be identified with the contents of beliefs. See Dretske, *Seeing and Knowing*, ch. 2.

one's experience, and different scenes would have caused different experiences, enabling the perceiver to usefully discriminate between alternative scenes.

I propose that an explanation of what we experience when we look at pictures will depend upon an account of the objects of perception, of what we experience when we look upon the world. For instance, the rough account of the objects of perception sketched in the previous paragraph suggests the following account of pictorial experience. I enjoy an experience as of a tomato when I look at a picture of a tomato because the picture was caused by a tomato and its design features are systematically alterable in accordance with changes in the tomato's appearance. As we shall see, this account is not only rough, it is also incomplete.

In the remainder of this chapter I will endeavour to elaborate and add to the rough account. I begin by describing Kendall Walton's views about our experience of photographs, showing that they are predicated upon the rough account of perceptual objects. I then argue, *contra* Walton, that what explains our experience of photographs explains our experience of all pictures.

9.3 Seeing-Through

If any pictures embody perceptual information that is caused by and counterfactually dependent upon their subjects, then photographs do. In a paper on photographic realism, Walton contends that when we look at photographs we actually see their subjects; photographs are representations *through* which we see the world; they are 'transparent'.[5] By this he means that 'we *see*, quite literally, our dead relatives themselves when we look at photographs of them'.[6] We see things through photographs just as we see things through eyeglasses, mirrors, binoculars, or television screens.

However, Walton also contends that we do not see the world through non-photographic pictures; hand-made pictures are not transparent. In looking at Holbein's portrait of Henry VIII we do *seem* to see him, but this is due to the fact that when we look at the painting we

---

[5] Kendall Walton, 'Transparent Pictures: On the Nature of Photographic Realism', *Critical Inquiry*, 11 (1984), 246–77. It should be noted that transparency does not imply invisibility—we can see a transparent medium through which we see the world.

[6] Ibid. 251–2.

make-believe seeing its subject—it is fictional that we see the king
through the painting (on make-believe, see Sect. 4.2). By contrast, seeing
the subject of a photograph is not make-believe seeing—we literally
see Casals in Karsh's photograph.

Why are photographs transparent and hand-made pictures opaque?
One answer is that photographs have different design features from
drawn pictures. But photo-realist painting can be indistinguishable from
photography, and some photographs strive for painterly effects. Nor
does the difference lie in accuracy of content, for photographs can
misinform and paintings can be highly accurate. Some theorists have
hoped to distinguish photographs from other pictures on the grounds
that photographs are the result of mechanical processes, while other
pictures are the products of human endeavour.[7] This is close, but not
quite right—photographs are obviously the products of human intervention in numerous ways.

Walton argues that where the mechanical origin of photographs
does make a crucial difference is in the counterfactual dependence of
photographs on their subjects. The following counterfactual statement
is true of most photographs: had its subject's visual properties been
different, then the photograph's content would have been different.
And when such a counterfactual dependence exists between photograph
and subject, it is as a result of the operation of the photographic mechanism. Granted, the contents of any picture can be counterfactually dependent on its subject's properties, but, in the case of hand-drawn
pictures, Walton maintains that the counterfactual dependence is mediated by the picture-maker's beliefs. A difference in the scene to be
represented would have made a difference in the content of the picture
only because it would have made a difference in the artist's beliefs, and
thereby in the way she drew. What a sketch shows depends on what the
artist believes she sees, whether or not she is correct, so that the actual
scene is in a way irrelevant. What a photograph shows is simply what
caused the image on the emulsion, and the photographer's beliefs are
irrelevant.

Walton's view is that 'in order to see through the picture to the scene
depicted, the viewer must have visual experiences which do not depend on the picture-maker's beliefs in the way that paintings do'.[8]
Seeing-through requires the existence of patterns of *belief-independent*

    [7] e.g. André Bazin, 'The Ontology of the Photographic Image', in *What is Cinema?*,
trans. Hugh Gray (Berkeley and Los Angeles: University of California Press, 1967), I.
12–13.   [8] Walton, 'Transparent Pictures', 264.

counterfactual dependence between a picture's content (and, by extension, experience of that content) and properties of the scene represented. Obviously, the existence of belief-independent patterns of counterfactual dependence is not sufficient for seeing-through. The output of a computer programmed to write detailed descriptions of its environment is not transparent, even if the descriptions stand in suitable patterns of counterfactual dependence to what they describe. We do not see the scene the computer describes.

What more is required for seeing-through is, Walton suggests, the existence of certain correspondences between perception and pictures, on the one hand, and 'the way the world really is', on the other. As Walton conceives it, objects and properties are similar when they are difficult to discriminate. Thus the difficulties we have in making perceptual and pictorial discriminations reflect similarities between objects— when two experiences or two pictures are similar, their subjects are similar. This is not true of descriptions:

A *house* is easily confused with a *horse* or a *hearse*, when our information comes from a verbal description, as is a *cat* with a *cot*, a *madam* with a *madman*, *intellectuality* with *ineffectuality*, and so on. When we confront things directly or via pictures, houses are more apt to be confused with barns or woodsheds, cats with puppies, and so forth.[9]

Descriptions are not transparent, because similarities among descriptions do not parallel similarities among objects. Similarities among pictures, however, reflect real similarities among objects. Transparent media maintain real similarities.

In sum, Walton offers an analysis of seeing-through derived informally from the rough account of the objects of perception. A representation is transparent if and only if its content preserves both real similarity relations and a belief-independent pattern of counterfactual dependence on visual properties of its subject. Walton concludes that we only see through photographs; other pictures we make-believe seeing-through.

I believe transparency to be the key to explaining experiences of pictures of all kinds. My aim is therefore to show that there is as much reason to believe that we see through paintings and drawings as through photographs, and this is why we see their subjects in both. In the next section I challenge Walton's reasons for denying that non-photographic pictures maintain belief-independent patterns of

---

[9] Ibid. 270.

counterfactual dependence on their subjects; Section 9.5 takes up the real similarity requirement.

9.4 Belief, Content, and Drawing

The difference between seeing-through photographs and not seeing-through other pictures does not concern the way they look, for they can look the same. Nevertheless, the discovery that we have mistaken a painting for a photograph is supposed to transform our experience of and attitude towards it. This strikes me as implausible.

Suppose a computer connected to a robot equipped with a paintbrush is able to replicate a pot of irises in the manner of Van Gogh. On Walton's view, both this picture and a photograph would be transparent. And were the picture made by a human who reliably followed a computer's meticulous paint-by-number instructions, my experience would shift from one of actually seeing irises to make-believedly seeing irises. It does not seem to me that my experience of these pictures differs in the way Walton describes—I believe I see irises in photograph and painting alike. To complicate matters, many photographs are made with *some* human intervention, so that viewers do not always know whether or *to what degree* a picture is the product of purely mechanical processes.[10] Our impression of seeing-through a picture should, on this view, be weakened by the suspicion that it has been touched up. If Walton is right about the distinctiveness of photographic experience, my intuitions require significant revision.

One way to defend my intuitions is to challenge the inference that since hand-made pictures maintain belief-dependent patterns of counterfactual dependence on their subjects, they are not transparent. What is it about belief-mediated patterns of counterfactual dependence that renders some pictures non-transparent?

An obvious answer is that they are likely to be less reliable, but Walton rightly resists connecting transparency with reliability. After all, photographs need be no more reliable or accurate than other kinds of pictures. Walton's rationale for the non-transparency of belief-dependent representations consists in an appeal to intuitions about what counts as seeing. He asks us to imagine a person who has visual experiences fed to his

---

[10] See William J. Mitchell, 'When Is Seeing Believing?', *Scientific American*, 270/2 (February 1994), 68–73; and Mark Roskill and David Carrier, *Truth and Falsehood in Visual Images* (Amherst, Mass.: University of Massachusetts Press, 1983), 71–109.

optic nerve by a neurosurgeon. The surgeon is careful to preserve suitable patterns of counterfactual dependence by ensuring that the patient has those visual experiences that he would have had were he seeing with his own eyes. Walton thinks our intuitions confirm that the patient in this case does not really see, and the reason is that his experiences are mediated by the surgeon's beliefs. By contrast, somebody fitted with a prosthetic eye which delivers information not mediated by beliefs does see.

But not everybody would agree that a person whose experiences depend on the surgeon's beliefs does not see. Suppose that Malebranche was right, and that a Supreme Being causes us to have visual experiences that are veridical and maintain suitable patterns of counterfactual dependence on the scenes before our eyes.[11] Surely we would still see, despite the fact that our experiences are mediated by the beliefs of the demiurge. In that case there is no reason to deny pictures are transparent on the ground that they are mediated by the beliefs of their makers.

Whether or not the belief-dependence of drawings entails that they are not transparent, there is reason to doubt that the relations of counterfactual dependence between drawings and their subjects are in actuality belief-dependent.

Walton does not deny that the content of experience of hand-made pictures is independent of the *viewer*'s beliefs; what he holds is that it depends on the *artist*'s beliefs. There is no difference in what is drawn without a difference in the artist's beliefs. This implies a conception of what is involved in drawing that I believe to be mistaken, since it is at odds with the idea I derived from Evans that pictures are information-transmitting devices.

The operation of an information system capitalizes on the existence of regular patterns of causal links between the system's inputs and outputs. Thus, if picturing is an informational system, then not only are pictures caused by their sources, but they are caused in ways that are typical of picturing. Imagine that, for some unknown reason, your breathing on a mirror caused an image to be formed from mist of an object that you are looking at.[12] This is an example of what has been called a 'deviant causal chain'.[13] An information system is by definition a

[11] Gregory Currie, 'Photography, Painting and Perception', *Journal of Aesthetics and Art Criticism*, 49 (1991), 24–5.

[12] Cf. Wollheim, 'On Drawing an Object', 24.

[13] Christopher Peacocke, *Holistic Explanation: Action, Space, Interpretation* (Oxford: Oxford University Press, 1979), 55.

system of non-deviant causal chains. Pictures, if they are outputs of an information system, must be caused by their sources in non-deviant ways. As we saw in Chapter 5, a signal trait of informational states is their belief-independence. In the case of pictures, this is manifest in two ways. First, what a picture represents is its source, the object or scene that played the required role in its production. A hand-made picture's subject is no more determined by the artist's intentions or beliefs than is a photograph's. Of course, what viewers identify as a picture's source may not in fact be its source—an identification may be 'ill-grounded'— but this goes equally for photographs. Neither a drawing nor a photograph whose subject is unrecognizable depicts it. So in this respect there is no disanalogy between drawings and photographs: if they represent their sources, they do so independently of the beliefs of their makers.

Second, drawing a picture, like understanding one, depends on the exercise of a psychological skill—namely recognition—and, as I have argued at length, we can recognize objects without the benefit of beliefs about their properties. Drawing is simply applied recognition. In order to draw, you are required only to make marks that are recognizably of the object whose appearance is guiding your drawing movements. A belief that one is drawing Piccadilly Circus is not required in order to make an object that can be recognized as of Piccadilly Circus; nor is a belief that one is drawing something with such-and-such features required to make a picture recognizable as of something with such features. Of course, this is not to deny that artists often have beliefs, even true beliefs, about what they are drawing. I merely maintain that having beliefs about an object or scene is not a prerequisite for drawing the object or scene.

Walton's conception of drawing as necessarily mediated by beliefs is further eroded by the fact that making a picture is making something with non-conceptual content. Entertaining a belief about an object requires having a concept of that object. But if neither making nor interpreting pictures requires the use of concepts, it cannot require having beliefs.

Before I explain why pictorial content is non-conceptual, it will help to briefly consider the case of perception. It was an original feature of Evans's conception of the information system that informational states are non-conceptual. Peacocke fleshed out and systematized Evans's arguments in discussing the non-conceptual content of perceptual states.[14]

---

[14] Peacocke, 'Perceptual Content', 298–317.

A content is conceptual if in grasping or experiencing it one must possess concepts of the properties it represents the world as having. If one *need not* possess concepts of these properties, then the content is non-conceptual. Peacocke's arguments turn on Frege's principle that two modes of presentation are identical if and only if the thought that the objects or properties presented are identical is uninformative. Here are two ways to know the length of a room: by looking at it or by learning from a surveyor that it is 25 feet long. These two contents are distinct, because seeing its length might dispose you to different beliefs from those you might have on the basis of knowing its length in feet. You might, for example, believe that a certain table will fit the room if you have only seen it, while you may believe that a 25-foot carpet will fit in the room only by consulting the surveyor. Moreover, you can rationally wonder whether *that length* is 25 feet, and the statement that it is will be informative. The contents of the two states differ by Frege's criterion.

If the content of the experience of the room's length is not a length in feet, it is probably specified by something like 'the visual angle subtended under such-and-such conditions'. But having a visual experience with a content as of that length obviously does not depend on having a concept of any such technical property. The content is non-conceptual. Similar points can be made about other properties represented in experience. For example, the capacity to see a full, continuous spectrum of colours is one which does not require the possession of concepts of every colour seen or of wavelengths of light.

Humans are able to discriminate and respond differentially to properties of their environment for which they need not have concepts. The non-conceptuality of the contents of experience is a consequence of the fact that experience depends on perceptual capacities whose operation is independent of our beliefs and whose structure is displayed not through patterns of beliefs but through differential responses.[15]

The content of experience of a picture's design properties is obviously non-conceptual. Neither artist nor viewer need have concepts of every or any design property in order to experience a picture's design. One may be able to draw and distinguish between two shapes without conceiving of one as a 1,000-sided figure and the other as a 998-sided figure. The Fabbrica di San Pietro, mosaic-tile supplier to the Vatican, maintains an inventory of more than twenty-eight thousand colours of

---

[15] Evans, *Varieties of Reference*, 155.

tile, all of which, I imagine, we can discriminate and use pictorially, though few of which we possess concepts of. Pictorial contents are also non-conceptual. Of course, to be able to recognize the subject of a picture under a dynamic range of aspects, including pictorial ones, is to have a concept of it. But the exercise of recognition skills engages sensitivities to aspects and properties of objects of which we need not, and usually do not, have concepts. Canaletto's painting represents its subject as having a rich set of properties, and thereby has the potential to trigger a recognition capacity for the Piazza San Marco and its inhabitants; but triggering such a capacity does not require concepts of every represented property comprising the aspect under which the Piazza is recognizable.

In so far as it is a recognition-based skill, drawing does not require that the properties of what is drawn be conceptualized. To draw is simply to be guided by the appearance of an object in marking a surface which will present an aspect that is recognizable as of that object. This requires a mastery of techniques of drawing gained through practice. The artist looks at an object, marks a surface, checks to see whether the result is recognizable as of the object, and then revises the drawing until a recognizable aspect emerges. Any competent draughtsman can draw shapes that are recognizable aspects of a given shape under given conditions, but neither the draughtsman skilled in drawing in perspective nor a naïve viewer need have a concept of just that trapezoid in order for it to be recognizable as of a square. In drawing, the eye and the hand work together, perhaps bypassing the mind, or rather that portion of the mind that deals in concepts and beliefs.

I see no reason why an artist *must* bring to bear *any* concepts about the content of a picture he is making. It is possible to draw something, guided by the look of the thing, and to produce a recognizable aspect of it, without having a concept of it. Let me put forward, however, two points of clarification.

First, I am not arguing that drawing is merely replicating or imitating what the artist sees. Translation from three dimensions into two always transforms what is drawn, as it is drawn. But these transformations can be, and usually are, accomplished at a sub-personal level under the guidance of perceptual processes of recognition. They need not be mediated, as Gombrich would put it, by the artist's 'mental set'. The argument that making a picture embodying a non-visual aspect necessarily engages the artist's beliefs is a remnant of the view that non-Albertian pictorial styles originate in the 'conceptual' rather than the 'perceptual'. I have been arguing that all systems of depiction are rooted in the dynamism of recognition.

Moreover, none of this should be taken to deny that artists frequently do conceptualize and form beliefs about what they draw. But what properties they conceptualize is a matter of choice, purpose, and the concepts they possess. The contents of mental states by virtue of which drawings are made are non-conceptual, because they need not engage our conceptual repertoire. If there is any parallel between depiction, perception, and the world, it is that the properties represented by the first and possessed by the last are not limited by our conceptual resources.

To recap, Walton argues that photographs are transparent in part because they maintain belief-independent counterfactual relations with their subjects. This argument appeals to the role of counterfactual relations in fixing the objects of perception. But Walton also holds that we do not see through drawings, because they maintain belief-dependent counterfactual relations with their subjects. I have tried to show that it is a mistake to think that a difference in a hand-made picture's subject would have made a difference in its content *only because* it would have made a difference in the artist's beliefs. First, pictorial contents are belief-independent because they are non-conceptual, and there are no beliefs without concepts. If the contents of pictures are not dependent on their makers' beliefs, then *a fortiori* their counterfactual relations with their subjects are not belief-dependent. A difference in an object may make a difference in a picture of it simply by affecting the artist's experience and thus the way she drew. Both hand-made pictures and photographs maintain belief-independent patterns of counterfactual dependence on their subjects.

This is not to say that there is no difference between photographs and other pictures. A photograph can be made without human aid; non-photographs need a human perceiver who has visual experiences which guide her in making the picture. Indeed, drawings might be described as perceiver-dependent pictures. But once what it is to perceive so as to draw has been distanced from having beliefs, the camera–perceiver distinction carries little weight. To perceive is to gather and convey information, much as a camera does.

9.5 *Isomorphism and Similarity*

Patterns of counterfactual dependence do not suffice for transparency. A computer might write descriptions of video input that maintain the required dependencies, but we would not 'see through' the descriptions to what they describe. Walton additionally requires that transparent media preserve 'real similarity' relations. 'Real similarity' is a combination of two ideas. First, he hints that certain similarities are 'real' in so far as they play a privileged role in certain explanations of the world. Second, he does not posit a first-order similarity between transparent media and the world; rather, he suggests that there is a second-order correspondence between similarities among design properties of transparent representations and similarities among the properties they represent their subjects as having. I follow usage in cognitive science by calling this correspondence a 'second-order isomorphism'.[16]

It will come as no surprise that I see several difficulties with the claim that transparency is the product of real similarities. Before launching a critique, though, I wish to acknowledge what I take to be the motivation for the appeal to real similarity. What seems wrong with the idea that a computer description is transparent is not that it is written by a computer, but that the description does not represent *visually*. Walton's suggestion that both pictures and vision represent by similar means might be thought of as an attempt to capture this intuition.

What is wrong with real similarity? To begin with, I am not convinced that certain similarity relations can be singled out as 'real'. Everything is similar to everything else in some respect, and the relative importance of any specific relation of similarity depends on context and purpose. Moreover, Walton grants that 'real' similarities may vary with 'conceptual scheme'. If this is so, then what is to stop description–world similarities from being deemed 'real' in some scheme? At any rate, there is no need to pursue this metaphysical question, since the weight of Walton's account of transparency falls not on the reality of real similarity but on the notion of second-order isomorphism.

Everything, as a latter-day Goodman might admit, is second-order isomorphic to everything else. And pictures undoubtedly do preserve second-order isomorphisms. There are always correspondences between the articulation of pictures' design properties and the articulation of the visual properties they attribute to their subjects. These correspondences need not be, and usually are not, one-to-one. Combinations of design

[16] See Roger Shepard and Susan Chipman, 'Second-Order Isomorphism of Internal Representation: Shapes of States', *Cognitive Psychology*, 1 (1970), 1–17; and Stephen E. Palmer, 'Fundamental Aspects of Cognitive Representation', in Eleanor Rorsch and Barbara B. Lloyd (eds.), *Cognition and Categorization* (Hillsdale, NJ: Lawrence Erlbaum, 1978), 290–4.

features may correspond holistically with pictorial properties, and vice versa. In the 'happy face', for instance, a dot stands for an eye only in the context of the rest of the design. The precise forms taken by these articulations I would of course attribute to the processes of recognition underlying how pictures represent in different systems (see Sect. 7.5). My objection is that second-order isomorphism is not sufficient for pictorial transparency, because non-transparent media also preserve second-order isomorphisms. For instance, as Gregory Currie points out, the errors in discrimination we make in reading a thermometer correspond with those we make in judging temperature (and the height of the column of mercury is counterfactually dependent on temperature to boot), yet we do not see the temperature through the thermometer.[17] In fact, any analogue measure, by definition, preserves some second-order isomorphism with properties of what it measures. The errors we make in discriminating properties represented by analogue clocks, speedometers, and bathroom scales correspond with errors we make in judging time, speed, and weight.

Non-analogue representations can also preserve the required isomorphisms. A description, for instance, may maintain second-order isomorphisms between similar-sounding words and visual, aural, olfactory, and gustatory features of objects. Imagine a language in which similar-sounding words denote similar properties. In such a language similarities among words are second-order isomorphic to similarities among properties of what they symbolize. But although a computer might be programmed to issue descriptions of its environment written in this language, it does not follow that we see, hear, or smell through the computer's print-outs. Surely no computer description written in any language can be transparent.

One might be tempted to respond that the difference between transparent and non-transparent media is that the former maintain more than just a second-order isomorphism with the properties they attribute to their subjects. One might insist, in other words, that design properties of transparent media be first-order similar to the properties represented. This is not true of my imaginary language—sounds do not resemble colours or smells. Pictures, by contrast, would be transparent, because they resemble their subjects.

Despite my general scepticism about theoretical appeals to similarity, I do not think that this is, on the face of it, a bad response. A resemblance

---

[17] Currie, 'Photography, Painting and Perception', 25.

theory of pictorial experience is not subject to the objections that we saw could be levelled against the resemblance theory of depiction. While I have urged that pictorial similarity does not explain depiction, I have not denied that we experience pictures as similar to the world. Rather, I have urged that pictorial similarity, in the terminology of Chapter 1, is representation-dependent—what picture–subject similarities we notice depends on the processes by which we identify what is depicted. Since the aspect-recognition theory does not depend on a theory of pictorial experience, it would not be circular for a theory of pictorial experience to avail itself of the fact that pictures are experienced as similar to their subjects.

Nevertheless, I counsel against this strategy. It seems to me difficult, if not impossible, to disentangle the notion that we experience pictures as similar to the scenes they represent from the notion that when we look at pictures we experience them as of the scenes they represent. An account of pictorial experience is likely to be one and the same as an account of experienced pictorial similarity.

9.6 Pictures as Visual Prostheses

I suggested that the principal motivation for requiring a real similarity between pictures and objects is that pictures represent the visual world by visual means. It may be that pictures are transparent in part because they employ visual properties to represent objects as having properties normally perceived visually. The general principle would be that transparent media are those whose design properties are perceivable through the same sense modality as are the properties comprising their contents. A voice on a radio is transparent in part because radios represent voices aurally and voices are normally perceived aurally; we do not see heat through thermometers, because they represent visually and heat is not something we normally see.

That an account of the objects of perception must incorporate an account of the various sense modalities is not a novel thought. Alvin Goldman remarks that 'perception is always perception *in a modality*. We never *just* perceive; we either hear, or see, or smell, etc. A theory of perceptual objects must therefore be a theory of our perceptual modality concepts.'[18] However, philosophy has made little attempt at or

---

[18] Alvin I. Goldman, 'Perceptual Objects', *Synthese*, 35 (1977), 260. Goldman's view is roughly that since different causes of an experience stand in different relations to perceiver and environment, (1) those relations that generate the most true beliefs are constitutive of the modality, and (2) the objects to which they stand are what we perceive.

progress towards a complete explanation of perceptual modality; nor can I undertake such a task here. Instead, I will briefly outline one simple, plausible account of perceptual modality, that advanced by Dretske, indicating its potential contribution to an account of pictorial experience.[19] Dretske, like Goldman, recognizes that a theory of perceptual objects requires an account of perceptual modalities and what distinguishes them. He begins by assuming that perception consists in a causal chain of information-bearing states culminating in an experience. The information borne by any of these states may be said to be given primary representation relative to the other states. Suppose one state represents something as *F* and a preceding or subsequent state represents it as *G*. *F* gets 'primary representation' relative to *G* if and only if the representation of something's being *G* depends on the informational relationship between *F* and *G* but not vice versa.[20] Those properties given primary representation within an informational system are the system's 'proper qualities'.

A perceptual modality, Dretske argues, can be defined by its proper qualities, and the object of a perceptual experience is simply the object whose properties are the modality's proper qualities. Thus a visitor pushes the doorbell, the bell sounds, and you are informed that there is a visitor at the door. This information is represented in an experience whose object is the ringing of the bell, not the button being pushed or the presence of the visitor, because the information that the button was pushed and that the visitor has arrived depends on the information that the bell rang, not vice versa. The sound of the bell is among hearing's proper qualities.

Similarly, what we see are those things whose properties are the proper qualities constitutive of vision—colours, shapes, orientations, distances, texture gradients, and other properties that get primary representation. It is possible to convey information about time visually, by means of the orientation of hands on the dial of a clock, but this information about time depends on the orientation of the hands on the dial, not vice versa. Time is not a proper quality of vision, so looking

---

[19] Dretske, *Knowledge and the Flow of Information*, 153–68. For alternative accounts, see Goldman, 'Perceptual Objects'; David Lewis, 'Veridical Hallucination and Prosthetic Vision', in Jonathan Dancy (ed.), *Perceptual Knowledge* (Oxford: Oxford University Press, 1988), 79–91; and Brian O'Shaughnessy, 'Seeing the Light', *Proceedings of the Aristotelian Society*, 85 (1985), 193–218.
[20] Dretske, *Knowledge and the Flow of Information*, 159–60.

at a clock, we do not see time. It is the information about the spatial configuration of the clock face that gets primary representation in vision, so it is the clock face that we see.[21]

Certainly, in looking at a picture, one thing we see is its marked, coloured surface, for pictorial design properties are by definition among the proper qualities of vision. But since pictures also convey information (or misinformation) concerning features of their subjects that are also among the proper qualities of vision, we also see the things that are represented as having those properties. Pictorial experience, therefore, is twofold. We see pictures in part because they are comprised of properties that number among the proper qualities of vision. And we see through pictures in part because they represent their subjects as having properties constitutive of vision. Pictures are visual prostheses in the sense that they represent the visual world through visual properties.

My review of Dretske's account is intended as an illustration of the way in which a theory of the visual sense modality and the objects of vision can contribute to an account of pictorial experience. The details of Dretske's account of perceptual objects are ultimately irrelevant for my purpose. What is really at stake is the principle that whatever explains why we see certain objects as having certain kinds of properties also explains why, when looking at a picture's designed surface, we see its subject as having the same kinds of properties.

In sum, we see things through pictures because the conditions under which they represent parallel the conditions under which we experience the objects of visual perception. In particular, pictures are transparent because they are caused by, counterfactually dependent upon, and second-order isomorphic with properties of their subjects that are constitutive of the visual sense modality.

A parallel account can be given of other transparent media. In listening to the radio, I hear the sound produced by the speakers, but I also hear 'through' the speakers to the sound of the orchestra recorded for broadcast. This is because the sound of the speakers is caused by and is counterfactually dependent on the sound of the orchestra, there is a second-order isomorphism between properties of each, and the speakers

---

[21] Dretske, *Knowledge and the Flow of Information*, 162. Dretske adds that more proximal states are not represented in experience because of the operation of constancy filters. I take for granted that whatever explains why we do not see a retinal image of a tomato when we look at a tomato also explains why we do not see a retinal image of a tomato (or a picture of a tomato) when we look at a picture of a tomato.

represent through sound what is normally represented through sound. Similarly, I see through the image on the television screen to the golf game in Florida because the game is a cause of the image, the image is counterfactually dependent on the game, there is an isomorphism between them, and the television visually represents visual properties. I believe that the four conditions I have provided are sufficient for pictorial seeing-through. Imagine a perceiver who looks at a picture and sees an array of coloured patches caused by an elephant. If he recognizes the array as of an elephant, then he will see articulated correspondences between parts of the picture's design and visual features that the elephant is represented as having. Moreover, the elephant would have been represented differently if it had different features (taking into account the limits of visual acuity and the chance of misrepresentation). What more could there be to experiencing the picture as of an elephant? Someone who sees the coloured array, recognizes the elephant, and can point out which parts of the array correspond to body, trunk, ears, tail, and limbs, but who nevertheless denies seeing the elephant in the picture, is like a person with blindsight. It is probably best to say that she enjoys an experience as of an elephant without knowing that she does.

By representing the visual world visually, pictures also extend what we see. We use them to see through to objects which cannot be seen by ordinary means. Many pictures enable us to see objects that are distant in time or space; some represent objects as having combinations of properties that they could not be seen to have by plain sight. One of the virtues of pictorial representation is that it enables viewers to see what would otherwise be invisible.

PART FOUR
Applications

10

Fictive Pictures

THIS chapter and the next extend the aspect-recognition theory to two special kinds of pictures, both of which are prominent among art pictures. In pictures of fictional subjects, the topic of this chapter, the pictorial informational system is put to imaginative use, allowing us to entertain make-believe thoughts about things that do not exist. Pictorial variations, the topic of Chapter 11, illustrate one way in which the aspectual content characteristic of depiction can itself become the focus of artful picture-making. Fictive pictures and pictorial variations not only shed light on the implications of the aspect-recognition theory for our understanding of art pictures, they also add to our understanding of the logic of depiction.

10.1 Fiction as Description

A fictive picture is one whose subject does not exist. But on standard accounts of reference, a representation can refer only to an object that does exist. This is the gist of Goodman's first thesis. Thus imagine that there hangs, at the offices of the Society for Epistemological Naturalists, a portrait of Quine's fictional philosophical antagonist, Wyman. Although the picture represents Wyman, it cannot refer to him, for he does not exist. Goodman reminds us that if a fictive picture denotes anything, it denotes the empty set. What is worse, if *Wyman* denotes the empty set, then what it denotes is the same as what a picture of Pegasus denotes, as what a polaroid picture of a yeti denotes, or as what Dr Strangelove's passport picture denotes—all denote the empty set. But what it is to represent each of these is patently not the same. Goodman dramatizes this thought: 'we can distinguish centaurs from unicorns and mermaids, and Don Quixote from Winston Churchill and Rip van Winkle. . . . And yet, and yet, there are no centaurs, there is no Don Quixote.'[1]

---

[1] Goodman and Elgin, *Reconceptions in Philosophy*, 85.

Goodman's solution to the problem of fictive representation is to construe it not as a kind of reference, but as a kind of predication. Although the portrait of Wyman *purports* to represent by referring to Wyman, it actually represents only by being a Wyman-picture. Thus differences between pictures which represent 'different' fictional subjects are differences in content rather than reference. *Wyman* and *A Yeti* both denote the empty set, but whereas the former is a wrong-headed-philosopher-picture, the latter is a Himalayan-hominid-picture, and we can distinguish a big-footed hominid from Rip van Winkle or the Man of la Mancha only because we can distinguish yeti-pictures from Rip-van-Winkle-pictures and Don-Quixote-pictures.

The fact that, as Goodman recognizes, fictive pictures purport to denote suggests a constraint on any explanation of fictive depiction: it should explain how fictive pictures seem to refer. To profit from this principle, we might consider the following observation. The purported referentiality of fictive pictures probably indicates that there are parallels between the mechanisms of fictional and non-fictional representation. Thus we should consider what a picture of Wyman or a manticore has in common with a picture of Quine or a domestic feline.

This injunction finds an echo in G. E. Moore's discussion of thinking about imaginary objects. For Moore, 'what is meant by saying that when I conceive of one property ϕ that it belongs to only one thing & you of another χ that it belongs to only one thing [and] we are nevertheless conceiving the *same* imaginary object' depends on the kind of relation that holds between ϕ and χ.[2] By extension, if two pictures with different contents represent the same fictive object, then there must be some relation between them that explains their shared subject. This implies the following rule: two pictures represent the same fictional object if and only if, were the object to exist, both would represent the same object. I call this 'Moore's constraint'.

Goodman's theory of fictive reference as pictorial predication does not explain purported reference in a way that satisfies Moore's constraint. It is curious to note an asymmetry between what he says about fictive reference and about ordinary reference. Goodman insisted, in his third thesis, that what a picture refers to is independent of what content it has. Thus, on the one hand, what a picture refers to has nothing to do with its content, while on the other, what a fictive picture purports to refer to has entirely to do with its content. To represent Wyman is

---

[2] G. E. Moore, ' "Real" and "Imaginary" ', in Casimir Lewy (ed.), *Lectures on Philosophy* (London: George Allen and Unwin, 1966), 31; see also Evans, *Varieties of Reference*, 368.

just to be a Wyman-picture, but being a Quine-picture is neither necessary nor sufficient for representing Quine.

At any rate, I have rejected Goodman's claim that pictorial reference
is independent of content, arguing that what a picture refers to does
indeed depend on its content. And as long as we have set aside the
independence thesis, it is worth considering a descriptivist version of
the proposal that fictive depiction depends on pictorial content.[3] On this
view, a Wyman-picture is simply a such-and-such-picture, though the
description 'the such-and-such' is empty. This tactic appears to accommodate Moore's rule, explaining fictive depiction as a special case of
ordinary descriptive depiction. Viewers understand empty descriptions
in the same way that they understand descriptions which are satisfied.

The description account of fictive representation also encourages an
analysis of fictional reference as reference to possible objects, and this has
some intuitive appeal. A picture of a unicorn is not true of any existing
species of animal, but it might be thought to accurately describe one that
might have existed. Though there is no Dr Strangelove, perhaps a picture
of him describes a person who might have been. Thus John Bennett argues
that fictive pictures match objects that exist in possible worlds but not the
actual world. He writes that 'many pictures which are soandso pictures
will have empty extensions in the actual world. They are soandso pictures
because everything in their extensions at any possible world is a soandso.'[4]

The idea that fictive symbols denote possible objects has a distinguished lineage—it was championed by Kripke in his seminal paper
'Semantical Considerations in Modal Logic', for instance.[5] But quite
apart from questions about the adequacy of matching accounts of depiction, and despite its natural appeal, there are serious doubts as to
whether fictive depiction can be understood as depiction of possible
objects, and some of these doubts were raised by Kripke himself.[6]

Not surprisingly, one difficulty is that posed by the possibility of misrepresentation in fictive pictures. If a picture denotes whatever matches

---

[3] See Nicholas Wolterstorff, *Works and Worlds of Art* (Oxford: Oxford University
Press, 1980), esp. 142–9. Wolterstorff's descriptive account of fictional terms as delin-
eating kinds, including person-kinds, may be abstracted from his Platonist ontology,
particularly the views that fictional characters 'exist' independently of their being delin-
eated in representations.

[4] John G. Bennett, 'Depiction and Convention', *Monist*, 58 (1974), 255–68.

[5] Saul Kripke, 'Semantical Considerations in Modal Logic', *Acta Philosophica Fennica*,
16 (1963), 83–94.

[6] See Saul Kripke, 'Empty Reference', the Shearman Memorial Lectures, University
College, London, 1973; and David Kaplan, 'Bob and Carol and Ted and Alice', in Jaako
Hintikka, Julius Moravesik, and Patrick Suppes (eds.), *Approaches to Natural Language*
(Dordrecht: Reidel, 1973), 505–8.

its content, it cannot misrepresent its subject; yet it is possible to mis-represent Wyman or a manticore, just as it is possible to misrepresent Quine or kitty. Moreover, if different pictures represent their fictional subjects as having different properties, how can they represent the same thing? Surely, pictures of Dr Strangelove that misrepresent him in dif-ferent ways—some as blond, some as Nigerian, others as quite sane—represent the same fictional object as is represented in the movie still of Dr Strangelove, though none is true of the same objects in the same possible worlds. This difficulty may not be irresolvable, though a solution calls for a theory of trans-world identity for possible objects.

Assuming we have such a theory, a further difficulty with the description theory of fiction is that an actual object, even if it fits all the right descriptions, does not normally qualify as the subject of a fictive picture. Suppose that, unbeknownst to Sellars and Kubrick, a man did exist who, as it happens, looked like and did the things attributed to Dr Strangelove. Does a still of Dr Strangelove from Kubrick's film refer to the 'real' Strangelove, of whose existence Sellars and Kubrick had no inkling? The answer is obviously no. The discovery that there was a person who did all that Sellars and Kubrick attributed to their Strangelove would not show that *their* Strangelove 'really' existed. How can a picture refer to possible objects with certain properties without also referring to actual objects with those properties?

A theory of fictive depiction must explain how fictive pictures pur-port to refer, showing, as Moore's constraint requires, how purported reference mimics and is parasitic upon actual reference. The description account promises to meet this requirement by proposing that fictive representation is a special case of an ordinary referential mechanism. However, in the majority of cases, fictive pictures do not represent *whatever* happens to match their content. If a Wyman-picture is a pic-ture of a philosopher of a certain description, it does not follow that the picture would represent any philosopher who happened to match that description. An explanation of fictive reference, like that of ordinary pictorial reference, must explain how a fictive picture can be targeted, as it were, on some fictional object. But how can this be possible? Nothing has causal ties with objects that do not exist.

10.2   Fiction and Pretence

The exercise of an element of pretence would seem to account for fictive pictures and their purported reference while accommodating

Moore's rule without fuss. One might think that whatever relations obtain between a picture and its subject in non-fictive depiction are simply pretended to obtain in fictive depiction. If an artist can depict something by making a representation embodying visual information from it, then an artist can depict a yeti by pretending to make a representation embodying visual information from a yeti.

According to standard accounts of literary fiction as pretence, acts of pretence suspend, yet rely upon, the mechanisms governing non-fictive reference. Thus John Searle argues that pretended reference depends on a kind of illocutionary act with the following characteristics.[7] To pretend to refer is to act in such a way that it is as if one were referring, by using expressions that would, according to the conventional rules governing the language, count as referring expressions. But pretending to refer demands a suspension of the convention that somebody who is using such expressions is in fact referring to objects. Thus the suspension of conventions of reference in pretended reference is itself a convention governing fictional discourse. Finally, one must intend to act as if one were referring and to invoke the conventions of fiction, and one must intend that the pretence be recognized—pretence is not deception.

Clearly no account according to which pretence piggybacks on the fact that the meanings of referring devices are conventional can be of much use in explaining fictive depiction. We require an account of pretence which accommodates the fact that understanding pictures depends on perceptual skills rather than knowledge of representational conventions. Moore's constraint suggests that the mechanisms of purported fictional depiction parallel those of basic picturing. But it remains mysterious how fictive pictures can be reconciled with the causal elements of information-based depiction.

I believe that Kendall Walton's analysis of pretence as an activity embedded in games of make-believe provides the tools we need for an account of fictive depiction as pretence.[8] As we saw in Chapter 4, Walton claims that all pictures are fictions—all are props in games of make-believe. To make believe is simply to imagine that some non-existent state of affairs is the case. In a game of make-believe, one's imaginings are regulated by (possibly conventional) rules that constitute the game.

---

[7] John Searle, *Expression and Meaning* (Cambridge: Cambridge University Press, 1979), esp. 65–9.
[8] My account of fictive depiction as make-believe is modelled on Evans's account of linguistic fiction as make-believe, in Evans, *Varieties of Reference*, 353–68.

Some games have props, objects about which the games prescribe
certain imaginings. In the game of mud pies, for example, lumps of
mud are props which we are directed to imagine are pies. Just so,
pictures are props in games of make-believe whose rules prescribe that
we imagine that our act of looking at them is looking at, noticing,
recognizing, and visually examining their subjects. *Piazza San Marco*
depicts the Piazza San Marco because it has certain features (a surface
marked and coloured in a particular way), and in the picturing game
we are to imagine that looking at anything with these features is looking at the Piazza San Marco. Walton provides a convenient notation:
'*p**(MB)' means '*p* is make-believedly true'. Thus when we look at
Piazza San Marco, we *see Piazza San Marco*(MB)—it is make-
believedly true that we see the piazza.

However, if the aspect-recognition theory is correct, *seeing Piazza
San Marco*(MB) in a painting just is seeing the Piazza San Marco,
albeit via a pictorial aspect. Provided we interpret them correctly, we
do not need to make-believe or imagine seeing most pictures' subjects—
we just do see them—therefore nothing is gained by construing pictures
as fictions. But since we cannot see, or refer to, objects that do not
exist, it might be useful to consider pictures of non-existent objects as
as invoking make-believe. This suggestion certainly conforms with the
general parallel I have drawn since Chapter 3 between pictorial and
linguistic representation. Make-believe may explain only fictive pictures, as it may explain only fictive words.

As part of his fiction-theory of pictures, Walton gives the following
account of reference in games of make-believe.[9] A φ-representation
refers to an object or kind only if it is a prop in a game of make-believe
in which the object or kind *exists*(MB) and *is uniquely φ*(MB).
Bracketing Walton's contention that all pictures are fictions, we are left
with the following account of fictive pictures: a φ-picture of Wyman is
a prop in a game of make-believe in which *Wyman exists*(MB) and
Wyman is uniquely φ(MB). The inadequacies of the suggestion that
fictive pictures function as descriptions are by now familiar. Luckily,
there is nothing in the need to explain pretended reference as make-
believe reference that commits us to the description view. Fictional
reference may well depend on make-believe causal or informational
connections.

[9] Walton, 'Pictures and Make-Believe', 312–14.

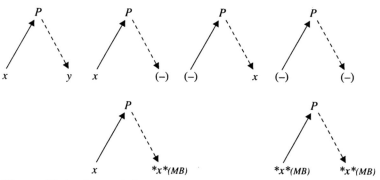

Fig. 24. Fictional groundedness

10.3 Pretence and the Information System

Pictures provide visual information derived from objects on the basis of which those objects can be identified, and recognition plays an essential role in all pictorial identifications. However, any pictorial identification may be ill-grounded, and it is the possibility of ill-groundedness that underlies the existence of fictive pictures.

Evans inventoried four varieties of ill-grounded identification. Ill-grounded identification results when a picture embodies information from one object and is recognized as of another, as is my Divine-picture 'of' Queen Victoria (Fig. 24, top left). Or an identification is ill-grounded when a picture either has a source and is identified as of nothing, or lacks a source and is identified as of something—examples are an infant's squiggle of its mother or my absent-minded doodle that is the spitting image of Parfit in Venice (Fig. 24, top middle left and right). Finally, identifications are ill-grounded when a picture has no source and elicits no identifications (Fig. 24, top right).

Fictive depiction is a variation on the fourth kind of ill-groundedness (Fig. 24, bottom right). A picture purportedly representing Wyman does not in fact have a source; nor can viewers identify it as of anything, for it has no subject for them to identify. I propose that a picture does, though, *have a source*(MB) and is *identifiable as of Wyman*(MB). Thus, while fictive pictures actually elicit ill-grounded representations of the fourth type, they are none the less *well-grounded*(MB).

The importance of classifying fictive pictures as a variation of the fourth type of ill-groundedness is evident if we acknowledge that although some fictive pictures might be recognizable as of real objects, they do not usually represent them. Imagine that there exists, somewhere in Wyoming, a philosopher who holds all the views that Quine attributes to Wyman and who is easily recognizable in the various portraits 'of' Wyman. Do Quine's writings and the portrait at the Society for Epistemological Naturalists denote the Wyoming Wyman?

To answer this question, we would want to distinguish two possibilities. One is that, unbeknownst to Quine and his readers, a figure taken to be mythic really existed, and the real Wyman was in fact the source of the information contained in representations of him (see Fig. 24, bottom left). In this case, the representations do denote him, and our identifications of Wyman-pictures have been, unwittingly, well grounded (thus it is possible to identify an object without knowing it). Since fictive pictures by definition lack sources, Wyman-pictures only appear to be fictional.

Of course, the more likely possibility is that the Wyoming Wyman was not the source of the apparent information put in circulation by Quine, and any resemblances are entirely fortuitous. Identifications of Wyman-pictures as of the real Wyman are instances of the third type of ill-groundedness, and only an *identification*(MB) of the picture as of a fictive Wyman is *well-grounded*(MB). The corollary is that viewers understand the picture as a fiction only if they *identify it as of Wyman*(MB).

Ill-grounded identifications of the first and second types can occur only *within* fictional contexts. It is possible to so misrepresent a picture of a fictional object that it is *not identifiable as of anything*(MB). If someone produced a white-snowman-camouflaged-against-the-snowy-Himalayas-picture of a yeti, the picture would not be *recognizable*(MB) as of a yeti, so it would precipitate *ill-grounded identifications*(MB). It is also possible to make a picture purportedly of one fictional object which is *mis-identifiable*(MB) as of another. An illustration of Holmes might show a mustachioed detective of obvious Gallic ancestry. If the illustration is *of Holmes*(MB) but is *recognizable as of Poirot*(MB), the identification is *ill-grounded*(MB). This kind of *ill-groundedness*(MB) is a consequence of the possibility of misrepresentation.

One might think that some identifications sustaining fictive depiction are ill-grounded in the second way. That is, some fictive pictures have sources, though their fictive subjects are not the same as their sources. A photograph of Dr Strangelove is a case in point. This picture has a source, Peter Sellars, though it is not meant to represent Sellars, or at least not primarily, and when the picture is taken to be a picture of Dr Strangelove, it has not been identified as of its actual source.

As we saw in Chapter 8, pictures can have tangled pedigrees—they can have multiple sources—and this is true of fictive pictures as well as non-fictive ones. It is helpful to draw upon the distinction between primary and secondary sources. An object is a picture's primary source if its role in the picture's production did not depend on the nature of the information derived from the picture's other sources, if any. Something is a picture's secondary source if its role in the picture's production depended on the nature of information derived from its primary sources.

Although fictive pictures necessarily lack primary sources, they may have secondary sources—and nothing but the threat of obscurity prevents a picture from having *secondary sources*(MB). Peter Sellars is the secondary source of Strangelove-pictures because his role in the picture's production hinged on his suitability as a conduit for *information*(MB) about Dr Strangelove. Identifying a fictive picture's secondary source, if it has one, is not a precondition for understanding it. It is not necessary to identify Sellars as the source of a picture of Dr Strangelove in order to *identify it as of that fictional character*(MB).

What remains to be seen is how we are able to *identify*(MB) fictive pictures' subjects on the basis of *information from them*(MB). Evans argues that linguistic fictions depend on a game of make-believe sustained by an initial supposition that information which has no source but which has a content apparently of something is of what it appears to be of.[10] Fictive pictures also depend on a pretence to the effect that the apparent information they contain is as it appears. This pretence may also be thought of as a suppression of disbelief about the authenticity of the information. Under its auspices, viewers allow their thinking to be controlled by apparent information just as if they did not mistrust it.

The pretence that groundless information is information from actual objects takes advantage of the belief-independence of states of the informational system. I have maintained that the perceptual informational states into which we are put by pictures are insulated from higher-order cognitive states. Looking at a picture, it seems as if we see Wyman, and since the content of this state is unaffected by doubts concerning its accuracy, it is all the easier to suppress disbelief. As Evans remarks,

---

[10] Evans, *Varieties of Reference*, 355, 359–60.

'one can let the automatic and habitual responses of one's cognitive system take over and produce the make-believe thoughts, emotions, and reactions which playing the game normally requires'.[11]

This accounts for the evident difference between games of make-believe involving perceptual information and games like mud pies. Whereas mud pies requires that players make an effort to entertain false beliefs, games of pictorial fictioneering are relatively effortless. It is easy to indulge the pretence that things are as they appear. *Seeing Wyman*(MB) in a picture does not require a belief that Wyman is there or that he has such-and-such properties, in the way that *seeing a pie*(MB) requires that one wilfully make believe that a pat of mud is a pie. The perceptual processes in virtue of which we identify pictures' subjects take on the burden that must be played by imagination in ordinary games of make-believe.

Things are as they appear in pictures because pictures trigger recognitional abilities, as well as other abilities to identify objects on the basis of their appearance. Nothing prevents the development of recognition abilities triggered exclusively by groundless information. That is, suitable perceivers can possess an ability to recognize yeti, an ability sometimes triggered by pictures of yeti, but never leading to a well-grounded identification. Games of pictorial fictioneering not only depend on the possibility of groundless recognition, they exploit and foster it. We make pictures *designed* to trigger recognition of non-existent objects.

The acquisition of recognition abilities for fictive objects largely parallels the acquisition of recognition abilities for actual objects. Recognitional abilities for fictive objects can be introduced through verbal testimony about fictional objects. Quine's descriptions of Wyman could generate a dossier of apparent information enabling some perceivers who are willing to indulge the appropriate pretence to recognize Wyman in pictures. Recognition abilities may also originate with fictive pictures themselves—familiarity with pictures *of yetis*(MB) enables us to recognize yetis, and consequently to *identify pictures as of yetis*(MB). After all, it is not possible to be acquainted with a fictional character, so pictures and stories must be responsible for initiating abilities to *identify*(MB) fictional objects.

I am arguing that the very recognitional abilities that explain how we identify pictures of actual objects explain the make-believe identifications that are the core of games of pictorial fiction-making. This is what

[11] Evans, *Varieties of Reference*, 359.

accommodates Moore's principle that the conditions under which two pictures depict the same fictive object should parallel those under which two pictures depict the same actual object. The mechanisms by which we make-believe identifying apparent sources of information are those by which we actually identify sources of real information. It follows that the conditions under which two pictures are fictively coextensive exactly parallel those under which two pictures are really coextensive. Pictures of Wyman are pictures of the same fictive philosopher only if they embody *information*(MB) recognizable as of the same *source*(MB), just as two pictures represent Quine only if they embody information that can be recognized as of the same man.

Being able to *recognize*(MB) a picture's *source*(MB) is the same as being able to recognize its *source*(MB). Imagine that although the yeti-pictures with which we are familiar are hoaxes, yetis do exist and are the source of the stories about Himalayan hominids that led to the hoaxes. Not only would it turn out that pictures of yetis in fact have sources, but our identifications of them would be well grounded, as they would depend on abilities to recognize real yetis.

While the recognitional and descriptive pictorial identifications, or, really, mis-identifications, that we indulge in when playing the pictorial fiction game come automatically, the pretence that things are as they appear is deliberate. It follows that there is a distinction between attitudes that we may describe as fictive and mythic. Whereas in playing a fiction game, one does not believe that a yeti shook hands with Sir Edmund Hillary but merely allows one's thoughts, for the sake of the game, to be guided by information to that effect; in myth, information to that effect causes one to believe that Hillary met a yeti. In both cases, one's thoughts are controlled by the information; in myth, deceptive information is given credence.

Understanding a fictive picture as a picture with a fictive subject imposes the following demands on viewers. Viewers must first identify the picture's make-believe source on the basis of apparent information from it. That is, they must make a *well-grounded*(MB) identification of its fictive subject. This requires that viewers treat the apparent information as if it were from an actual object by engaging in a pretence. That they engage in a pretence means that they are aware that the picture is fictive, and are conniving in the pretence that it denotes. Those who are genuinely misled by a fictive picture, believing that its subject exists, are not engaging in such a pretence, and have not grasped the picture as a fictive picture.

It is not required, on this account, that a fictive picture be intended to be fictive. An artist may believe that Wyman exists and make a picture 'of' him without engaging in a pretence about the origin of the information that the picture contains. Viewers may understand the picture as fictive nevertheless, pretending that the apparent information has the source its maker believed it had. Viewers who meet the conditions that I have listed understand a fictive picture, whether they know that the artist meant it to denote its subject or whether they know that she meant it to convey apparent information to be taken as denoting its subject. Once again we see that the meaning of pictures, including fictive ones, is independent of the artist's, or anybody else's, beliefs. Pictures' status as perceptual mechanisms is the foundation of their function as fictions.

11

Picturing Pictures

I WANT to conclude with a discussion of a class of pictures that test the resources of any theory of depiction. Pictures that represent other pictures rather than, or in addition to, representing ordinary objects pose puzzles about the domain of the relation 'is a picture of' and also about the point of pictorial representation. How can a picture depict another? And what could be the meaning of a picture of another?

11.1 Variation Meaning

The most conspicuous of the many ways in which pictures represent other pictures is by variation. Whereas allusions are often veiled, and copies, especially in the form of photographic reproductions, are too common to draw attention, variations—from Duchamps's *L.H.O.O.Q.*, to Picasso's meditations on the masters, to Lichtenstein's revisions of Picasso's variations—declare themselves to be pictures of pictures, and so pose challenges to viewers and theorists alike.

The challenge to viewers has to do with the special character of 'variation experience', involving as it does identification of a picture *as a variation of another*, and not as an ordinary picture of some scene. Variation identification is distinguished by the way it depends upon and is infused by experience of another picture, the variation's original. A variation invites reflective viewers to make connections with its original, to mark their similarities and differences, to observe the interplay between the formal and representational properties of each, and, in sum, to ponder why this variation was made of that original in that particular manner.

The challenge to the theorist is to explain the challenge to the viewer. First of all, this calls for an account of 'variation meaning'—of how meaning accrues to a picture when it represents another picture in a particular way. We can think of a variation's meaning *qua* variation roughly as what a suitable viewer learns from the fact that it is a variation. In addition, the theorist must explain how a picture can be a variation—how one picture can represent another in the first place. We should expect that the means by which variations represent their originals are in some way an extension of the means by which ordinary pictures represent their subjects. A theory of variation will parallel a theory of depiction. In keeping with the scope of this book, I shall limit what I have to say to figurative variations of figurative pictures.[1] Theories of variation and variation meaning are not, of course, unrelated to each other. The adequacy of any theory of variation meaning is to be measured in part by its treatment of what constitutes our grasp of the fact that a picture is a variation, namely the special character of variation experience. A theory of variation meaning which obscures or distorts this experience is an inadequate one. But that we do identify one picture as of another is due to the fact that one picture can represent another, and this is to be explained by a theory of variation. Thus an account of variation meaning that does justice to the character of variation experience depends on an adequate account of variation.

I maintain that the available accounts of variation meaning are inadequate, because they are predicated upon theories of variation that are also inadequate. By contrast, an account of variation inspired by the aspect-recognition theory is more amenable to an adequate account of variation meaning. As a start, I outline and assess two models of variation meaning. One comes from Wollheim's _Painting as an Art_, where it is illustrated with reference to some of Picasso's variations on Manet's _Déjeuner sur l' herbe_.[2] The source of the other conception is art-historical and critical writing on variations.

11.2 Meaning and Explanation

While it is unlikely that historians and critics who study variations take themselves to be explaining the meaning that variations hold for ordinary viewers, we may nevertheless consider whether historical and critical explanations of variations provide a serviceable model of variation meaning. For this purpose, an exhaustive survey of the historical and critical literature is not necessary. I will stay with Wollheim's Picassian theme in a case study of extended interpretations by Douglas Cooper of Picasso's _Déjeuners_ and by Leo Steinberg of Picasso's variations on

---

[1] I ignore non-representational variations on non-representational works, non-representational variations on representational works, and representational variations on non-representational works.   [2] Wollheim, _Painting as an Art_, 231–48.

Delacroix's *Femmes d'Alger*.[3] The choice of studies of Picasso is particularly appropriate in view of his interest in making variations.

Cooper's introduction to the printed edition of Picasso's *Déjeuners* has an air of apologetic, and so must be read against a background of art-historical and critical anxiety, even disdain, about variation. Since variation is thought to be an offshoot of student practice of copying the masters, variations are easily dismissed as mere technical studies. This attitude was evident in the scandalized responses of critics to the discovery of Manet's borrowings (including the *Déjeuner* itself), which were attributed to a lack of imagination.[4] A contemporary hold-over is John Berger, who dismisses Picasso's variations as 'no more than exercises in painting—such as one might expect a serious young man to carry out, but not an old man who has gained his freedom to be himself'.[5] Throughout his discussion of Picasso's *Déjeuners*, Cooper is at pains to establish the legitimacy of Picasso's variations within the artist's *œuvre*.

The corner-stone of Cooper's account of Picasso's variations is that 'it matters little that an artist takes over the work of another and uses it as a spring-board for his imagination so long as he has the ability to transform it by his creativity into a new and purely personal image'.[6] Accordingly, Cooper argues that the *Déjeuner* provided Picasso with an opportunity to apply his discoveries concerning form and expression to great effect. It allowed him to revisit some of the themes and characters with which he had long been engaged. Manet's scenario is repeatedly reworked, each of its players being replaced by a succession of familiar Picassian types—bathers, the artist and his model, the monumental woman, the sleeper, the monkey, the youth—who explore the picture's dramatic and expressive possibilities (e.g. Fig. 25). Cooper goes on to document in detail the way in which Picasso's concerns find expression in many versions of his *Déjeuners*.

Whereas the *Déjeuner* stimulated Picasso's ideas on matters of subject

[3] Douglas Cooper, *Pablo Picasso: Les Déjeuners* (Paris: Éditions Cercle d'Art, 1962), 5–35; and Leo Steinberg, 'The Algerian Women and Picasso at Large', in *Other Criteria*, 124–234.

[4] John Rewald, *The History of Impressionism*, 2nd edn. (New York: Museum of Modern Art, 1946), 151. But for a more complex picture of conceptions of originality and imitation in this period, see Richard Shiff, 'The Original, the Imitation, the Copy, and the Spontaneous Classic: Theory and Painting in Nineteenth-Century France', *Yale French Studies*, 66 (1984), 27–54.

[5] John Berger, *The Success and Failure of Picasso*, rev. edn. (New York: Pantheon, 1989), 183. [6] Cooper, *Picasso: Les Déjeuners*, 7. The translations are mine.

Fig. 25. Pablo Picasso, *Déjeuners*, 22 August 1961

and expression, his variations on other pictures served him in other ways. Courbet and El Greco contributed formal problems, Cranach the possibilities of androgynous figures, Poussin an opportunity to undertake subjects forbidden since Courbet, and Delacroix's *Femmes d'Alger* an opportunity to test the pictorial language which he had developed since cubism.[7] In each case, however, it is by incorporating an earlier image into his project and stylistic repertoire that a variation gains a place in his *œuvre*. Michel Leiris compares making a variation with making oneself at home in someone else's house, 'not altering and correcting as if you are finding fault with your landlord, but—in all simplicity—furnishing the place to make it cosier and more congenial to your habits and tasks'.[8]

Leo Steinberg's essay, 'The Algerian Women and Picasso at Large', a masterful analysis of Picasso's versions of Delacroix's *Femmes d'Alger*, subscribes to the same explanatory principles as Cooper. We are to explain a variation as part of a larger context, namely the concerns and individual resources of the artist. The attraction of the *Femmes d'Alger* as material for variation lay, for Picasso, in its potential to

---

[7] Cooper, *Picasso: Les Déjeuners*, 25–8.

[8] Michel Leiris, 'Picasso et les Ménines de Velasquez', in *Picasso: Les Ménines* (Paris: Galeries Louise Leiris, 1959), n.p.

explore pictorial problems which had long preoccupied him. The *Femmes'* erotic content and compositional manœuvrability, and the link between them, particularly attracted Picasso (Fig. 26). Throughout his career, Picasso sought to evoke robust, erotically charged figures as complex three-dimensional objects on a flat surface, to fashion sensuous images not distorted by the demands of an all-seeing representation. The goal was to reconcile a traditional figurative mode of representation with the ideal of omnispection developed after cubism, and to do so in a way which re-embodies fragmented cubist images and preserves their erotic appeal. In the *Femmes d'Alger*, the problem was primarily how to pose the sleeping figure occupying the lower right of the canvas as simultaneously prone and supine. Each version of the *Femmes d'Alger* introduces and wields with greater dexterity some of the tools in Picasso's stylistic repertoire: the use of visual ambiguity, multiple viewpoints, and what Steinberg calls the principle of anatomy by assemblage. The result is a 'unique coincidence which is at once diagram and embrace' (Fig. 27).[9] Picasso's *Femmes* may be understood as a manifestation of the distinctively Picassian equation of representation and the erotic.[10]

Cooper and Steinberg both seek to explain Picasso's variations by situating them within the context of the artist's individual style and concerns. The distinctive place of any individual work within this context depends on its contribution to developments in the artist's *œuvre*.

This approach, with its roots in traditional historical and critical methodology, certainly explains why a particular picture was chosen as material for variation and then given a particular kind of treatment. However, such accounts do not explain the features of a picture which comprise its distinctive meaning as a variation. Exactly the same points could be made about these pictures regardless of their being variations. Moreover, in looking at a picture such as the *Femmes d'Alger*, most sensitive, informed viewers do not, and probably were not intended to, experience the depiction of the sleeping figure as a solution to formal and representational problems in Picasso's *œuvre*. We have seen that an account of variation meaning must acknowledge the distinctive content of viewers' experience of variations, but these historical narratives do not allow for the prominence of the original in that experience. Indeed,

---

[9] Steinberg, 'Algerian Women', 234.

[10] See Robert Rosenblum, 'Picasso and the Anatomy of Eroticism', in Theodore Bowie and Cornelia V. Christensen (eds.), *Studies in Erotic Art* (New York: Basic Books, 1970), 337–50.

Fig. 26. Eugène Delacroix, *Femmes d'Alger*, 1834

Fig. 27. Pablo Picasso, *Femmes d'Alger*, version O, 14 February 1955

they exclude identification of the variation's original as part of variation experience, relegating it to the status of a stimulus to the artist's
imagination. All that is of significance in a variation is brought to it by
the artist; nothing, really, is contributed by the original.

This conclusion should come as no surprise in light of Steinberg's
conviction that viewers rarely experience variations as variations.
Steinberg claims that the identification of a variation's source, like the
identification of the sources of allusions or influences, is a specialist
skill.[11] Whereas artists, critics, and historians may locate a variation's
source and derive some pleasure from being privy to the artistic process, the outsider is anxious 'to relate art at once to the phenomenal
world and the realm of experience, to see the image as an immediate
response to its ostensible object'.[12] In looking at Picasso's *Femmes*,
most viewers see only a harem scene. It follows that the meaning of a
variation to ordinary viewers is its meaning as an ordinary picture, and
is exhausted by its ostensible subject-matter. Of course, since pictures
themselves are constituents of the visual realm, the claim that they
cannot be the ostensible subjects of pictures is surprising and requires
substantiation.

11.3 Variation Meaning as Secondary Meaning

Richard Wollheim, in *Painting as an Art*, proffers an account of variation meaning as a kind of 'secondary meaning'. A picture's 'primary
meaning' is what we grasp when we understand what it represents, its
subject and its content in my jargon. Wollheim describes his as a psychological account of meaning, because its ingredients are the mental
state of the artist, the way in which this mental state caused her to paint,
and the experience that the resulting picture induces in suitable specta-
tors.[13] Pictorial meaning is primary meaning, because it is made available to viewers through the experience they have when looking at the
picture as its maker intended.

A picture's secondary meaning is what we understand when we learn
what the *act of making the picture* meant to the person who made it.
Secondary meaning also fits within Wollheim's psychological account

[11] Leo Steinberg, 'The Glorious Company', in *Art about Art*, by Jean Lipman and
Richard Marshall (New York: E. P. Dutton, 1978), 8–31.   [12] Ibid. 15.
[13] I have criticized each of these elements, in Sects. 8.3, 9.4, and 2.3 respectively.

of meaning, as it is a product of the artist's mental state, the way this caused him or her to paint, and the resulting experience enjoyed by suitable viewers. As to the last of these, Wollheim grants that secondary meaning is mediated by primary meaning—what a picture meant to the person who made it must be revealed by the look of the picture. According to Wollheim, the meaning of a variation as a variation is a species of secondary meaning, consisting in a revelation of what the act of making a picture of another picture meant to the artist.[14] For a picture to have meaning as a variation, its look must disclose the artist's feelings, thoughts, and emotions about the fact that it is a variation. But although this meaning is mediated by the work's pictorial content, variation meaning is not a species of pictorial meaning. The reason is straightforward: a variation's meaning cannot be identified with the image it borrows from its original, for this belongs as much to the original as to the variation, and a variation's meaning as a variation is not something it shares with its original.

Wollheim illustrates his account of variation meaning as secondary meaning in an explication of Picasso's *Déjeuners* series. Cooper and Steinberg are right that these pictures subject Manet's material to radical manipulations consistent with Picasso's artistic enterprise, but their significance lies in what the manipulations indicate about Picasso's attitude to the fact that he is making pictures after one by Manet. In particular, they express Picasso's wish, born of envy, to identify himself with his predecessor by appropriating the master's work.

The rationale for this interpretation refers to the way in which Picasso transformed the original *Déjeuner*. Whereas in Manet we find an air of abstraction and secretiveness, indeterminate space, horizontality, sensuous pleasure, and modernity, in Picasso's variations we find the alert, remorseless stare, structured space, verticality, austerity, and timelessness. Whereas Manet shows artists relaxing from their work, Picasso represents the strenuous work needed for visual apprehension. Art, for Picasso, is a labour of vision, and unlike passive copying, variation is work. It is because great painting is, for Picasso, visual work that the manipulations to which he subjects the *Déjeuner* bring him closer to Manet. In looking at the variations, we see Picasso's transformations as work, and thereby come to understand that through this work Picasso enviously attempts to identify with Manet.

Wollheim's reading of Picasso nicely illustrates his contention that

---

[14] Wollheim, *Painting as an Art*, 187–90, 246.

variation meaning is secondary meaning, not primary. To grasp a variation's meaning as a variation is to understand what the borrowing meant to the artist. To grasp that the artist figure in Picasso's *Déjeuners* has piercing eyes is to grasp part of what it represents; but though these piercing eyes are a clue to what making the picture meant to Picasso, they are not part of its variation meaning. Understanding a variation as a variation is not grasping its look or its content, but rather the mental state of its maker.

One worry that might be raised about this account is that it appears that secondary meaning, paradoxically, need not be intended—Picasso probably did not wish to put his envy on display in his variations on Manet—and Wollheim concedes that 'most forms of secondary meaning are unconscious'.[15] But unless some sense can be made of the notion of unconscious intentions, this obviously offends Wollheim's principle that meaning is always something intended. Nevertheless, I set aside this worry. After all, my own position has been that a picture's meaning does not depend on its maker's intentions, and this is not inconsistent with the possibility that a painter is unaware of the meanings she creates.

Much more troublesome is the fact that revealing what making it meant to the artist is neither necessary nor sufficient for a variation to have meaning as a variation. A picture may provide for an experience of itself as of another picture and as related to its source in a variety of ways without conveying anything of what the fact that the picture is a variation meant to its maker. Indeed, there might be nothing that the fact that a variation is a variation means to the artist beyond the picture's complex relations to its original. The idea that making a variation is inevitably psychologically revealing assumes that the anxiety of influence that Cooper and Steinberg are responding to is pervasive. But it is, in fact, symptomatic of art only in a particular time and place.

Finally, like Cooper's and Steinberg's, Wollheim's account does not do justice to the character of variation experience. Since variation experience depends on the contents of both variation and original and the relationships between them, what is essential to understanding a variation is identifying its relationships with its original on the basis of visual encounter with both. But grasp of these relationships is not what Wollheim identifies as essential to understanding a variation's meaning. I do not dispute that pictures often have secondary meanings; what I

---

15 Ibid. 246.

doubt is that variation meaning is *always* secondary meaning. What is wrong with Wollheim's account is that it takes variation meaning always to be a form of secondary meaning rather than pictorial meaning.

11.4 Theories of Variation

Both the accounts of variation discussed so far share the view that understanding a variation does not consist in just grasping its pictorial content. Steinberg and Wollheim acknowledge the reasoning underlying this view: Wollheim defines variation meaning as secondary meaning because a variation's subject-matter belongs equally to its original, and Steinberg subscribes to a similar view of the 'motif' or 'image' that a variation borrows from its antecedent. All art, Steinberg claims, is a modification of earlier art, for the art of the past provides artists with a repository of images which are available for reuse. In order to explain a variation's meaning, we cannot refer to its subject-matter, for that is shared with an earlier picture. We must look to such extra-pictorial factors as themes in the artist's *œuvre* or the content of the artist's mental states.

The train of thought underlying the two accounts of variation meaning is, briefly, this. A picture represents another by sharing its content. But if variation and original share content, then variation meaning cannot inhere in pictorial content, for a variation *qua* variation does not have the same meaning as its original. Therefore variation meaning is not pictorial.

In this section I turn from theories of variation meaning to theories of variation—of what it is to be a variation—in the hope that the latter might shed light on the former. To begin, I focus on the assumption that a picture represents another by sharing content with it.

It seems natural to suppose that what makes a picture a variation is precisely that it reproduces its original's subject-matter. According to what I call the 'matching theory' of variation, a variation represents its original only if it represents what its original represents, or, put another way, if its content matches its original's. However, the matching of content between two pictures does not suffice for one to be a variation of the other. The match might be fortuitous. Moreover, the relation of matching is a symmetric one, while 'is a variation of' is not. Obviously what is missing is the causal relationship between a variation and its original. A picture is a variation of an original only if the original's appearance played a causal role in the variation's production. This explains the asymmetry of variation: Manet's *Déjeuner* cannot be a variation of Picasso's variations, because the former is not causally dependent on the latter.[16]

Some might favour intentional dependence over causal dependence: a picture is a variation of an original only if it is intended to be a variation of that original. However, intentional dependence cannot replace causal dependence. An intention to create a variation on Parrhasius's famous but lost *trompe-l'œil* draperies cannot succeed, no matter what degree of match one may be lucky enough to achieve, for the simple reason that Parrhasius's picture no longer has causal power. Moreover, the intentional requirement implies, I believe wrongly, that a work made by an artist influenced by a picture he has seen but forgotten is not a variation because it was not intended as one.

If variation entails causation plus matching, then how do variations differ from copies (and forgeries)? We distinguish between a young artist's copy of an old master for training purposes and a mature artist's variations on an earlier work, a difference that is not simply a matter of the purpose for which each was made. It is tempting to suggest that whereas a copy matches its subject closely, a variation matches it more loosely.[17] The difficulty with this proposal is that there is no way to fix just how much matching is required for copying. Copies are rarely, if ever, perfect—Rubens's copy of Titian's *Bacchanal with Sleeping Ariadne* is very much a Rubenesque Titian, for instance. Moreover, the matching standard effaces the distinction between a variation and a poor copy. Poor copies are only fair imitations of their models, but they are copies none the less.

Perhaps the difference between a copy (or forgery) and a variation is this. Whereas copies aim to attain a high degree of match with their originals, variations are free to depart from the strictures of similarity. Copies' mismatches with their originals are always contrary to intention whereas variations' mismatches need not be. Forgeries, which are a special case of copies, show this most clearly. This does not imply that variations cannot closely match their originals. What it does imply is

---

[16] We can imagine pictures which are variations of each other: two painters engage in a pictorial 'duet', simultaneously making pictures of each other's pictures. This is not a counter-example to the causal condition, for in this case, variation is symmetric along with causal dependence.

[17] See Göran Hermerén, *Influence in Art and Literature* (Princeton: Princeton University Press, 1975), 63–8.

that the differences between a copy and its original are always contrary to the copyist's intention of making a perfect imitation—probably stemming from either imperfect mastery of technique (in the case of poor copies) or the inevitability of individual style (in the case of masterful copies).

In short, then, a picture is a copy of an original if and only if its content matches its original's, the match is causally dependent on the original's appearance, and any mismatch is contrary to intention. A picture is a variation on an original if and only if its content matches that of its original to a sufficient degree, and this match is causally dependent on its original's appearance.

The matching theory of variation does not require that content of variation and original match perfectly, but rather leaves room for them to differ. Nevertheless, if it is to explain how a variation is identified as of its original, then it does make understanding what the variation represents dependent on noticing its match with its original. Dissimilarities in content do not undermine a picture's status as a variation, but they do not contribute to identifying what it represents. As long as what makes a picture a variation is sharing of content and variation and original do not share meaning, then it is no surprise that accounts of variation meaning neglect the possibility that a variation's meaning lies in the way its content departs from that of its original.

In his essay 'Variations on Variation', Goodman is sensitive to the need for an account of variation that explains how variations represent their antecedents by means of differences in content, not just matched contents.[18] Variations refer to their originals by exemplification of some shared features and by 'contrastive exemplification' of some features not shared.

'Exemplification' has a precise meaning in Goodman's technical vocabulary. A picture exemplifies a feature when it both has that feature and refers to it. It does not exemplify all the features it has, but only those to which it also refers. The paradigm of exemplification is a tailor's swatch. A swatch possesses a certain colour, texture, weave, and weight, and by referring to these properties it functions as a sample suitable for selecting fabrics. But the swatch does not exemplify all the fabric's properties (e.g. size), since it does not refer to all of them. Those properties to which the swatch does refer are those in virtue of which it serves as a sample.

[18] Nelson Goodman, 'Variations on Variation—Or Picasso back to Bach', in *Reconceptions in Philosophy*, 74–6.

Thus a variation refers to its original by referring to properties that both possess—particularly by referring to shared contents.[19] But, as we have seen, a variation does not share all its properties with its original, so Goodman allows that a variation may refer to its original by contrastive exemplification of properties they do not share. This requirement is an important one, since it was the view that a variation represents its original only on the basis of shared features that gave rise to inadequate accounts of variation meaning. Proposing that a variation refers to its original as much through contrasting features as shared ones promises an improved account of variation meaning.

But what is *contrastive* exemplification? According to Goodman, two pictures contrastively exemplify a property when they refer to a property that belongs literally to one and figuratively to the other. No doubt both a variation and its original literally exemplify many properties, some of which they co-exemplify, and they may figuratively exemplify properties in tandem as well. But why must what one exemplifies literally correspond with what the other exemplifies metaphorically? Let us grant that Picasso's *Femmes d'Alger* paintings exemplify omniscient vision. Does it follow that they are variations because the original by Delacroix metaphorically exemplifies omniscient vision? What could this mean? Evidence of a correspondence between metaphorical and literal exemplification among contrasting features is absent in Goodman's own analysis of Picasso's variations on Velázquez's *Las Meninas*.[20] In these pictures Goodman sees, for instance, the Infanta as devitalized and made to express at first inner turmoil then courage, but these qualities are not, it seems to me, ones referred to and metaphorically possessed by Velázquez's original. No doubt contrastive exemplification exists and can be important in variation, but it does not explain all, or even many, of the significant differences in content between variation and original.

11.5 Artful Aspects

Neglect of the possibility that variation meaning might be pictorial meaning originates with the view that a picture represents another by

[19] Exemplification of shared content is a special case of exemplification of shared properties. Goodman's more general formulation encompasses abstract variations, which have no pictorial contents to share. Abstract variations may refer to shared expressive, manifestational, or design properties.

[20] Goodman, 'Variations on Variation', 76–81.

sharing subject-matter with it. For this reason, Goodman's idea that a variation can refer to its original by contrastive exemplification of properties they do not share is a step in the right direction. I suggest that a theory of variation modelled on the aspect-recognition theory successfully executes Goodman's strategy, providing for a more adequate conception of variation meaning.

The information that pictures convey is information which feeds into abilities to recognize objects under remarkably different guises. We may recognize an object seen from one point of view on the basis of having seen it from different points of view; we may recognize objects seen in distorting conditions, whether natural or induced through optical technology; and most impressively, we can recognize objects as they change over time. Although recognition is usually accompanied by an experience of similarity, objects recognized are not experienced as similar to objects previously seen in uniform ways. Pictures present a diverse range of recognizable aspects of objects and kinds of objects. This much is familiar.

In addition to objects and kinds of objects, a third type of entity that pictures sometimes depict is other pictures. Consider Picasso's *Déjeuners* (see Fig. 25). In interpreting this picture, we clearly make use of an ability to recognize kinds of objects—there are some trees, some artists, and so on. Sometimes recognition abilities for individuals also come into play, as in Picasso's witty recreations of Rembrandt's self-portraits, which denote Rembrandt on the basis of a recognition ability generated by the original self-portraits. In addition to being able to recognize the objects which are the subjects of Manet's, Rembrandt's, and Picasso's pictures, we can recognize the pictures by Manet and Rembrandt on which Picasso executed variations. I call this kind of recognition 'variation-recognition'.

As the examples I have chosen amply demonstrate, variation-recognition is dynamic. A variation is no mere copy, and attempts to assimilate variation to copying disregard a large and increasingly important body of artistic achievement. Some variations may simply present aspects belonging to different projective systems—one imagines Vermeers in reversed perspective—but others make fuller use of the resources of recognition.

Variation-recognition is not reducible to subject-recognition. While we have seen that variation and original need not have the same content and need not present similar aspects of their subjects, one might think that a variation and its original must at least present recognizable, albeit different, aspects of the same subject. Both Picasso's and Manet's *Déjeuners* are recognizably of picnickers, for instance. Thus we might explain one picture's representing the other by the fact that both present recognizable aspects of the same object. But this is neither necessary nor sufficient for variation. In the first place, coextensive pictures need not be variations of each other. Moreover, a variation need not present an *independently* recognizable aspect of the subject of its original. Identification of the subject held in common between variation and original may depend on first knowing what the original depicts.

For instance, nobody could recognize the faceless figure in Francis Bacon's study of Velázquez's *Innocent X* as of that particular pope, but an art-historically sophisticated viewer will be able to recognize Bacon's painting as a picture of a pope and as a variation of Velzáquez's picture. By identifying it as a variation on *Innocent X*, it is possible to identify Bacon's picture as of Innocent X. Auerbach's versions of Titian's *Bacchus and Ariadne* are a more extreme case. These pictures are in my opinion barely pictorial—they certainly do not present recognizable aspects of Bacchus's arrival at Naxos—but they are recognizable, to a suitable viewer, as of Titian's picture, and can thereby be identified as of the scene it represents.

The Bacon, in a moderate way, and the Auerbach, in a more striking way, demonstrate the following principles. Variation-recognition cannot be reduced to the ability to recognize the objects and kinds of objects that originals take as their subjects. And if a variation need not present a recognizable aspect of its original's subject, what it must do is present a recognizable aspect of its original's aspect of its subject. But the relation 'is an aspect of' is not transitive, so that the fact that a variation presents an aspect of its original's aspect of its subject does not entail that the variation presents an aspect of its original's subject. Variations are not just pictures of the same things as their originals: they are pictures that present aspects of the aspects presented by their originals. It is in this sense that Picasso's pictures not only depict picnickers and Rembrandt; they depict Manet's *Déjeuner* and Rembrandt's self-portraits.

Variation-recognition provides a way to forge informational links between one picture and another, or one picture and many others. Just as an ordinary picture may be recognizable as of an individual object or a kind of object, so a pictorial variation may be recognizable as of a single original or a general type of picture. Whereas we identify one of Picasso's *Déjeuners* as a variation on a single picture, Manet's

Déjeuner, on the basis of information derived from Manet's picture, Picasso's Rembrandt self-portraits derive information from no single Rembrandt self-portrait, and so are identifiable not as variations on particular Rembrandt self-portraits, but rather as variations on the 'genre' (if we can call it that) of Rembrandt self-portraits.

In each case there is a possibility of ill-groundedness. An identification of Manet's *Déjeuner* as the source of Figure 25 is ill-grounded if, for example, the model for this picture was not Manet's picture. Furthermore, variation-recognition can be defeated in many of the same ways as can ordinary pictorial recognition. Variations can be ambiguous; they can present unusual aspects of their originals, and they can suffer at the hands of unskilled artists.

A representation is a pictorial variation of an original only if it embodies information derived from its original on the basis of which a suitable viewer can recognize it. This requires that the original play a causal role in the variation's production, since informational systems rest on causal processes. A complete account of variation must also explain what constitutes an intention to make a variation of another picture and the role, if any, that this intention plays in distinguishing variations from copies. However, the most important feature of an aspect-recognition theory of variation is that it describes a mechanism according to which both similarities and dissimilarities between the contents of variation and original are responsible for the one representing the other. It is this feature that grounds an adequate conception of variation meaning.

A theory of variation meaning is charged with explaining what the meaning of the fact that a picture depicts another can consist in. I have insisted that such a theory must locate variation meaning in the character of our experience of variations, which revolves around not only the variation but also its original and the relations between them. Reference to neither the artist's stylistic agenda nor her psychological attitude to the act of borrowing explains variation meaning in a way that does justice to our experience of variations as of other pictures. I propose that the meaning which variations have *as variations* lies in their complex aspectual relations with their originals and their originals' subjects. To understand a variation, as a variation, suitable viewers, those who can recognize the original under the relevant kinds of aspects, must actually identify the variation as an aspect of its original.

I have already argued that pictorial content is necessarily aspectual:

artists must select aspects of scenes and objects for representation. Different systems of representation, conveying different aspects, are sometimes preferred in different contexts to communicate different kinds of information. Thus does depiction have a historical and cultural dimension. But the selectivity of depiction is not something that viewers are usually aware of. An ordinary picture must select an aspect of its subject for representation, but that it has selected one aspect rather than another need not be part of what is communicated by the picture. Variations, by contrast, draw our attention not only to the aspects they present but also to the aspects that their originals present. When a picture represents another picture by presenting an aspect of it, then selectivity itself is 'thematized' and becomes part of the variation's meaning.

Of course, each variation has its own meaning as a variation. That is, the content of each, as an aspect of its original, draws our attention to different features of its original and its original's aspectual content. A different variation presenting a different aspect of the same original highlights different features of that original's aspectual content. Each of Picasso's versions of the *Déjeuner* has a different meaning as a variation, because it has a different primary meaning—this contrasts sharply with Wollheim's account, according to which each is equally an expression of envy.

It may be helpful to think of variations as drawing attention to horizons of pictorial possibilities, with different variations opening up different horizons.[21] By presenting different aspects of their originals, different variations reveal alternative sets of ways in which their originals might have treated their subjects. A variation is a picture whose content matches that of another in some respects and contrasts with it in others, and this matching and contrasting points up the stylistic and representational choices that its original embodies by contrast with chosen alternatives.

This account supports a surprising claim sometimes made on behalf of variations, namely that modern appropriations confer meaning on past works. For instance, one of Steinberg's theses in 'The Glorious Company' is that borrowings serve to revitalize and introduce into the contemporary era the work of past masters. Picasso seems to see his variations on the *Meninas* in just this way. Of his *Meninas* series, he reflects:

---

[21] Cf. Podro, 'Depiction and the Golden Calf', 181–2.

I would say to myself: suppose I were to move this figure a little to the right or a little to the left? . . . Almost certainly I would be tempted to modify the light or arrange it differently in view of the changed position of the figure. Gradually I would create a painting . . . sure to horrify the specialist in the copying of old masters. It would not be *The Maids of Honor* he saw when he looked at Velázquez' picture; it would be *my* Maids of Honor.[22]

One might wonder by what mechanism 'backwards meaning' can be bestowed. The answer is that a variation changes the way we look at its original in a quite specific sense, by drawing attention to the commitments and non-commitments made by its original which viewers might not otherwise have noticed and reflected upon.[23]

By no means do I wish to suggest that variation meaning, as I have described it, exhausts the meaning of a variation *as a picture* (rather than *as a variation*). A variation may have what Wollheim calls secondary meaning (as may any picture), and its secondary meaning may sometimes depend on its having a particular variation meaning. That is, a picture may convey its maker's attitude to it by setting up those complex aspectual relationships with another picture that endow it with variation meaning. Picasso's representation, in the *Déjeuners* series, of artists as vigorous, even aggressive, observers contrasts with Manet's picture of contemplative artists. This contrast is reflected in the system of representation chosen by each—Manet's pallid, static, and isolated figures become, in Picasso's graffiti-like drawings, energetic, tense, and dramatic. We can learn from Picasso's interpretation of Manet something about his attitude to his predecessor and to the work of making pictures; but we learn this through Picasso showing us the viewpoint that Manet takes to a subject and some of the alternatives. A picture's meaning as a variation sometimes gives it a secondary meaning.

In addition to claiming that variation meaning is a species of secondary meaning, Wollheim also holds that only pictures that reveal what making them meant to the artist have aesthetic significance. Thus, if variations have aesthetic significance, it is because they reveal something about the artist's attitude to the act of borrowing.

---

[22] Quoted by Jaime Sabartés, introduction to *Picasso: Variations on Velazquez' Painting 'The Maids of Honor'* (New York: Abrams, 1959), n.p.

[23] There might be conceptions of artistic activity according to which Picasso did, or might have, made Velázquez's *Meninas as we see it today*. Locutionary pictorial acts may not be those limited to the application of pigment to a surface. Perhaps what a curator does in hanging a picture in the midst of other pictures can endow it with meaning not intended by the artist and not inherent in the picture.

A tacit aim of this chapter has been to indicate, in a rough way, the foundations of an account of pictures' distinctive aesthetic significance. If there is a uniquely pictorial aesthetic, and if I am correct in maintaining that pictures are distinctive as a medium of representation because they are aspectual, then we should expect this aesthetic to be provoked by, and to centre on, pictures' aspectual structure. One way that pictures can generate aesthetic interest *qua* pictures is by thematizing their selectivity. Selectivity may be thematized in any picture; but in variations, pictorial selectivity is thematized in a complex yet concrete way that suffuses our experience of both variation and original.

An appreciation of the aspectual character of pictures and of the role of recognition in identifying pictorial aspects is therefore useful for explaining not only how pictures work in everyday communication and why they differ from one historical or social context to another, but also how they can function as an art-form unlike any other.

BIBLIOGRAPHY

ALBERTI, LEON BATTISTA, *On Painting*, trans. John R. Spencer, rev. edn. (New Haven: Yale University Press, 1966).

ALPERS, SVETLANA, *Rembrandt's Enterprise: The Studio and the Market* (Chicago: University of Chicago Press, 1988).

BACH, KENT, 'Part of What a Picture Is', *British Journal of Aesthetics*, 11 (1971), 119–37.

BALTRUŠAITIS, JURGIS, *Anamorphic Art*, trans. W. J. Strachan (Cambridge: Chadwych–Healey, 1977).

BAZIN, ANDRÉ, 'The Ontology of the Photographic Image', in *What is Cinema?*, trans. Hugh Gray (Berkeley and Los Angeles: University of California Press, 1967), i. 9–16.

BENNETT, JOHN G., 'Depiction and Convention', *Monist*, 58 (1974), 255–68.

BERGER, JOHN, *The Success and Failure of Picasso*, rev. edn. (New York: Pantheon, 1989).

BERNDT, RONALD M., *Australian Aboriginal Art* (New York: Macmillan, 1964).

BLACK, MAX, 'How Do Pictures Represent?', in Maurice Mandelbaum (ed.), *Art, Perception, and Reality* (Baltimore: Johns Hopkins University Press, 1972), 95–129.

BLOCK, NED, 'The Photographic Fallacy in the Debate about Mental Imagery', *Noûs*, 17 (1983), 651–61.

BOAS, FRANZ, *Primitive Art* (New York: Dover, 1955).

BROWN, ROGER, and HERRNSTEIN, RICHARD J., 'Icons and Images', in Ned Block (ed.), *Imagery* (Cambridge, Mass.: MIT Press, 1981), 19–49.

BRUCE, VICKI, 'Changing Faces: Visual and Non-Visual Coding Processes in Face Recognition', *British Journal of Psychology*, 73 (1982), 105–16.

—— , 'Recognizing Faces', *Philosophical Transactions of the Royal Society of London*, B302 (1983), 423–36.

BRYSON, NORMAN, *Vision and Painting: The Logic of the Gaze* (New Haven: Yale University Press, 1983).

CAREY, SUSAN, and DIAMOND, RHEA, 'From Piecemeal to Configurational Representation of Faces', *Science*, 195 (1977), 312–14.

COOPER, DOUGLAS, *Pablo Picasso: Les Déjeuners* (Paris: Éditions Cercle d'Art, 1962).

CURRIE, GREGORY, 'Photography, Painting and Perception', *Journal of Aesthetics and Art Criticism*, 49 (1991), 23–9.

CUSSINS, ADRIAN, 'The Connectionist Construction of Concepts', in Margaret Boden (ed.), *The Philosophy of Artificial Intelligence* (Oxford: Oxford University Press, 1990), 368–440.

DANTO, ARTHUR, 'Animals as Art Historians: Reflections on the Innocent Eye', in *Beyond the Brillo Box: The Visual Arts in Post-Historical Perspective* (New York: Farrar, Straus and Giroux, 1992), 15–31.

——, *Transfiguration of the Commonplace: A Philosophy of Art* (Cambridge, Mass.: Harvard University Press, 1981).

DAVIES, GRAHAM; ELLIS, HADYN; and SHEPHERD, JOHN, 'Face Recognition Accuracy as a Function of Mode of Representation', *Journal of Applied Psychology*, 63 (1978), 180–7.

DENNETT, DANIEL, *Content and Consciousness*, 2nd edn. (London: Routledge and Kegan Paul, 1986).

DEREGOWSKI, JAN B., 'Illusion and Culture', in R. L. Gregory and E. H. Gombrich (eds.), *Illusion in Art and Nature* (London: Duckworth, 1973), 161–91.

——, 'Pictorial Perception and Culture', in Richard Held (ed.), *Image, Object and Illusion* (San Francisco: W. H. Freeman, 1974), 79–85.

DEUCHAR, MARGARET, 'Are the Signs of Language Arbitrary?', in Horace Barlow, Colin Blakemore, and Miranda Weston-Smith (eds.), *Images and Understanding* (Cambridge: Cambridge University Press, 1990), 168–79.

DRETSKE, FRED, 'Conscious Experience', *Mind*, 102 (1993), 263–83.

——, *Knowledge and the Flow of Information* (Oxford: Basil Blackwell, 1981).

——, *Seeing and Knowing* (Chicago: University of Chicago Press, 1969).

DUMMETT, MICHAEL, *Frege: Philosophy of Language*, 2nd edn. (London: Duckworth, 1981).

——, 'What Is a Theory of Meaning?', in Samuel Guttenplan (ed.), *Mind and Language* (Oxford: Oxford University Press, 1975), 97–138.

EATON, MARCIA, 'Truth in Pictures', *Journal of Aesthetics and Art Criticism*, 39 (1980), 15–24.

ELLIS, HADYN D.; SHEPHERD, JOHN W.; and DAVIES, GRAHAM M., 'Identification of Familiar and Unfamiliar Faces from Internal and External Features: Some Implications for Theories of Face Recognition', *Perception*, 8 (1979), 431–9.

EVANS, GARETH, *The Varieties of Reference*, ed. John McDowell (Oxford: Oxford University Press, 1982).

FARAH, MARTHA J., *Visual Agnosia: Disorders of Object Recognition and What They Tell Us about Normal Vision* (Cambridge, Mass.: MIT Press, 1990).

FLEMING, NOEL, 'Recognizing and Seeing As', *Philosophical Review*, 66 (1957), 161–79.

FODOR, JERRY A., *The Language of Thought* (New York: Crowell, 1975).

——, *The Modularity of Mind* (Cambridge, Mass.: MIT Press, 1983).

FRAISSE, PAUL, and ELKIN, EDWIN H., 'Étude génétique de l'influence des modes de présentation sur le seuil de reconnaissance d'objets familiers', *L'Année psychologique*, 63 (1963), 1–22.

FRAZER, JAMES GEORGE, *The Golden Bough: A Study in Magic and Religion*, abridged edn. (New York: Macmillan, 1963).

230 *Bibliography*

GALLIE, W. B., 'Essentially Contested Concepts', *Proceedings of the Aristotelian Society*, 56 (1955), 167–98.

GIBSON, JAMES J., 'The Information Contained in Pictures', in Edward Reed and Rebecca Jones (eds.), *Reasons for Realism* (Hillsdale, NJ: Lawrence Erlbaum, 1982), 269–83.

——, 'The Visual Field and the Visual World', *Psychological Review*, 59 (1952), 149–51.

GOLDMAN, ALVIN I., 'Perceptual Objects', *Synthese*, 35 (1977), 257–84.

GOMBRICH, E. H., *Art and Illusion: A Study in the Psychology of Pictorial Representation*, 2nd edn. (Princeton: Princeton University Press, 1961).

——, 'Illusion and Art', in R. L. Gregory and E. H. Gombrich (eds.), *Illusion in Nature and Art* (London: Duckworth, 1973), 193–243.

——, *The Image and the Eye: Further Studies in the Psychology of Pictorial Representation* (Oxford: Phaidon, 1982).

——, 'Meditations on a Hobby Horse, or the Roots of Artistic Form', in *Meditations on a Hobby Horse*, 4th edn. (Chicago: University of Chicago Press, 1984), 1–11.

GOMBRICH, RICHARD, 'The Consecration of a Buddha Image', *Journal of Asian Studies*, 26 (1966), 23–36.

GOODMAN, NELSON, *Languages of Art: An Approach to a Theory of Symbols*, 2nd edn. (Indianapolis: Hackett, 1976).

——, *Problems and Projects* (Indianapolis: Bobbs–Merrill, 1972).

——, and ELGIN, CATHERINE, *Reconceptions in Philosophy and Other Arts and Sciences* (London: Routledge and Kegan Paul, 1988).

GREGORY, RICHARD, 'The Confounded Eye', in R. L. Gregory and E. H. Gombrich (eds.), *Illusion in Nature and Art* (London: Duckworth, 1973), 49–69.

HAGEN, MARGARET A., *Varieties of Realism: Geometries of Representational Art* (Cambridge: Cambridge University Press, 1986).

HAUGELAND, JOHN, 'Analog and Analog', in J. I. Biro and R. W. Shahan (eds.), *Mind, Brain and Function* (Brighton: Harvester, 1982), 213–25.

HERMERÉN, GÖRAN, *Influence in Art and Literature* (Princeton: Princeton University Press, 1975).

HOCHBERG, J., and BROOKS, V., 'Pictorial Recognition as an Unlearned Ability: A Study of One Child's Performance', *American Journal of Psychology*, 75 (1962), 624–8.

HOCKNEY, DAVID, *On Photography* (New York: André Emmerich Gallery, 1983).

HYSLOP, ALEC, 'Seeing Through Seeing-in', *British Journal of Aesthetics*, 26 (1986), 371–9.

JONES, REBECCA K., and HAGEN, MARGARET A., 'A Perspective on Cross-Cultural Picture Perception', in Margaret A. Hagen (ed.), *The Perception of Pictures* (New York: Academic Press, 1980), ii. 193–226.

KAPLAN, DAVID, 'Bob and Carol and Ted and Alice', in Jaako Hintikka, Julius Moravesik, and Patrick Suppes (eds.), *Approaches to Natural Language* (Dordrecht: Reidel, 1973), 490–518.

——, 'Quantifying In', in Donald Davidson and Jaako Hintikka (eds.), *Words and Objections*, rev. edn. (Dordrecht: Reidel, 1975), 206–42.

KORSMEYER, CAROLYN, 'Pictorial Assertion', *Journal of Aesthetics and Art Criticism*, 43 (1985), 257–65.

KRIPKE, SAUL, 'Empty Reference', the Shearman Memorial Lectures, University College, London, 1973.

——, *Naming and Necessity*, rev. edn. (Oxford: Basil Blackwell, 1980).

——, 'Semantical Considerations in Modal Logic', *Acta Philosophica Fennica*, 16 (1963), 83–94.

——, 'Speaker's Reference and Semantic Reference', in Peter A. French, Theodore E. Uehling, Jr., and Howard K. Wettstein (eds.), *Contemporary Perspectives in the Philosophy of Language* (Minneapolis: University of Minnesota Press, 1979), 6–27.

KUBOVY, MICHAEL, *The Psychology of Perspective and Renaissance Art* (Cambridge: Cambridge University Press, 1986).

LEIRIS, MICHEL, 'Picasso et les Ménines de Velasquez', in *Picasso: Les Ménines* (Paris: Galeries Louise Leiris, 1959).

LEONARDO DA VINCI, *On Painting*, trans. Martin Kemp and Margaret Walker (New Haven: Yale University Press, 1989).

LÉVI-STRAUSS, CLAUDE, *The Way of the Masks*, trans. Sylvia Modelski (Seattle: University of Washington Press, 1982).

LEWIS, DAVID, 'Analog and Digital', *Noûs*, 5 (1971), 321–7.

——, *Convention* (Cambridge, Mass.: Harvard University Press, 1969).

——, 'Languages and Language', in Keith Gunderson (ed.), *Language, Mind, and Knowledge*, Minnesota Studies in the Philosophy of Science, 7 (Minneapolis: University of Minnesota Press, 1975), 3–35.

——, 'Veridical Hallucination and Prosthetic Vision', in Jonathan Dancy (ed.), *Perceptual Knowledge* (Oxford: Oxford University Press, 1988), 79–91.

LOPES, DOMINIC, 'Pictorial Realism', *Journal of Aesthetics and Art Criticism*, 53 (1995), 277–85.

——, 'Pictures, Styles, and Purposes', *British Journal of Aesthetics*, 32 (1992), 330–41.

MANNS, JAMES W., 'Representation, Relativism, and Resemblance', *British Journal of Aesthetics*, 11 (1971), 281–7.

MARR, DAVID, *Vision* (New York: W. H. Freeman, 1982).

MAYNARD, PATRICK, 'Depiction, Vision and Convention', *American Philosophical Quarterly*, 9 (1972), 243–50.

——, 'Drawing and Shooting: Causality in Depiction', *Journal of Aesthetics and Art Criticism*, 44 (1985), 115–29.

MILLIKAN, RUTH GARRETT, 'Perceptual Content and Fregean Myth', *Mind*, 100 (1991), 439–59.

MITCHELL, WILLIAM J., 'When Is Seeing Believing?', *Scientific American*, 270/2 (February 1994), 68–73.

MOORE, G. E., ' "Real" and "Imaginary" ', in Casimir Lewy (ed.), *Lectures on Philosophy* (London: George Allen and Unwin, 1966), 20–43.

NEANDER, KAREN, 'Pictorial Representation: A Matter of Resemblance', *British Journal of Aesthetics*, 27 (1987), 213–26.

NOVITZ, DAVID, 'Picturing', *Journal of Aesthetics and Art Criticism*, 34 (1975), 144–55.

O'SHAUGHNESSY, BRIAN, 'Seeing the Light', *Proceedings of the Aristotelian Society*, 85 (1985), 193–218.

PALLIS, C. A., 'Impaired Identification of Faces and Places with Agnosia for Colors', *Journal of Neurology, Neurosurgery and Psychiatry*, 18 (1955), 218–24.

PALMER, STEPHEN E., 'Fundamental Aspects of Cognitive Representation', in Eleanor Rorsch and Barbara B. Lloyd (eds.), *Cognition and Categorization* (Hillsdale, NJ: Lawrence Erlbaum, 1978), 259–303.

PATEMAN, TREVOR, 'Transparent and Translucent Icons', *British Journal of Aesthetics*, 26 (1986), 380–2.

PEACOCKE, CHRISTOPHER, 'Depiction', *Philosophical Review*, 96 (1987), 383–410.

——, *Holistic Explanation: Action, Space, Interpretation* (Oxford: Oxford University Press, 1979).

——, 'Perceptual Content', in Joseph Almog, John Perry, and Howard K. Wettstein (eds.), *Themes from Kaplan* (New York: Oxford University Press, 1989), 297–329.

——, *Sense and Content* (Oxford: Oxford University Press, 1983).

——, *A Study of Concepts* (Cambridge, Mass.: MIT Press, 1992).

PIRENNE, M. H., *Optics, Painting and Photography*, with a foreword by Michael Polyani (Cambridge: Cambridge University Press, 1970).

PODRO, MICHAEL, 'Depiction and the Golden Calf', in Norman Bryson, Michael Ann Holly, and Keith Moxley (eds.), *Visual Theory: Painting and Interpretation*, (New York: Harper Collins, 1991), 163–89.

PONCE DE LÉON, *The Columbus Gallery* (New York: Ponce de Léon, 1893).

PRICE, H. H., *Thinking and Experience* (Cambridge: Cambridge University Press, 1962).

PUTNAM, HILARY, 'The Meaning of "Meaning" ', in *Mind, Language and Reality* (Cambridge: Cambridge University Press, 1975), 215–75.

PYLYSHYN, ZENON, 'The Imagery Debate: Analog Media Versus Tacit Knowledge', in Ned Block (ed.), *Imagery* (Cambridge, Mass.: MIT Press, 1981), 151–206.

REWALD, JOHN, *The History of Impressionism*, 2nd edn. (New York: Museum of Modern Art, 1946).

ROBINSON, JENEFER, 'Some Remarks on Goodman's Language Theory of Pictures', *British Journal of Aesthetics*, 19 (1979), 63–75.

——, 'Two Theories of Representation', *Erkenntnis*, 12 (1978), 37–53.

ROSENBLUM, ROBERT, 'Picasso and the Anatomy of Eroticism', in Theodore Bowie and Cornelia V. Christensen (eds.), *Studies in Erotic Art* (New York: Basic Books, 1970), 337–50.

ROSKILL, MARK, 'Recognition and Identification', *Critical Inquiry*, 3 (1977), 709–23.

—— and CARRIER, DAVID, *Truth and Falsehood in Visual Images* (Amherst, Mass.: University of Massachusetts Press, 1983).

ROSS, STEPHANIE, 'Caricature', *Monist*, 58 (1974), 285–93.

RYAN, T. A., and SCHWARTZ, CAROL B., 'Speed of Perception as a Function of Mode of Representation', *American Journal of Psychology*, 79 (1956), 60–9.

SABARTÉS, JAIME, *Picasso: Variations on Velazquez' Painting 'The Maids of Honor'* (New York: Abrams, 1959).

SAVILE, ANTHONY, 'Nelson Goodman's *Languages of Art*', *British Journal of Aesthetics*, 11 (1971), 3–12.

SCHIER, FLINT, *Deeper into Pictures: An Essay on Pictorial Representation* (Cambridge: Cambridge University Press, 1986).

SCHWARTZ, ROBERT, 'Imagery—There's More to it than Meets the Eye', in Ned Block (ed.), *Imagery* (Cambridge, Mass.: MIT Press, 1981), 109–30.

——, 'Representation and Resemblance', *Philosophical Forum*, 5 (1974), 499–512.

SEAMON, JOHN G., 'Dynamic Facial Recognition: Examination of a Natural Phenomenon', *American Journal of Psychology*, 95 (1982), 363–81.

SEARLE, JOHN, *'Expression and Meaning* (Cambridge: Cambridge University Press, 1979).

——, *'Las Meninas* and the Paradoxes of Pictorial Representation', in W. J. T. Mitchell (ed.), *The Language of Images* (Chicago: University of Chicago Press, 1980), 247–65.

——, 'Proper Names', in Peter Strawson (ed.), *Philosophical Logic* (Oxford: Oxford University Press, 1959), 89–96.

SHEPARD, ROGER, and CHIPMAN, SUSAN, 'Second-Order Isomorphism of Internal Representation: Shapes of States', *Cognitive Psychology*, 1 (1970), 1–17.

SHIFF, RICHARD, 'The Original, the Imitation, the Copy, and the Spontaneous Classic: Theory and Painting in Nineteenth-Century France', *Yale French Studies*, 66 (1984), 27–54.

STEINBERG, LEO, 'The Algerian Women and Picasso at Large', in *Other Criteria* (London: Oxford University Press, 1972), 124–234.

——, 'The Eye Is a Part of the Mind', in *Other Criteria*, 289–306.

——, 'The Glorious Company', in *Art about Art*, by Jean Lipman and Richard Marshall (New York: E. P. Dutton, 1978), 8–31.

SWEARER, DONALD K., 'Hypostasizing the Buddha: Buddha Image Consecration Ceremonies in Northern Thailand', *History of Religions*, 34 (1995), 263–80.

TRAVEL, D., and DAMASIO, A. R., 'Knowledge without Awareness: An Autonomic Index of Facial Recognition by Prosopagnosics', *Science*, 228 (1985), 453–5.

TULVING, ENDEL, *Elements of Episodic Memory* (Oxford: Oxford University Press, 1983).

URMSON, J. O., 'Recognition', *Proceedings of the Aristotelian Society*, 56 (1955), 259–80.

WALTON, KENDALL, 'Are Representations Symbols?', *Monist*, 58 (1974), 236–54.

——, 'Categories of Art', *Philosophical Review*, 79 (1970), 334–67.

——, 'Fearing Fictions', *Journal of Philosophy*, 75 (1978), 5–27.

——, *Mimesis as Make-Believe: On the Foundations of the Representational Arts* (Cambridge, Mass.: Harvard University Press, 1990).

——, 'Pictures and Make-Believe', *Philosophical Review*, 82 (1973), 283–319.

——, 'Transparent Pictures: On the Nature of Photographic Realism', *Critical Inquiry*, 11 (1984), 246–77.

WEISKRANTZ, LAWRENCE, *Blindsight: A Case Study and Implications* (Oxford: Oxford University Press, 1986).

——, *et al.*, 'Visual Capacity in the Hemaniopic Field Following a Restricted Occipital Ablation', *Brain*, 97 (1974), 709–28.

WILKERSON, TERENCE, 'Representation, Illusion, and Aspects', *British Journal of Aesthetics*, 18 (1978), 45–58.

WILLATS, JOHN, 'The Draughtsman's Contract: How an Artist Creates an Image', in Horace Barlow, Colin Blakemore, and Miranda Weston-Smith (eds.), *Images and Understanding* (Cambridge: Cambridge University Press, 1990), 235–54.

WILSON, CATHERINE, 'Illusion and Representation', *British Journal of Aesthetics*, 22 (1988), 211–21.

WITTGENSTEIN, LUDWIG, *Philosophical Investigations*, trans. G. E. M. Anscombe, 2nd edn. (Oxford: Basil Blackwell, 1958).

WOLLHEIM, RICHARD, *On Art and the Mind* (London: Allen Lane, 1973).

——, *Painting as an Art* (London: Thames and Hudson, 1988).

——, 'Seeing-as, Seeing-in, and Pictorial Representation', in *Art and its Objects*, 2nd edn. (Cambridge: Cambridge University Press, 1980), 205–26.

WOLTERSTORFF, NICHOLAS, *Works and Worlds of Art* (Oxford: Oxford University Press, 1980).

ZIMMER, HEINRICH, *The Art of Indian Asia* (Princeton: Princeton University Press, 1955).

PICTURE CREDITS

Fig. 1 gift of Mrs Barbara Hutton, © 1995 Board of Trustees, National Gallery of Art, Washington, DC. Fig. 2 from Franz Boas, *Primitive Art* (New York: Dover, 1955). Fig. 3 reprinted by permission of the Putnam Berkley Group from *The Perigee Visual Dictionary of Signing* by Rod R. Butterworth and Mickey Flodin, copyright © 1991 by Rod R. Butterworth and Mickey Flodin. Figs. 4, 6, 19, and 22 by Ron Plath. Figs. 6 and 24 by Prose & Contexts dtp. Fig. 7 Alinari/Art Resource, NY. Fig. 8 Giraudon/Art Resource, NY, © 1995 Artists Rights Society (ARS), New York/SPADEM, Paris. Fig. 9 from Luke Taylor, 'Seeing the "Inside": Kunwinjku Paintings and the Symbol of the Divided Body', in Howard Morphy (ed.), *Animals into Art* (London and Boston: Unwin Hyman, 1989), 376. Fig. 11 from *Journal of Social Psychology*, 52 (1960), 186; reprinted with permission of the Helen Dwight Reid Educational Foundation; published by Heldref Publications, 1319 Eighteenth St NW, Washington, DC 20036–1802, © 1960. Fig. 13 gift of Mrs John W. Simpson, © 1995 Board of Trustees, National Gallery of Art, Washington, DC. Fig. 14 NASA. Figs. 15 and 23 Foto Marburg/Art Resource, NY. Figs. 17, 25, and 27 © 1995 Artists Rights Society (ARS), New York/SPADEM, Paris. Fig. 20 The Seattle Art Museum, Eugene Fuller Memorial Collection, photo credit: Paul Macapia. Fig. 21 oil on two canvases, 72 × 240″, © David Hockney. Fig. 26 Giraudon/Art Resource, NY.

INDEX

UNIVERSITIES AT MEDWAY LIBRARY

Printed in the United Kingdom
by Lightning Source UK Ltd.
121247UK00001BA/155